Think Like a Champion

A Guide to Championship Performance for Student-Athletes

Dick DeVenzio

www.pgcbasketball.com

Third Edition

Think Like a Champion: A Guide to Championship Performance for Student-Athletes
Published by PGC Basketball

For more information about our books, visit our website at https://pgcbasketball.com.

Library of Congress Control Number: 2006925177

ISBN-13: 978-0-9839380-1-9

Original publication date: 1996

For information, purchases or permissions, go to:
https://pgcbasketball.com

Cover Design by Priyanka Kodikal

Special thanks for assistance to Huck DeVenzio.

Huck is the author's older brother, editor, advisor, and trusted friend. His help was important in every phase of production.

CHAMPIONSHIPS
are **not** won on the
night of a *BIG EVENT,*
but **years** before
by ATHLETES
who *COMMIT*
themselves **daily** to
CHAMPIONSHIP
PRINCIPLES.

Chuck DeVenzio, a very successful baseball and basketball coach from the 1940s, once astounded his players, his assistant coaches, and his son (the author of this book) when he said, just before a big game, *"I hope the floor is real slippery tonight or the ball has too much air."*

Why did he hope for bad conditions? He wanted the other team to be distracted, to be bothered by the conditions, and to have excuses for failures throughout the game. And what about his own team?

He never worried about conditions having a negative impact on his teams. He spent every day of his coaching life teaching athletes to be tough, to accept whatever conditions existed, and to adapt, not to make excuses. *"You have to* ***embrace the conditions,"*** he said, *"not complain about them."*

Table of Contents

A list of the 112 chapters follows

Contents by Chapter

Introduction to Athletes

Let's Sit Down and Talk Sports

I just want you to understand what this book is about, why it was written, and how it might be able to help you.

Mostly, I wanted you to have a book you could sit down with and read for just a few minutes at a time—before going to bed at night, on the bus on the way to a game, or maybe on a day you just don't feel like continuing to practice—and get something worthwhile from it, something *you* can really use on your quest to become a sports champion.

I wanted a book you could read from the beginning but which you could also open to any page—in the middle or near the end or anywhere—and get something that might help you in a game or in practice, or in planning and preparation. I also wanted to produce a book that covers enough different, commonly-experienced situations that you would be able to find some solid advice or at least some food for thought—easily—whenever you are looking for something specific.

I hope this book can be like a good friend at times, and like a wise teacher at other times.

Can a book really do all these things? What makes me think I can write such a book or that I am qualified to tell *you* what to do?

First, I have no intention of telling you what to do. Nor am I sure I can write a book that will help you have a more successful athletic career. But here is why I feel somewhat qualified to try.

I think it would be fair to say that I come from "a great sports family." Like me, my two brothers played college basketball. (They weren't big stars, but they got there.) We all made our way through Little League and high school sports because of a father who was a great coach. I use that word "great" carefully. My father was a great coach. He coached for forty years and I don't think he ever had a losing season. He knew how to win and he knew how to communicate his intensity and his knowledge to his players—regardless of whether he was coaching baseball, basketball, volleyball, table tennis (all of which he did) or any other sport.

Perhaps even more important, he especially knew how to communicate desire. I grew up wanting to be the best basketball player in America, and I worked diligently for a long time to achieve that. I never quite made it. [*Dick DeVenzio was a first team Parade Magazine All-American during his senior year at Ambridge High School and MVP of that year's big national all star game, the Dapper Dan Roundball Classic.* – editor] But I did make a pretty good effort at out-practicing everyone in America. Of course, I have no way of knowing if anyone during my era actually practiced harder than I did, but not many could have practiced *much* harder. I used virtually all of my time from age twelve to twenty to become the very best basketball player I could possibly become. Doing that included daily weight and agility training, running and conditioning, charted skill practice and development, and a lot of thinking, reading, practicing, planning, and dreaming.

Along the way I had the benefit of coaching not only from my father but also from some of the top people in my sport. Chuck Daly, the well-known commentator and coach of the original Olympic Dream Team in Barcelona in 1992, was an assistant coach at Duke during my time there. Hubie Brown, also a former pro coach and current commentator, was also an assistant at Duke then. Additionally, I have had the opportunity to play in many foreign countries and to have coached in five different languages (Spanish, French, Dutch, Papiamento, and English). In other words, I've played and coached in a variety of places under many conditions, and I never just went through the motions. That wasn't my style. I gave a great deal of effort and thought to those experiences.

If nothing else, I can assure you of this: I have given thousands of hours of thought to the meaning of athletics. I have spent most of my life analyzing and thinking about sports. In addition to basketball, I have played a lot of tennis, baseball, softball and ping-pong; and I have been an avid observer of dozens of sports, particularly football, hockey, golf, wrestling, soccer, swimming, gymnastics, volleyball, track & field, and boxing. The Summer and Winter Olympics give spectators the opportunity to witness a variety of other sports and to realize that competitors in all sports, even at the highest levels, have a lot in common—the need for practice, dedication, persistent effort, good coaching, overcoming obstacles, coming from behind, etc.

In a nutshell, my observations and experiences over the past several decades convince me that, having played and coached at very high levels in basketball, I may have some worthwhile things to say about general issues in all sports.

Whether it be graciously winning, struggling to handle defeat, coming back from an injury, or being criticized by a coach or a fan, many essentials are common to nearly all athletes in every sport. Therefore, I feel no need to pretend to be an expert in all sports. I merely claim to be a person who has played and coached one sport at high levels and who has thought a lot about sports in general. So, though I don't know enough about most sports to help with techniques or strategies, and since I'm not likely to appear at one of your games or tournaments to help cheer you on, I will try to give you my best in the only format I know where I might be able to help you reach your goals and fulfill your dreams. In this book, I want to talk to you like a friend and help you think about sports. As a former athlete, a motivational speaker, an author of several books, and a teacher, coach, and camp director, I feel I have had sufficient experience to be able to talk sports with you—intelligently. I hope you agree and enjoy the conversations.

Introduction to Parents and Coaches

Too Many Commentators, Not Enough Coaches

My goal is to reach out to athletes all across the nation (and maybe beyond) and talk to them about the right way to approach sports—the way of the true champion. It is my feeling that the majority of athletes today don't get firmly grounded in the ideas, concepts, and attitudes that lead to championship performance. Instead, too often they get a skewed notion of what a tough competitor is and what sports are all about. I think I know why this skewing happens.

Today's young athletes watch a lot more TV than athletes did a generation ago, and they see a lot more sports. They also get exposed to a lot more commentary. That's where I think the problems begin. When I was growing up, the primary exposure to sports concepts and attitudes came from direct association with coaches. Today, the primary exposure comes from association with TV commentators—millionaires armed with isolated cameras and videotape (instant) replays and nine different camera angles and the job requirement to explain—or create—events.

As a result, it is not at all uncommon to see over and over again, even during the fourth quarter of a close game, the replay of a "big call" or "crucial play" that happened in the first quarter.

This may be wonderful for fans and sideline quarterbacks and would-be commentators—to hash and rehash over a call in the first quarter that may have decided the outcome of a game—but it is terrible if this view of sports is adopted by an athlete.

The idea of thinking of a first quarter play in the fourth quarter, or ever claiming that a first quarter call could decide the outcome of a game, is totally against the teaching of any good coach. Coaches, rightfully, teach athletes to forget the past immediately and focus fully on the performance now and on anticipating what is about to happen. In fact, the best coaches teach athletes to expect some bad calls, factor them in, and still prepare to win. Any deviation at all from this kind of focus and anticipation is a prescription for failure as well as for skewed values. Good coaches simply don't allow it. But athletes, taking their cue so often from TV, learn otherwise. They question referees' calls constantly—and think they ought to—and their focus is often on things completely removed from performance.

This book will try to wage a kind of holy war for the hearts and minds of athletes against the incessant commentary aimed at fans, controversy, and TV ratings points. Hopefully it will show athletes the error of a misguided focus in a variety of settings and inspire them to think like—and be—true champions.

Preface

How to Use This Book Effectively

I hope you don't try to read this book quickly from start to finish, page by page. I'm afraid it will bore you to death and begin to sound terribly repetitious. That was my impression as I proofread, but I decided not to change it. Here's why.

I wrote this book thinking of athletes who have a lot to do and don't have much time to read books not related to schoolwork. In other words, I wrote it thinking that athletes would keep it by their beds and use it as a reference; they'd find a topic of interest and maybe read for five or ten minutes each night before going to bed. As a result, I tried to make each section short, yet complete in itself. I didn't want to make readers keep referring to another page, so I decided to be somewhat repetitious.

For example, I have included a section on "Playing Hard" as well as a section on "Work Ethic." The two are quite different in some ways, but similar in others. Rather than write one and refer you to the other, I tried to make each complete by itself. As long as you read them a few days apart, I think you will find them both useful and somewhat interesting. But if you read them back to back, I fear you might say something like, "Okay Man, enough already, I heard you the first time."

There are a lot of great books in the world. I don't expect nor want you to read mine for two straight hours or as though you are in a race to finish. On the contrary, I hope you will read this book little by little, over a period of time, and let the ideas sink in. Particularly, I wanted to make the book easy to browse through for a few minutes before a game, before practice, or before going out on your own to lift weights or run. If you read in this way, I think you will be positively influenced to think and perform like a champion.

—Dick DeVenzio, 1996

Think Like a Champion

1.
Academics

The whole concept of striving for athletic success and maximizing ability and eating right and sleeping well and thinking straight and competing hard becomes ridiculous if it's all done on a shortsighted journey that leaves you nowhere at its end.

In America, academics have become almost synonymous with athletics or, if not actually synonymous, then try harmonious, or "inextricably linked."

There are several reasons for this. Since major college sports became so popular (even before pro sports in football and basketball), the concept of student-athlete became linked in everyone's mind because, at least on paper, an athlete *had* to be a student. He had to hit the books in order to be eligible to play. Of course, this situation still exists. And now high schools are raising their standards. If an athlete wants to play, he has to maintain some particular grade point average.

At one time, people created sports in order to get students interested in coming to school. But now that sports are so important and so well established, they are looked upon as a privilege; you can't participate in them unless you're already doing well in school. It doesn't necessarily have to be this way, but in America this is how it is. It is a big historical shift. But what does this mean to you? No use spending much time considering whether it's good or bad, it just is.

Nearly all the way up on your way to the pros—where you

can be a complete idiot as long as you can do the sport well—you *have* to be a student in order to be an athlete. That means, whether you like it or not, in most sports you will be forced to be attentive to academic affairs in order to do your thing in sports.

This isn't very likely to change since America has always had a commitment to education. The idea of democracy requires that the citizens of the nation be intelligent and informed so they can rule themselves. In other words, the commitment to education is likely to grow with time, not go away.

Even a pro athlete, who I have said can be an idiot as long as he can hit home runs or run a football or blast a serve in tennis, has a stake in education. It is true that once an athlete becomes a paid professional, he or she does not have to meet any particular academic standards. But the athlete has other concerns too, like money and television and intelligence.

Pro sports are as tightly tied to television as collegiate sports are to education. Perhaps more so. Pro sports depend for their very existence on television. And television requires that an athlete have a certain education or at least the appearance of one. The big stars, the ones who make the real big money and who get the commercial opportunities and become celebrities, are those who can speak and think and sort through all the con artists and schemers along the way.

And speaking of con artists and schemers... if you have little education and are not smart enough to see through a bad deal or read and understand a complicated contract, how likely are you to hold onto all that money being thrown at you? America is filled with former sports stars, literally thousands of them, who once made a lot of money in sports but today have nearly nothing to show for their past accomplishments except memories and trophies and newspaper articles. Where did all the money go? To lawyers and agents and financial "counselors," and to grand schemes to multiply that money.

Reality ought to be clear to you. *It makes sense to get as much education and to become as smart as you possibly can, regardless of your situation, your interests, or your earnings.*

What does this mean to you? It means that even if you make it to the top of the world in your sport, you still need to develop self-discipline. You need to know how to act, how to read, how to think, how to negotiate, and how to recognize and make good deals for yourself. And you can certainly expect that you will need these abilities even more "at the bottom" or any place where your athletic abilities are not so spectacular that other inadequacies can at times be overlooked.

For everyone who is not destined to become a millionaire pro athlete (and even for those who are) there will be a growing need to be intelligent in order to have a decent standard of living in the twenty first century. Why say this? Why be concerned about it here? Because the whole concept of striving for athletic success and maximizing ability and eating right and sleeping well and thinking straight and competing hard becomes ridiculous if it's all done on a shortsighted journey that leaves you nowhere at its end.

If a menial job and a poor future are at the end of all your hustle, determination, and effort, then anyone who urged such things on you would be your enemy and a kook, a lunatic.

Anyone would look at all that effort and determination and training, and ask with true astonishment, "Why? Why did you do all that? What good did it do you? Didn't anyone with some intelligence and experience caution you that it might all be a big waste of time, a tragic distraction in the grand scheme of things?"

To blaze through your sports career, picking up trophies and awards and competing for championships but paying no attention to lifelong opportunities and educational priorities, would be as stupid as walking to a field to practice your sport and not stopping to pick up a thousand dollar bill that blew by you on the street.

"Hey, why don't you pick up that money?"

"Can't. I'm on my way to practice."

"Yeah, but you have to eat, don't you? You have equipment to buy, don't you? I mean, you need money, don't you?"

"Yeah, but I'll worry about that later. Ri ght now, I'm focusing on sports."

"Hey, wait. Focus is great. But the thousand bucks are right there for the taking. Just reach down and grab 'em. Don't be crazy."

"Can't. I'm just thinking sports right now."

You wouldn't do it. You wouldn't be *that* focused. You wouldn't be *that* crazy. And neither should you be crazy enough to be so focused on your sport that you don't take advantage of the educational opportunities in your lap right now.

Every young athlete, by law, has to go to school. Most of the athletes who read this book will be in some sort of school—junior high, high school, or college. That means you will be sitting somewhere seven or eight hours a day in some building with the chance to learn and get ahead sitting right there with you. You are surrounded by books, professors, libraries, laboratories. All you have to do is respond. Like bending down and picking up the money. You just have to be there, listen, learn, try. Make the most of it.

Sure, focus on your sport. But grab every opportunity along the way. *Passing up opportunities is stupid.*

Academics *are* important. These are not just words spoken by parents and principals. If you're bored with school, there's a cure for that (see "Boredom"). If you're not so good in school, there's a cure for that (see "Being a Student"). If you're not very good at taking tests, you can be (see "Interviews"). If you're just confused about this whole thing called education and academics, you can find your way out (see "Getting Organized," "Goal Setting," and "Positive Places").

But, as is true with sports, you have to get tough. You have to have the right attitude. You have to bypass obstacles. You have to stop making excuses for failures and start finding reasons for success. And you can.

2.
Acknowledging Fans

They don't take two steps out of their way to acknowledge these fans. Most of them don't even look up or nod.

There are very few athletes in the world who would get an A on a report card that measures how well they acknowledge fans.

When you pause to consider the importance of fans in sports, you begin to realize how badly most athletes are failing in this area and how much athletes take this aspect of their sporting lives for granted.

Imagine the end of the season, the big game, the clash everyone's been waiting for, and this guy has a meeting, and that person has a toothache, and this family has a birthday party, and that group thinks the weather may be too bad—so everyone stays home.

Big game? Can you imagine the feeling of the players, accustomed to getting so much attention, when suddenly no one showed up for the big one?

It has become customary for athletes to mouth words about the fact that they don't even notice the fans, that they don't play for fans, that fans, in fact, are something you need to learn to put out of your mind, to ignore. Of course in certain situations—when opposing fans are taunting or trying to distract you—it is necessary to concentrate on the task at hand and to perform well in spite of them. But ignore them? No way. Opposing fans should propel you.

Think back on all the championship celebrations you have seen on TV where athletes talk about having the "best fans in the world" and about how important the fan support was to the success of the team. Think of all the times you have watched star football players raise their hands during big games, trying to get the fans to make more noise. Think of all the times you have heard coaches and commentators talk about the importance of keeping the fans out of a game or getting the fans into a game.

Fan support can make a tremendous difference, and it should be cultivated. If you don't have any fans supporting your team, you should get some. (Any team can. It's easy. See "Invitations.") And if you already have fans, you should be grateful. You should acknowledge them in a variety of ways and make constant efforts to let them know you appreciate their support.

When was the last time you thanked a fan for coming to one of your games? When was the last time you thanked fifty fans for coming to your games? When was the last time you wrote a thank you letter to a fan? When was the last time your team put on a demonstration for your special fans?

Demonstration? Thank you letter? To a fan?

Yeah, you're right. These are ideas most athletes haven't even thought about. Almost no one does. Let me give another example of athletes ignoring fans and losing a valuable opportunity that could make a difference to your team and perhaps to your future.

Cruising Through Hotel Lobbies

During my life in sports I have witnessed the following scene literally hundreds of times, as a player, as a coach, as a fan, and as an uninvolved observer. Early in my career I was oblivious. I didn't even know I was on stage or that a play was going on. Unfortunately, that's the way most athletes are today, oblivious. Here's the scene:

A group of athletes is assembled in a hotel lobby far from home. They are usually college athletes but could be high school athletes as well. They have achieved some success somewhere or would not have made it to the point of being on a team that travels and spends money to stay overnight in hotels. The circumstances are not crucial; the team is away from home, in a hotel. Perhaps they are on their way to work out before the game, or perhaps they are assembled in order to eat a pre-game meal. Maybe they are headed to the game or on their way to bed for the night.

Whatever the situation, the players walk through the hotel lobby. Some fans are talking in a corner or just standing around near the registration desk. Sometimes those fans are particularly evident because they are wearing school colors, or carrying a banner or other article that makes it clear they are there to root for the team.

So what happens? The athletes walk by.

What? That's right. The athletes walk by.

Think about this. The athletes walk by. They go on their way. They don't walk over to the fans. They don't take two steps out of their way to acknowledge these fans. Most of them don't even look up or nod. Typically, they focus on their teammates, trading insults, hitting each other with inside jokes. They are being watched and no one has taught them to take the focus off their own shyness and nervousness and to shine it back on the fans.

No one has taught them to be mirrors, reflecting the glory or acknowledgment back on the fans who are giving it out.

Every player ought to be looking up, walking over, shaking hands and engaging these special people in conversations. These fans, wearing your school colors, could have done a thousand things instead of going to watch you play. But there they are, standing in the lobby of your hotel, paying homage to your achievements and efforts with their presence. And you don't even look up and acknowledge them?

Who the hell do you think you are?

It's a very appropriate question.

Even if you are merely a selfish jerk you ought to realize that it would be time well spent to talk with these people. They obviously have some wherewithal; they have the money and the desire to stop working and spend some time traveling and attending a mere game. No doubt they also run businesses or have some influence in their community. They could probably give you a summer job, or help you get started in a career.

Most athletes are too ignorant to even be aware of their

own self-interest. Whether you are motivated by selfishness or gratitude, those fans hanging out in the lobby of your hotel—those fans who came a long way *just to see you*— deserve your attention. If you're too dumb to realize you owe them a thank you, at least you ought to be smart enough to realize there might be an advantage in knowing them. You may never again be in so favorable a position to make influential friends, to make positive impressions, and to further your own career possibilities.

Try walking up to people in a strange hotel lobby when you are *not* on a team, and see the reaction. If they don't back away and avoid you entirely, people will probably roll their eyes, be suspicious, and question your every word.

When you are on a team and those special people are there to see you perform, every tiny positive action you take will be magnified a hundredfold. Veer off, say hello, thank them for coming so far. "You came all that way, just to see us play?" One question like that will have dozens of people gossiping for the rest of the trip about "what a fine young man" (or woman) you are.

Do you have your life and your opportunities so well mapped out that you can ignore the opportunity to have dozens of well-connected people spreading good words about you? Most of us don't. And most of us realize that, under typical circumstances, it is much more likely negatives will spread about you than positives.

But *not* when you are walking through hotel lobbies. *Not* when you are part of a team. ***Not*** when people have made a special effort to see you play. And *not* when you do what hundreds of thousands of other athletes routinely fail to do—acknowledge the people around you who are adding importance to the sport and event you are engaged in.

I have given this speech to athletes all over the nation and many of them have the same response. Once it sinks in that they really are in an exalted position and ought to respond to it, they get fearful. "But what would I say?"

Say? Say anything. *Just thank them for coming.* Express the sincere appreciation you ought to feel for the fact that they came a long way just to watch you and your team perform. Ask them if they had a nice trip, if they are staying in this same hotel, if they have ever been there before… or don't ask them a thing. Just thank them and stand there and be quiet.

And guess what? Once they get over the shock of realizing that an athlete has acted like a reasonable person, they will be more than happy to do the talking. Ninety-nine times out of a hundred they will start asking you questions or start telling you all about their children, their families, their lives.

As long as you act grateful and are interested in them, they will be happy to do the talking. (If you haven't learned this basic lesson of life yet, it is time.) If you want to take this a step farther, just act curious about them. Ask any question that pops into your mind. Where are they from? When did they leave? How long did it take them? Do they go to every game? With whom did they come? Did they see the past game? Are they going to the next one? Did they read about such and such in the paper?

You don't need things to *say*. You just need a few questions to ask, any questions, so they get the sense that you are curious. They will do the rest. Trust me. A bit of acknowledgment will pay dividends over and over, plus it ought to be a joy for you (as it is for most people) to be in a position to be able to brighten others' lives through simple attention and curiosity.

Don't wait until you are the nation's leading movie star or sports hero. It isn't necessary. If you are on a team, if you are an active athlete competing in scheduled events, that is enough all by itself. Many people on the fringes envy your privileged position and will be buoyed by your attention. Why not give it to them?

3.
Acknowledging Friends

It shouldn't be possible to do so much with so little effort, but timing and circumstances are often critical in life, and this is one of those rare times when you can control and use timing and circumstances to your advantage.

You will probably never again be in a position to delight and honor your special friends and family the way you can as an athlete or performer. The phenomenon of acknowledgment is so strange it's almost funny. Let me give just one example.

Most of you see your mother every day. She can talk to you any time she wants. Most of the time she tells you to do things and scolds you when you fail to do them. You are anything but a big shot to her. She knows you inside and out. You may be the athlete getting your name and picture in the paper, but she knows you as the athlete who leaves your bedroom all messed up. In other words, there should be no way to impress your mother just because you happen to have a uniform on. But you can!

When your mother arrives at a game and you are running around warming up, take two seconds to say hi to her. People will notice. She will, whether you see it or not, puff up with pride. And she will feel better about you, about herself, and about life.

It shouldn't be possible to do so much with so little effort, but timing and circumstances are often critical in life and this is one of those rare times when you can control and use timing and circumstances to your advantage.

Does your fraternity come into a game together? Can you flash the guys some special sign? Do your friends come in together? How about your history professor? (Or don't you want a two-second switch from a C to a B?)

No use spending any extra time trying to reemphasize this. *The results of acknowledging the special people in your life, under the special circumstances of being the performer in the spotlight, are simply incredible.* And you are a complete fool not to take advantage of this phenomenon.

It makes no sense that people, particularly your family and friends, should be so flattered by your attention just because you happen to be "on stage" at a particular time. But they are.

The rest is up to you.

4.

Adverse Circumstances: A Chance to Show off!

Oh, sure, you would have won if it hadn't rained. Well, big deal. It rained.

During the course of any athlete's season, there will be many adverse circumstances to deal with. To many athletes, these circumstances come as a big surprise and cause great distress. Their performance suffers. They "would-a" won or they "could-a" done well, but the circumstances...

What a shame that those athletes don't have a great coach reminding them every day that adverse circumstances are normal, expected, awaited, and to be viewed simply as a chance to show off—in the best way possible.

Oh sure, you would have won if it hadn't rained. Well, big deal. It rained. And you suddenly had the opportunity to demonstrate that you could win in spite of the rain. The opportunity to win the admiration of teammates, coaches, and true sports fans suddenly increased when it rained, but you used the rain as a justification for losing instead of seizing the moment to magnify the admiration that could have come from winning.

No tennis player wants to be down two sets to none, or down two games to none, nor does any athlete *want* to be behind going into the fourth quarter or the ninth inning or the final rotation, but when you find yourself in those circumstances—and you will—you have an opportunity to adopt whatever attitude you choose.

Big tennis match. Down 2–0 in sets. Down 5–0 in games. Down Love–40. Match point. Seemingly impossible odds against you. But there's nothing impossible about the attitude you choose. You can choose to think, "Oh no, this is it," or you can choose to focus on what an incredible comeback it would be if you could win now.

Everyone would talk about it. Unbelievable. Incredible. Awesome.

Unbelievable comebacks and accomplishments begin with an attitude that says, "These conditions are about as bad as they can get. What an opportunity! If I can just pull this off."

Having this attitude doesn't mean you are suddenly going to reverse every tide and go on to win every game. But it should mean that you will play the next point and every point thereafter as well as possible with enthusiasm, pride, and aggressiveness. With an opportunistic attitude you aren't crippled by the circumstances, you welcome them as a chance to show what you are made of. If you lose, you lose. But you sure aren't going to help your opponent win by focusing on the negatives.

When you think about sports and the psychology involved, and about all the frustrations that can be witnessed any time you turn on the TV or go to a field, it ought to be apparent what a tremendous advantage you would have if you simply decided, right now, to *start viewing every negative circumstance as an opportunity.*

It rained. Your opponent got a lucky break. Your star player got injured. Your coach got thrown out. Your feet have blisters. Your dog just died. Choose your woes. They are inevitable. They are also an opportunity to show off. An opportunity for you to define the true meaning of athletics. An opportunity for you to feel proud, strong, and special. And, often, a special opportunity for you to experience a turning point and perhaps pull off an upset or a comeback you could not have accomplished on your own.

Remember that even so-called great athletes often get flustered and lose their cool and blow sure wins after suffering some defeat that "never should have happened." In other words, the next time—any time—you face adverse circumstances, don't throw in the towel. Take advantage of those circumstances. They just may be a passport to your finest moments in sports.

5.
Analyzing Performance

Does one inch in the last second, one way or the other, really dictate that the post-game responses are so dramatically different?

It's the last of the ninth, one run behind, one man on, two outs, the wind up, the pitch, a long high drive, deep left center field, going way back, way back...

Or would you prefer the ball to have been snapped, no time left on the clock, last play of the game, five point deficit, but a long pass into the end zone, both the wide receiver and the strong safety about to leap...

Or you hear the buzzer go off, the referee signals that the shot has been released in time, one point deficit, if it goes in, you win (if it misses you lose)...

You understand the situation. The ball is in the air. Heads you win, tails you lose. Does the ball sail over the fence, get snatched in the end zone, swish through the hoop... or is it caught on the warning track, deflected out of bounds, or air balled?

The outcome is in the hands of the gods. May I suggest a fantasy? Let's have the post-game talks right now. Stop the ball in mid-flight, stop the players, stop the spin of the earth, and let's talk about things. With the game's outcome still unknown, no one can say "we made the big plays when we needed them." No one can say "we did what it took to win." No one needs to throw things or talk about what might have been. If only this, if only that.

Coaches, reporters, parents, athletes…go ahead. Talk about it now. What was good? What was bad? What needs to be improved for next game? What can be learned?

Got it? Everyone finished? Okay. Time-in. Spin on, Earth. Move, folks. Go, balls. Kerplunk!

Are you aware of how dramatically the post-game commentary changes depending on whether one last-second ball is an inch one way or another? Over the fence, there are celebrations, congratulations, champagne in the showers. Remember that play. *All* those great plays. What an awesome game.

Of course, an inch short (or simply in the other locker room) everything is completely different. Tears, disappointment, failure, self-doubt, second guessing, dissension, blaming. Those refs…Johnny…the coach…darn, if only this, if only that. That one play. And that other. And that other. Why me? Why us? Not again. It ain't fair. "We just didn't get it done." "We didn't have what it took." "We blew it at crunch time." "We'd beat them nine out of ten times."

Does one inch in the last second, one way or the other, really dictate that the post-game responses are so dramatically different? Welcome to the world. Winning and losing. Champ or chump.

You can't do much about the rest of the world. It isn't likely to change very much. But personally, on your own, you ought to be influenced by this insight if you haven't already given it a great deal of thought. *After most wins, you really aren't entitled to all the congratulations you get* nor to the focus on all the good things that happened. And after most losses, you really don't deserve all the criticism or the anguish of realizing that so many plays—if only just one had gone differently—cost you the victory.

Before we re-spun the globe, no one was crying, no one squirting champagne. There were, as in most games, some good plays and bad plays, some good calls and bad calls.

Can you remember the last time you watched a victory celebration and the coaches and players essentially credited the referees with the victory? "It was the refs. They did it. They won it for us." Yet nearly everyone in the world has heard losers, after almost every loss, cite the referees as one of the primary culprits. "Gawd, those refs!"

It sounds stupid. And it is. Post-game commentary usually is.

Most games contain several good plays, several bad plays, and a lot of mediocre plays. Athletes need to see games as they are, regardless of what happens in the last second or two. Heroes are rarely as great as post-game commentators wish to make them; and scapegoats are rarely as guilty as the talk show lynch mobs would have you believe.

Seeing games as they are ought to make it a lot easier for you to be gracious when you win, and calmer and philosophic when you lose. Not bad things to be.

6.
Attitude

The referee blows a call. So what? The other team cheats. Big deal. None of these external events needs to change who you are, how you act, what you are proud of...

Attitude means a lot of things these days. Sometimes, by itself, it means a bad attitude. Sometimes it means a way of carrying yourself with self-respect and flair. It means different things to different people. So here, let's talk about what it means to have the right attitude, the right way, or the best way, to carry yourself and to approach your sport and your life.

This subject is crucial. It's everything. With the right attitude you can overcome any obstacle, surmount any fate.

You lost the big game. So what? You know what that means. If you have everything in perspective, you realize that losing a game, any game, is not the end of the world. It's the same if you win the big game. So what? You haven't gained eternal life. You won a game. You win some, you lose some.

So, what's so important about attitude? Having a great attitude or the right attitude means understanding the big picture, realizing and having a special sense about winning and losing games and playing games and how you act and how hard you work and how you relate with teammates and how you respond to the coach and how you react to negative events. It's all there.

With the right attitude, you don't need the perfect blueprint. You don't need to be able to anticipate every tiny detail or every incident that might come up in a game, because your attitude prepares you in general, for everything, and therefore you are fully prepared for anything.

If this sounds like double-talk, it isn't. A great attitude, the right attitude, is nothing more than a way of seeing yourself with a kind of self-pride and nobility; that vision, that feeling dictates what you do in every situation.

Once you have this special attitude about yourself, the whole range of things that can happen externally doesn't matter much. So someone tries to draw you into a fight, plays dirty, or taunts. So what? That's his problem. He doesn't see the big picture. He isn't filled with pride. He doesn't have the vision. Because when you have it, you rise above all that. You let yourself be amused by those things, perhaps, but you don't get drawn into them.

The referee blows a call. So what? The other team cheats. Big deal. None of these external events needs to change who you are, how you act, what you are proud of.

Attitude is internal. It is, therefore, not the clothes you wear but the feeling you have wearing them. It is, therefore, not winning every championship but the way you go about playing the games, competing, trying, striving. Are you yelling and screaming at a referee or umpire? What does that say about your attitude? You may think it shows that you are a great competitor who got a bad call, but what it really says is that you let someone else determine your mood, you let someone else decide your actions, you let someone else decide your cool.

If you were an artist that would be like giving someone else the brush and the paint and letting that person decide what would go on your canvas. How stupid. If you're an artist, you grab the brush, you choose the paint, you make the picture.

Why let someone else have control over who you are? Why not have more self-pride than that? Why not be more competitive than that?

Yes, competitive. If you are a real competitor you don't let others control you. *You* decide how you want to act. Do you want to walk out onto a field and kick dirt and throw things? Then why wait till the umpire makes a bad call? Why not do it before the game or between innings? Or after? Why wait for a cue from an umpire? Why let the umpire control you?

Reacting to calls and external events is not attitude and it's not competitiveness, it's weakness. Instead, take pride in deciding for yourself what you do, how you act, how you respond. You have the ability right now, while sitting down and reading a book, to decide how you want to react to situations you will face this year and for the rest of your career. How will you respond to taunts, to criticism, to bad calls, to punches, to cheaters, to fans, to reporters?

Why leave it up to others? As an athlete, as a proud athlete, I would never want others to think they are in charge of my actions. I want it to be clear to everyone—fans, teammates, opponents, everyone—that I am the grand decider. I decide.

What attitude have *you* decided upon?

Attitude is pride. It's toughness. It's cool. It's baaad. You name it what you like. Just make sure you have it. Attitude. The toughness to make your own decision, the pride to act the way you have decided to act, to be what you decide to be...under every circumstance *they* can throw at you.

7.
Being a Student

Anyone who spends many hours a day in school ought to find a way to enjoy that time.

Being a student is a lot like being an athlete. To be the real thing you emulate the stars. Too few, however, are making any effort to emulate outstanding scholars. Plus, we don't see many outstanding scholars on TV on Saturday afternoons...or do we?

In a sense, nearly everyone we ever see on TV is a scholar of some type, someone who has made it through the ranks, graduated from high school, usually from college, and nearly always from some schools of hard knocks.

A lot of people want to be on TV so there is fierce competition, just like in sports. A commentator or newscaster has passed by a lot of others who aspired to that position. The same is true usually for the people being interviewed. Politicians, entertainers, business leaders.

What do you notice when you see people on TV? In general they appear to be organized, articulate, purposeful. Their appearance reflects a certain self-pride. If they are holding some papers, books, or a briefcase, there is often further evidence of purpose and pride.

How many students have you seen toss books in lockers, get papers scrunched up and torn, turn in homework assignments that look hastily thrown together? These aren't terrible crimes but they don't imitate what top scholars do. Scholars are proud of their efforts, just like athletes. That means their books and papers are going to receive star treatment. They strive for excellence in a library or meeting room just like athletes are doing on a field.

If you don't currently have a sense of what it's like to be a real student, try a few experiments. Put new covers on your books and put them on neatly (or get someone else to do it.) so they look good. Then keep them clean and neatly stacked wherever they are. Get a separate folder or large envelope for your papers and assignments so they have little chance of getting torn or dirty. Keep a calendar that shows clearly when tests are coming up or papers are due.

Go to each class with the idea of listening carefully to what's going on. If the material is interesting, rejoice! But if it's boring, listen carefully and ask, "How can anyone find this stuff interesting?" (Some people do find it interesting; it's just a matter of finding out why.)

In each of your classes make sure you have an overview. That means make sure you understand why you have that class and what the material covers, so that each day the work for that day is placed in a larger context.

Most important of all, try just walking around like a real student. Walk into class like someone who is eager to learn—even if you aren't—and take some notes as though you want to be able to recall that information later—even if you don't. Sit and look the teacher in the eye and pretend, if necessary, that the things in your book are of great interest.

It's not necessary to do all this as a big lie. Doing it as an act will be fine. Do it as an experiment. Just try it. Tell your friends, if that will help, and make a joke out of it. But try it.

Acting like a real student makes it easier to *be* a real student. (Just as thinking and acting like a champion makes it easier to become a champion.) And regardless of what some of your friends may think, *anyone who spends many hours a day in school ought to find a way to enjoy that time and make the most of it.*

For those of you who already are conscientious in school, don't pat yourself on the back. See if you can raise yourself up a level the way good athletes do when attempting to be outstanding. Listen better, add more to the experience, take better or more memorable notes. Define what the ideal student would be and strive for that as an experiment. And see how you like it.

There is a definite, undeniably good feeling that comes from the pursuit of excellence in whatever you do. In school, we learn all sorts of non-excellent behaviors along the way because most of us want to get in our daily quota of talking with friends, messing around, telling and laughing at jokes, etc. There's nothing unusual about this. However, sometime, you need to make a break from all of these extraneous behaviors and start focusing your efforts.

Separate your student time from your friend-making and joke-telling time. Sure, you can tell a joke and laugh during a class. Everyone enjoys these things from time to time. But just make sure you don't joke and laugh and distract yourself on a regular basis.

Some students get all the way through elementary school maintaining the notion that one of their primary goals is to disrupt a teacher, get in as many jokes as possible, talk to friends as much as possible, and stay "off task" as long as possible. This probably isn't your problem. But would you say you are typically in a classroom experimenting with excellence? Nearly every student, like every athlete, can increase his level of participation, his effort, his enthusiasm, his leadership. Why not you?

The better you are at a sport or a school subject, the more you like it and the more you are able to work at it diligently and effectively. If there's a subject you hate, get better at it and keep pretending for awhile. Try acting as if you like it for just a couple of weeks. You may truly be astonished at what happens. The habit of excellence can become enjoyably addictive.

8.
Bench-Warming

Don't let "them" make you feel uneasy for wanting to drop off a team. And don't let yourself resort to bench antics to get through an unhappy situation.

This section may not include advice that a typical coach is looking for, but a lot of athletes need to examine this issue carefully.

There are thousands of stories about bench antics, the subtle and not so subtle things athletes do on benches because they are unhappy not playing in games. Some athletes sit back, hands behind their heads, stretched out and showing a posture like they are relaxing at the beach instead of participating in a big, important game. Others make noises, make an effort not to pay attention to what's going on, or talk about things totally unrelated to the events on the field.

This is a not-much-talked-about subject but one that plenty of athletes are familiar with, which is why I think some thoughts are appropriate here even if they are controversial. A lot of athletes should seriously consider removing themselves from teams instead of riding the bench, giving the endeavor less than their best, and often even engaging in antics they are not proud of.

If you believe you deserve to be playing, obviously it isn't going to be fun sitting on the bench. Nor does it make sense to sit a bench indefinitely. The very definition of an athlete, as I see it, is one who *plays* a sport. If you find yourself sitting on the bench on your team, you have to ask yourself some questions.

Have you been patient enough? You can't expect, in anything you do, that things will always turn your way immediately. Make sure you give yourself adequate time.

What might you do differently? Talk to your coach. Explain your feelings. Find out your coach's feelings. Find out what you can do to alter the situation so you can play.

What does the future hold for you? If you have to put in a year sitting on the bench but it's clear that you will be playing full time in the future, it may be well worth sitting there and paying your dues.

If you decide it's worth paying your dues, then pay them well. Be attentive. Be involved. Learn all you can. Be encouraging to your teammates. Sit near the coach. Listen to all he or she says, and think about what you would do if you were playing. What could you do to reduce the coach's frustrations? What are the players doing who are pleasing her?

If you have decided you are in a dues paying situation, give it everything you have. But if the situation isn't clear, if the future isn't certain, it may be wise for you to remove yourself and get yourself in a better situation.

It's a big world out there. If you aren't lead guitarist, you may be first sax. If you aren't playing on the basketball team, perhaps it would be better for you to spend the winter preparing to be the star of the baseball team. The sooner you realize that your time is valuable, the better your life is likely to be. Why sit a bench and go through the motions when you could be playing some other sport, or devoting your time to some other activity?

As you can see, I'm not a fan of bench-sitting. As a coach I played everyone on the bench in every game, except for those who I clearly defined as "future players." Then I gave those future players a choice and let them know I would not be upset if they dropped off the team and came back next year. If they opted to stay on, their continuation would be frown-less, antic-less, and with their parents' full understanding that they weren't going to be playing this year.

Either understand your situation fully and be happy with it and make the most of it, or don't be involved at all.

While a coach may like having the security of big numbers to facilitate practicing and to be covered in case of injuries, that's not your problem. In your brief life you want to make sure you are fully and constructively engaged in whatever activities you are involved in. Being on the periphery isn't where you want to be for very long. No sport is that important.

I would rather play the tuba in the Podunk band than sit the bench on the Duke University basketball team. But everyone's different. You have to decide what you're willing to do and not do, and how long you can continue to give your best efforts to whatever it is you are doing.

Sports teams have a limited amount of joy to disperse. There is just not enough on a basketball team to distribute it to fifteen people. There is not enough joy on a football team to distribute it to seventy-five people. There is not enough joy on a baseball team to distribute it to twenty people.

As you probably know, there are a lot of basketball teams with fifteen players, a lot of football teams with seventy-five players, and a lot of baseball teams with twenty players. If you are a pro, the money you are making may increase the joy sufficiently that it doesn't matter if you aren't playing.

But if you aren't making money and you're still sitting the bench, you ought to look for a better opportunity. Isn't there another league you can get in? A different sport you could play? A different activity you could enjoy?

It's your life. If you are happy sitting the bench well then of course, sit there. And continue to enjoy yourself. But if you are not happy, don't feel as though you're crazy and don't bother asking yourself what's wrong with *you*. Most athletes don't like sitting the bench. In an ideal world there would be no bench-sitting. Everyone would play, just as you do when you wake up on a Saturday morning and call some friends to go to a park. A few here and there wait their turns to play but all go to the field with that intention. And they all play, except for the ones who said, "Nah, I don't want to play, but maybe I'll come down to watch."

Hey if you want to watch and you're comfortable with that, watch. If you want to play a sport, you have to find an opportunity for yourself.

Don't let "them" make you feel uneasy for wanting to drop off a team. And don't let yourself resort to bench antics to get through an unhappy situation. Sports are sports. When they are productive and enjoyable, squeeze them for every last drop. Enjoy them to the fullest. But when they become time-consuming and unproductive and not enjoyable, don't linger in a state of shock. Not all sports situations are good ones to be in. *Feel free to leave the unproductive situations*—not at the drop of a hat or at the first sign of difficulty or an obstacle but whenever you have a better use for your time and effort.

9.
Blame Yourself!

All sorts of things always go wrong. Big deal. We know that. That's the given in the athletic algebra. The only unknown is you.

It is apparently human nature to blame someone or something for failures and inadequacies. Typically, almost everyone blames the president or the governor or the mayor or the principal or the boss or the teacher...for whatever may have gone wrong. Athletes and fans, for the most part, do little to lift themselves beyond this phenomenon of scapegoatism. It's always someone else's fault, never yours.

In all fairness, however, since sports are so performance- and result-oriented and outcomes so definitive, coaches have probably done better than most others to reverse this tendency. Athletes are constantly being told not to blame others. They still do it, of course, but at least there is a lot of talk about the importance of not doing it.

Most every athlete has heard, many times, the idea that the player who messes up during the final play is NOT the player who lost the game. The game, we know, is won or lost throughout its duration, not just in the final seconds. This concept is so well known I hadn't planned to discuss it at all. There seems no reason to emphasize what has been said so often.

But if you seek excellence in athletics it is not merely necessary to avoid *saying* that someone is to blame for a failure or defeat, it is necessary to avoid *thinking* that someone is to blame.

I hope you grasp the immense difference in these two concepts. Many athletes congratulate themselves for not blaming a teammate in the course of actually blaming him. "I know one play doesn't lose a game, but that last fumble really hurt us." Flimsy disguise there. It fools no one.

Better, but still not adequate: "No one is to blame, we all had a part in it." (Thinking "That last fumble really hurt us.")

The avoidance of blame-placing is a start. But it's not enough. If you really want to be an athlete, a champion, work on your thinking. It really was *your* fault. What could *you* have done differently? Could you have shown more leadership before the game or been more encouraging in practice, thereby avoiding the critical point? How could you have helped your teammate hold onto the ball? Did you remind him, intelligently, not to fumble? (Note: If you simply told him to grip the ball with both hands, you may have actually contributed to making him more careful and less aggressive. Wouldn't it have helped him be tougher and to feel more aggressive if you had reminded him of how tough he is and of how much you'd hate to be the other team trying to get the ball from him?)

I am not claiming I know the best way to stop fumbles or to eliminate all other potential errors. But I am claiming that, if we are seeking excellence, we must search constantly for ways to improve, for ways to encourage, for ways to do whatever can be done to help teammates reach their potential and help the team win. When we stop searching and start to blame, or spend time thinking of blaming, we have lost another opportunity.

Ask yourself if you have reached the point in your athletic development where you can lead your team in scoring and play the best defense and still walk off a field having lost, feeling sincerely that the loss was ***your*** *fault.*

I am not talking about humbly *claiming* it was your fault or saying it was your fault in hopes that others will contradict your contention. I am talking about truly *feeling* it was your fault, because your focus is fully on what *you* must do. Meeting this demand isn't all that noble, selfless or wonderful for you. It is mere intelligence.

Teammates will make mistakes. No use being shocked by that. No use pointing it out. No use thinking about it. Reserves, starters, stars, and champions will all make mistakes. So will referees, umpires, and coaches. Playing conditions may not be right. All sorts of things always go wrong. Big deal. We know that. That's the given in the athletic algebra. The only unknown is you. What are *you* going to do? What could *you* have done better? Personally, with regard to your teammates, with regard to everything going on, how can you have the most positive impact possible?

Any other focus is a waste of time.

When you get to the point in your athletic career when you can walk off a field having been the big star but having emerged a loser, yet have your focus entirely on what *you* could have done better and how you can do better next time, you have arrived. You are an athlete. You think like a champion.

10.
Boredom in the Classroom

Going to school, if you listen to a lot of reformers, is supposed to be like playing Xbox or watching MTV...

If I were the principal of a school, and if I could hire all interesting, exciting, stimulating teachers, I wouldn't do it. I would instead hire a bunch of boring teachers to help train you for the life you are about to lead.

If there is one huge mistake being made whenever people talk these days about educational reform, it is the mistake of claiming that school subjects and teachers have to be more exciting, more relevant, more this and more that. Going to school, if you listen to a lot of reformers, is supposed to be like playing Xbox or watching MTV. But I don't buy it, and I don't think you should either.

It's not the subject's or teacher's responsibility to excite you, it's your responsibility to find ways to get excited. It's your responsibility to extract something interesting from subjects that initially seem boring. Learning to find excitement should be recognized as one of the primary purposes of school.

There are a couple of other issues here as well. First you have to realize that the less you know about a subject the more boring it is likely to seem. Or think of it this way: the presence of boredom usually indicates the ignorance of the person who is bored, not the lack of exciting content within the subject itself.

I like to use opera as an example because so many Americans are underexposed to this much-loved form of music. If, while switching channels someday, you happen to come upon a fat lady singing, you are likely to grunt something like "ugh," never stopping to think that there are thousands of people who have chosen that station and are sitting in front of their TV sets in admiration of that talent and of the beauty and feeling in that music.

You may be bored by opera simply because your exposure to it has been insufficient for you to get from it what others get. Rather than go on and on with this subject (it's one of my favorites) I'll just conclude with five basic reasons for the boredom most students feel.

1. Ignorance or underexposure to particular subjects.
2. Wimpdom or wimphood, take your pick. (Just too wimpy to grapple with a subject and to give it time to become interesting.)
3. Failure to develop sufficient curiosity and attention span to be able to deal with the unknown.
4. Narrow-mindedness. Concluding that some subject or teacher is worthless for a superficial reason. "The teacher is fat" or "the teacher talks funny" or "I just don't like that stuff" or "I'll never need that stuff anyway."
5. Square-ness (the opposite of well-roundedness). You simply don't like much of anything and you don't even know that your attitudes make you about half a human being. Square folks are often proud of their square-ness, which even sharpens their corners, if you know what I mean.

You could group all five reasons above under the heading of "stupid" and you wouldn't be too far off. If you are bored with school, get with it, Wimp. You have a lot of deficiencies to work on. You ain't got time to be bored.

11.
Building Team Morale

It's worth whatever effort you put into it. Playing on a team with great morale is one of the very best experiences that life has to offer.

There are a lot of ways to build team morale but the methods are not as important as the desire. If your team consists of a group of players who don't care about playing on a real team, a lot of methods will fail. On the other hand if a group of players really wants to work together for a common goal, usually it can be accomplished.

With that said, I think it is still important to consider several factors that can have a positive or negative impact on team building. During the course of any season, given the variety of personalities and motivations within any group, dozens of turning points (we may wish to call them opportunities) will determine the closeness, the cohesiveness, and the morale of the team.

Many of those turning points will involve the top players, the ones not really competing for spots because they have already established themselves as being among the best on the team. These players, the least dispensable ones, typically determine the course of the team. They can of course be influenced by anyone, including the not-so-talented players who are quite dispensable from a talent standpoint.

If you want to influence the morale of your team, whether you are one of the stars or not, it is important to concentrate your attention on the stars. This is not to say that the others are not important. It is just to say that the stars will set the tone; therefore, they are the best place to put your attention if you really want to have an impact. If the stars are willing to play together, be friends, work together, the rest will fall into place. If the stars have dissension among them, don't like each other, and don't want to work together, things are going to be difficult.

Knowing this, it is important to try to set the right tone early in the season before bickering starts, before tempers flare, before animosities ever get a chance to develop. (These types of problems can be corrected, but it is much easier to avoid them initially than to reverse them after they occur.)

How do you set the right tone early? It's simple. Encourage each other. Talk to each other. Compliment each other. Notice and comment on the contributions of others. Avoid criticizing and negative comments. Leave those to the coach. And get in the habit of interrupting others' negatives and of butting in with your own positives. It makes a difference.

You may find yourself on a team where some of the others, particularly the stars, are not thinking the way you are. Perhaps the stars on your team are negative, perhaps they bicker, complain, and argue. Then what?

You have to gang up on them. First, find a teammate who thinks the way you do and join forces. Then, approach the next most like-minded player together, two against one, and talk about the need for more positive comments, for teamwork and a positive team atmosphere. When you get player number three, the three of you need to gang up on the fourth most approachable player.

Gang up on these individuals in private. Not in front of others or any place where outside influences can interfere. Even a player considered an arrogant star will usually have difficulty facing four or five or six teammates who are committed, forceful, and of like-purpose. We're all human. The star may initially act unimpressed by your efforts while he concentrates on defending his own actions. But few people, star athletes included, are as tough, unchanging, and arrogant as they may first appear. In other words, press on. Make your points, and try to enlist his help in building the concept of team. Reverse each negative he throws out.

It's the coach's fault.
We plan to talk to the coach.

It's those other guys.
We plan to talk to them.

Joe won't do this or that.
We plan to get Joe to do this or that.

On the field you work together to bring about the encouraging, positive atmosphere that you want. Off the field, you work to eliminate the bases for others' accusations and negatives. I am not trying to pretend this is easy, but it's worth whatever effort you put into it. Playing on a team with great morale is one of the very best experiences life has to offer. And playing on a team racked with dissension is one of the worst.

Sometimes it may help to bring two problem players together to work out their differences, but when you do that you often run the risk of creating even more animosity as new things get said and new issues and problems get raised. That's why I would first do it behind the scenes. One on one and, if possible, two or three or eight against one.

You always have one thing going for you regardless of how things may appear: *nearly everyone in the world enjoys playing on a team with good spirit and cohesion.* If certain players seem committed to bringing about precisely the opposite it isn't because they hate teamwork and good team feelings, it's because something has gotten in the way. Someone doesn't like someone else. One player feels that another player is trying to get all the glory or all the shots or all the girls or guys.

Typically many players, perhaps most, will feel that the coach isn't doing things properly, that they aren't getting enough playing time or they aren't being used properly. Certainly, there are abundant opportunities for unhappiness and discord on any team. At any given time, several players are likely to be feeling these kinds of negatives. The only way to deal with them is to be as aware of them as possible, to commit to being consistently positive and supportive of other players, and to get as many teammates as possible to do the same.

You won't solve every problem. But if you can get a significant number of players to go along, you will solve a lot of problems and probably promote pretty good team morale.

There is one more consideration: win!

Many more problems arise when a team is losing than when it is winning. Of course everyone can't always be on a winning team. But you can have a positive impact on your chances of playing on a happy, winning team through preparation. Practice diligently in the off-season, get your teammates to work out together, and build team spirit before the season even starts, when it's easier and there are no games to lose or coaches criticizing you.

Remember, too, that when you are ganging up on one player, since this initiative can take place in the off-season, don't go at him with the group's agenda. Find out what he thinks. Give him the sense from the beginning that he's not part of the problem but that you want him to be part of the solution. You want his help. You are not there to criticize or change him.

This is basic sales technique, or basic human interaction. Common sense. Call it what you like. You need it. Building a real team may require the techniques of sales manuals, of management principles, and of any other course on human relations. You can't just leave it to chance or expect good things to just fall into place. Like a good marriage (so I've been told) you have to work at it.

You have to work at building team morale. And it never stops, though once you get things going positively, it gets a lot easier. Once things start going downhill, it gets harder.

Most important, be active. Don't leave team morale up to the coach, or the team captain, or the star ,or oldest or toughest or meanest player. It is up to *you*. Few players do all they can. Even the ones who seem to contribute the most on the field seldom take time to find out behind the scenes what's bugging the players who aren't contributing to a positive atmosphere.

Finally, don't get discouraged because one guy is constantly sabotaging your efforts. Get your gang together and work on him. When you finally get him with you, you may be in a situation more gratifying than almost any other that life has to offer. So keep working at it. Don't give up. As Charlie Brown once said, "Nothing difficult is ever easy."

12.
Celebrating Early

You don't start celebrating when it seems impossible for them to come back...

How many times have you watched a team make a big play to take the lead near the end of a game and then see players jump around with the joy and glee of champions with time enough on the clock for the other team to win the game?

Athletes tend to view these situations at the ends of games much differently from coaches, so I think you ought to be fully aware of how coaches feel. It could keep you out of the local funeral home and your coach out of court in a murder trial.

Almost nothing bothers a good coach more than a premature celebration. In football, these kinds of celebrations can result in penalties which make it suddenly easier for the opposing team to come back. In basketball, a technical foul can do the same. But I am not even talking here about penalties or fouls or other potential negatives that can result from excessive celebrations. I am talking about the mindset involved.

Coaches, usually from painful personal experience, understand the full meaning of the phrase, *it's not over until the fat lady sings*. Or, *it's not over until the i's are dotted, the t's are crossed, and the check has cleared the bank*. There are many ways to say what experienced people recognize too well: you just never know what strange things can happen, and you never want to know in just what bizarre, unimaginable ways a seemingly certain victory can be snatched from your hands.

As my father/coach always said, *"Let the bizarre unimaginable things happen to* ***them****! We don't celebrate until we're in the locker room. Period."* There could be six seconds left, our team at the free throw line having just hit the basket that put us up by six. Up by six, only six seconds left, us at the line.

How could we possibly lose? That's how a player thinks. But the coach? The coach wonders why you would even ask such a question. "My gawd," he might say, "imagine how terrible it would be if we learned the answer." Isn't it possible for us to miss the free throw, for us to somehow foul them, for someone in the crowd to go berserk and get a technical foul called? Next thing you know, they're stealing an inbound pass or we're stepping on a line, they're hitting a three point shot at the buzzer and going out with a victory they never, never, never should have had. "You would live with that your entire life." That's what the coach thinks because many do indeed live with such memories.

Take Neil McGeachy, for example. He was an interim basketball coach at Duke University for one year in the 1970s. The team had seventeen seconds left on the clock in a game against their big rival, the University of North Carolina, and an eight point lead. Eight points. Back in those days there was no three-point shot. Impossible you say? Yeah, but it happened, to good players. A basket reduced their lead to six points. A steal and a quick basket cut it to four. And there were still about twelve seconds left. No way, right? I don't remember the details (fortunately, I didn't play in the game) but I remember a shot at the buzzer tying the game and the University of North Carolina winning in overtime.

Impossible? Seemingly so. But there are thousands of fans in the Carolinas who can tell you what happened second by second, and that was twenty years ago. People just don't forget a sure win turned into a loss. The players who played in that game will never forget it. The coach will live with that memory forever. It's not a happy one. It didn't need to happen. And it wouldn't have happened if the players had assumed it might.

When the team went up by eight with less than a half minute left, the fans went berserk. People were jumping around, and the players themselves had that celebratory feeling. You can't control people in the crowd but you certainly can control a team. And you don't celebrate until it's over. *You don't start celebrating when it* ***seems*** *impossible for them to come back. You start celebrating when it* ***is*** *impossible for them to come back.* What a difference.

If you are a young player this emphasis will mean even less to you. You simply haven't experienced enough amazing, incredible, no-way-it's-possible comebacks to have the proper reverence for what I am saying. The next time you have a twenty point lead with only three minutes left you will feel as though it's okay to celebrate then. So what if some guy in some book says not to?

And in that particular case, you may turn out right. You probably will. Most twenty point margins do stand up for three minutes. Incredible, unimaginable things just don't happen on a daily basis. You're right again. But if it happens to you just once...once is too many times.

As every coach will tell you, why take that chance? Why have to sit back later and anguish over how the impossible happened? Why not just take the easy way out, control your emotions, and play the game to the best of your ability right up until the buzzer goes off? Why not just decide right now that your victory celebrations will take place in the locker room, not on the field?

There's nothing wrong with a high five, a raised fist in the end zone, a hug at the end of the pool. If you think about it, you'll know what a premature celebration is, and you'll be smart not to engage in one, ever. Before the gun sounds, best to just go about the business of winning. You'll have plenty of time to celebrate after the game. But first things first. Mark the 'W' on the schedule, then do your dancing.

13.
Cheap Success

Ain't no one gonna be around to fix things when the breaks go against you, which they will soon enough.

There's no such thing, in reality, as cheap success. What I'm talking about here are those time when you manage to get lucky.

In tennis, your ball hits the net and just drops over. In basketball, you miss your aim by three feet but the ball banks in off the glass. In baseball, you swing with all your might and the ball rolls thirty-five feet down the third base line and just stops there.

Game, set, match. Two points. A single.

In tennis, people apologize. In basketball and baseball they smile with embarrassment. But I don't think any of that is necessary. In every sport, you'll get your share of bad breaks, too. Balls sail 330 feet over the wall, but just barely go foul. Balls that are hit or shot perfectly, or so it seems, just barely miss.

You can feel embarrassed by a lucky shot if you like, and I suppose that permits you to feel justified in throwing a tantrum when what-should-have-been doesn't pan out. But isn't it better to just realize that you'll get some good breaks and some bad breaks along the way? Why give them any attention at all? Focus fully on your performance and don't feel embarrassed when you get one you didn't really deserve. Ain't no one gonna be around to "fix" things when the breaks go against you, which they will soon enough. So take all the luck you can get, in stride. You deserve it. And more.

14.
Chess-Game Vision

The scene was a blur of action. Multi-colored shirts seemed to be rotating around the court and there seemed to be defenders everywhere…

One of the main reasons an athlete practices and plays over and over again is to learn to see the action unfold clearly, almost as if it were on camera in slow motion. This I call chess-game vision, essentially the ability to see the whole field or court at once, and watch a play unfold, slowly. It only happens with experience. In fact, sometimes you seem to have it on one level only to realize that you don't have it when you move up to the next level. Making this transition is often impossible for athletes who may excel in their backyards but can't seem to perform the same heroics on a school team. What exactly is this vision thing? It is hard to define, but I think a few examples may be useful to you.

Once at my summer basketball program for point guards a young athlete told me that the concepts I was teaching were good for drills but they couldn't be used in games because "the action in games happens too fast to do all that stuff." The idea of getting double-teamed and still looking for her four teammates—and perhaps calling one particular teammate into a better position to make a pass easier to complete—seemed just impossible to her. How could she be searching for her teammates and talking and choosing just the right one and then telling that one teammate to move, when two defenders were swiping and pushing and grabbing for the ball? "You only have five seconds before they blow the whistle for a tie-up," she said. Like most inexperienced athletes she failed to realize that good players do indeed do all that stuff (in a lot less than five seconds) and once you are experienced it doesn't seem as though the action happens so fast. The defenders' efforts don't seem so all-consuming, and your own teammates' positioning is something you're very aware of before the double-team even arrives. There is not only time to "do all that stuff," there's even time to motion to a different player to race down the opposite side before throwing the pass, and maybe still a few moments extra to pull a sandwich from your back pocket and catch a bite to eat.

During the first real basketball game I played in junior high school I had the sensation that I was on a merry-go-round. The scene was a blur of action. Multi-colored shirts seemed to be rotating around the court and there seemed to be defenders everywhere I looked. Dozens of them at least. Through most of the game my biggest worry was that I would get a pass and dribble to the wrong basket. I kept reminding myself which basket was ours. Ten years later it never occurred to me to wonder which basket was ours. If the other team had only four players back on defense, the imbalance would be as obvious as the sofa suddenly missing from your living room. By then it didn't take counting. For some basketball players, this kind of vision never comes. They spend their lives dribbling down courts unaware of even having an advantage. They rely strictly on talent. For others, the vision comes rather easily (though always after playing a lot of games).

Two of the best examples of this phenomenon come from professional football.

A star linebacker once explained this concept on TV without being asked about it while talking about the frustration of playing against super quarterback Joe Montana who played most of his career with the San Francisco 49ers.

"He could read defenses so well, you felt foolish lining up in some disguised coverage. When he took the snap, he seemed to see so clearly what we were doing that it felt just plain stupid to line up away from the positions we needed to be in. We never seemed to fool him at all. It was like he would drop back smiling at us, knowing immediately that we were already scrambling to recover into our designed coverage. Most quarterbacks would get confused and feel rushed by our disguises, but Montana just seemed to be out there playing the game in slow-motion, seeing everything we were doing before we even had a chance to do it."

An old NFL Highlights film contains a segment I have heard several times, caught by a sideline microphone near Terry Bradshaw of the Pittsburgh Steelers. Bradshaw would go on to lead the Steelers to four Super Bowl titles but at this point in his career he was just getting used to playing the fast-paced NFL game. His youthful exuberance was obvious as he excitedly told one of his teammates, a lineman I think, about his sudden revelation just after completing a touchdown pass. "It always seemed like people were running all over the place, and now suddenly I'm back there, and I can just see it all. I can see everything, like it all just slowed down." The teammate had hardly any reaction. He either didn't like Bradshaw or, more likely, just didn't understand the concept that Bradshaw was so excited about. A lineman may not have to see the whole picture unfold slowly. He may just have to knock down the man in front of him. I don't know. But the big guy did not share Bradshaw's excitement at all, though Bradshaw couldn't help sharing his joy. Something spectacular had happened. Bradshaw was more than just elated, his excitement was pouring out over like a flood. The game had suddenly, in an instant and for all time, slowed down for him. He was clearly astonished at his sudden change in vision.

If you haven't reached this point in your career, if you don't understand this concept, I can just say be patient and keep working at your sport. Because when it comes it seems to come all at once. You don't have it at all, and suddenly you have it completely. You'd think that something so important would come bit by bit but it doesn't. Terry Bradshaw's excited sideline chatter is enlightening. He was a college star. He had already started and played a whole year with the Steelers. He had already thrown some touchdown passes. But he didn't yet "see." He was out there doing his best, putting his wonderful ability into play and sometimes even credited with winning a big game, but he wasn't yet in control of the chess-game aspect of his sport. The game had not yet slowed down for him, although his photo was already on the covers of magazines. He was a star, but every game was a kind of crapshoot, with him hoping for the best, hoping to win with talent.

When you suddenly get the vision, you still don't have any guarantee of winning championships or awards, but it sure does feel good and it is certainly worth working and waiting for. It's a tremendous advantage when an athlete adds chess-game vision to talent.

15.
Choking

Not too many athletes or teams actually choke, though most teams gain and lose leads several times per game.

Choking may be the most talked-about, yet least substantive issue in sports. TV commentators and newspaper columnists, and of course talk show callers seem to love this concept. Almost anyone or any team that blows a lead is said to have choked. But statistics I have seen do not support this notion. If you check your team records you will probably find that you got behind by a dozen points in the first quarter as often as you lost twelve-point leads in the final quarter. Yet no one accuses a team that starts off badly as having choked. They simply didn't do well.

Athletes and teams often don't do well. End-of-game nervousness doesn't seem to cause more bad plays than occur any other time in the game, it simply gets more attention. In other words, *don't beat yourself up or consider yourself a choker just because you happen to lose a lead sometime.* Teams that go from three-point leads to six-point deficits early in a game rarely draw any conclusions from those nine-point swings. But teams and athletes that suffer a nine-point swing and lose a game near the end may label themselves chokers and actually contribute (because of their negative beliefs) to losing leads in the future when otherwise victories would have occurred.

Illogical thinking of this kind—creating fallacious casual relationships—can be dangerous in a variety of settings. Some athletes might blame a loss on seeing a black cat. "Yesterday I saw a black cat and today we lost."

No doubt about that one, is there? The fact that one team's offensive line outweighed the other team's defensive line by seventy pounds per man may also have had something to do with it.Be careful about the conclusions you draw and the labels you put on things. Not too many athletes or teams actually choke, though most teams gain and lose leads several times per game.

If you do fear choking, and fear that your muscles tighten and your nerves rattle and your performance suffers at the end of big games, here are a few things to consider.

1. Everyone gets nervous at the end of big games. No harm in that. It happens to even big stars. Remember (see the section on "Nervousness") nervousness is natural. Invite it in, don't try to avoid it. Embrace it. You can play well in spite of some rattling nerves. Athletes do it all the time.
2. Remind yourself what got you to where you are. If you have a lead near the end of a big game, how did you get it? Were you aggressive? Did you execute sharply? Whatever got you the lead is what can get you the victory. "Dance with who brung ya," as the old saying goes. Stick with what got you there. Doing what you've been doing doesn't guarantee you a victory but it certainly makes sense to concentrate on doing what has worked.
3. Take your attention off yourself and your own performance and concentrate on lifting and inspiring your teammates. Not only will your encouragement help them get past their jitters, the action and intensity of your efforts will likely have a positive impact on your jitters as well.
4. Remind yourself that you are playing a sport, that failure and defeat are not the worst things in the world. They happen to everyone. And even when you're down, you have a chance. At least go after it. Go for it. Carpe diem, seize the day. Put yourself in a frame of mind to seek a victory aggressively rather than to watch the clock, hoping the time ticks away before you have a chance to lose.

Most athletes and teams contribute to their own losses when they are tentative and hopeful instead of staying aggressive and demanding. Consider the running back who goes from wanting to slash through a line like a blazing bowling ball knocking down pins to concentrating on not fumbling. The difference in thinking is so dramatic that the fumble suddenly becomes more, not less, likely. Although it is natural at the end of a game you are winning to start thinking about not messing up, you have to think through that trap and get your mind back on splattering those pins against the walls.

Remember that what others may call choking is usually just a perfectly logical outcome based on nothing more than ability or lack of it. When a 50 percent free throw shooter goes to the line at the end of a big game, he has a 50 percent chance of missing. When he misses, did he choke? Maybe. But he misses often—at home, in warm ups, and at the beginning of games. So it can't be such a surprise, or necessarily a choke, when he misses at the end of a big game.

If you are an excellent shooter, chances are, even if you feel nervous you will succeed most of the time (not every time) at the end of big games. If you are a poor shooter feeling nervous you will likely fail most of the time at the end of big games, though occasionally you will surprise people and score.

Remember, too, that choking or not doing well at crunch time is also a function of experience. If you find yourself in the first big game of your life, you are indeed more likely to mess up than an athlete who has been in a dozen big games. There is no way around that. Just do the best you can and hope for luck. And if you lose or blow it, I'm sorry, but there are no guarantees of success for athletes. Sports success goes most often to athletes who persist, who overcome adversity, and who learn from failure. If you are lucky enough to be able to avoid having to learn the hard way, congratulations. Write a book. But console yourself if you do mess up. There are better days ahead, and just about every champion has had to say at one time or another, "Oh well, we'll get 'em next year."

Choking or not choking, when all is said and done, is tightly connected to the skills and habits you have developed over a long period of time. The grand coaches' cliché has practical meaning over and over again: the way you practice is the way you will (usually) play the game, beginning, middle and end. *If you want to limit the chances that you will choke in a big game, practice, practice, practice. Improve, improve, improve.* Develop a habit of diligence and excellence in practice every day, and it is very likely to carry you through the games.

16.
Coachability

You can try your best—after the season—to get the coach fired if you feel that strongly. But during the season...

Every coach is concerned with how coachable an athlete is. How concerned should a player be with a coach's coachability? I think it ought to be crucial to you, even if from a purely selfish standpoint.

If you happen to love your coach, love listening to his pep talks and philosophies, and want to do everything your coach says in the best possible way, you are lucky and will probably be able to listen attentively and flatteringly and do your best effortlessly. In other words, you are probably a joy to coach and you need not concern yourself further with this subject.

But what if you don't like your coach? What if you don't particularly agree with the things he says? What if you think he doesn't know what he's talking about?

My answer to all those questions is the same: So what? There is no need for your likes and dislikes, your personality preferences, and your philosophical tastes to get in the way of your performance in a sport. And be sure of this: if you are in constant conflict with your coach, and showing it, your performance will suffer. You won't get things done as well as possible when your focus is on conflict, and the coach won't instruct you and spend the time to make sure your abilities can be used fully.

You don't have to be a wimp to be coachable. You are free to disagree, to talk to your coach, to try to get him to see things your way. But once the talk is over, your job is to nod, accept, and do the best you can under the circumstances.

I'll go a step further. You can try your best—after the season—to get the coach fired if you feel that strongly. But during the season, your best course of action is to be as coachable as possible, to work with your coach to bring about the best results you can under the circumstances.

It's not a question of love and understanding, kindness and goodness and all that. It is mere practicality. If you are playing a sport it will be to your advantage to give your coach the feeling that you're working with him rather than against him. When he starts feeling that you're working against him he is going to do less than his best, or he is going to quit letting you play, or his own focus and performance will be even more distracted. (If he was bad to begin with, wait till you see how bad he'll get once he realizes you're against him.)

It doesn't have to be a joy to be coached in order for you to work toward being considered a joy to coach. In fact, in many ways it may be good for you to have a coach who forces you to make a big effort rather than having someone who is your idea of the perfect coach. The world, as you can no doubt guess, is hardly full of perfect coaches and bosses and supervisors, so why get so pushed out of shape simply because your coach isn't exactly what you hoped for?

And guess what? Very few players think they have the ideal coach, even those players who are coached by national celebrity coaches. After all, coaching is a tough profession. With all the time and intensity involved in a player-coach relationship, some problems along the way are inevitable. But don't let those problems allow you to lapse into negative thinking. Forget about the ideal coach and spend your time thinking about being the ideal player.

Consider your not-so-great coach as good training for life, and get on with it. Practice being coachable, and a joy to coach, and focus on the best performance possible.

17.
Communication

If you aren't trying to improve your communication skills and trying to have more of an impact on the atmosphere you are playing in, you are neglecting a big part of sport.

Good, intelligent communication is important in just about everything, not just sports. This is a very broad and important subject about which many books have been written, but I am going to touch on just a few ideas for you to consider.

The essential point to understand is that it is necessary to make a constant effort to improve your communication. Teammates need encouragement and help. Coaches need reinforcement and help. You can add much to your sports experience by being tuned in to your teammates and coaches and by knowing how to respond, what to say, how to say it. And communication skills, like sports skills, submit to practice. The more you practice them, the better they get.

If you are one of those athletes who just shuts up and plays, and claims you're not into a bunch of talk, think again. No one is demanding that you be into a bunch of talk. But you should be aware of how valuable communication is. The star has a concern, the star in a slump has another, the former star on the bench has another; and the reserves always have a special set of feelings and concerns. If you are oblivious to your teammates' issues or make no attempt to respond to any of them, you will soon be labeled a selfish player and you will be part of the problem yourself.

This does *not* mean you have to take each teammate by the hand and sympathize with every fragile feeling. It just means you have to be aware of what's going on around you and be willing to respond and communicate feelings and ideas. If you do this, your team will win more often. If you fail to do it, you will lose more often. It's that simple.

The complexity of human communication is what gives *Homo sapiens* special opportunities, enables us to be inspired, and lets us work together to accomplish a goal. If you aren't trying to improve your communication skills and aren't trying to have more of an impact on the atmosphere you are playing in, you are neglecting a big part of sport.

Talk to your teammates and coaches. Learn not only to say what you think and to express your thoughts clearly, but also to listen to your teammates and coaches and to understand what they are trying to express. This effort will serve you well off the field later in life, for your whole life. You can never be too good a communicator, and sports participation offers many excellent opportunities to use communication skills in order to improve performance. Let me give just one example.

Every practice or training session has tired, bored, unhappy, unfocused, and uninspired athletes...to varying degrees. To what extent can you turn them, your teammates, into energized, tuned-in, happy, focused, and excited athletes? Surely you realize that athletes who practice diligently will improve more and play better in games. So, how do you help make that happen? You communicate. You encourage. You notice things and respond. You *pick up your teammates constantly with whatever kinds of encouragement and urgings are most likely to work on them*. If you keep to yourself and remain quiet, you're fooling yourself. You are failing to do things that could, and constantly do, make a big difference in the results of future games. Your communication in games, of course, matters too. But never so much as it does during the preparation for those games.

Finally, let me close this section with a question that raises an entirely different issue. How well do you communicate with yourself? What do you tell yourself when you confront an obstacle, when things don't go the way you hoped, when people do things that initially disappoint you? How good are you at communicating with yourself, at getting yourself to respond intelligently and reasonably to whatever happens to you?

Are you accustomed to telling yourself, "I can handle this, this is just another obstacle to be overcome, no sweat, no big deal, I'll take care of it"? Communicating intelligently and inspiringly with yourself is even more important than communicating intelligently and inspiringly with your teammates. You're unlikely to be able to reach them if you can't reach yourself.

Remember, practice makes perfect. You have to practice communicating intelligently with yourself, and with others, if you want to be good at it. And you certainly ought to want to be good at it. Good communication is an essential ingredient of championship performance. Do you need some actual evidence to get you started? Before practice, talk with your teammates about specific tactics or skills to help them get focused and to get them to want to work hard. In the training room or at the start of practice use humor to get players' minds off sore feet or nagging injuries. Encourage them throughout a practice. Use specific names, compliment. Point out good things during and after practice to the team and to individuals. Notice things and comment on them. Everything will make a difference. Go for it!

18.
Complaining

Complaints nearly always sound just as foolish, and amusing, as they really are once they are replayed...

Have you ever stopped to consider the fact that it would be possible to go through your whole life without ever bothering to complain about anything? Many people have made commitments to do just that and they love the results. So would you.

When you catch yourself in the midst of a complaint, you know you are hardly at your very best. You're mumbling, whining, dragging life through the mud. The condition you're complaining about makes life bad enough. Why drag yourself down even further by complaining about it? Does this mean you have to smilingly accept everything that ever happens? Of course not. You are free to fight for your beliefs, to organize people to help you, to point out injustice, foolishness, stupidity, or evil whenever and wherever you find it. Just don't bother complaining about it.

This may seem more like a life lesson than a sports lesson, but it probably belongs in every book where excellence is a goal. Certainly it belongs in a sports book because sports seem to offer many opportunities for complaining. The weather, the conditions, the administration, the referees, the coaches, the field, the fans, the players. Every aspect of sports is ripe for complaining if that's what you choose to focus on. But let's assume you don't. I'm going to figure, if you've gotten this far in the book, that you've already made your commitment and your concern is what to do with your teammates and maybe even coaches who are often complaining.

What can you do? You can't avoid them, you are with them every day. And what if explaining this simple logic and offering some words of encouragement—or attempting to change the subject—just doesn't work on them? What can you do with teammates who complain?

Tape them!

So you don't cause ill feeling, tell them you are doing a paper for a sociology class or a study for a science project. Carry a mini recorder with you and be ready to turn on the tape any time they start complaining. When the tape is replayed, other people, even avid complainers, will enjoy it immensely. Complaints nearly always sounds just as foolish, and amusing, as they really are once they are replayed.

However, people can become very reluctant to complain when they know their complaints may be passed on to others. If you don't have your tape recorder with you, squint and tilt your head in some special way reserved only for "complaint recognition and recording." If they fail to get the message, beg them not to forget what they are saying so you can record it later for your paper.

And, hey, if none of this works, why not really write a paper? It will enable you to think of all those stupid comments with amusement and as research.

19.
Conditioning

Few athletes are overjoyed at the thought of conditioning. It's tough. It's demanding. It causes pain. But everyone has to do it.

Conditioning is crucial to success in every sport. The best technique and the most ability won't help you win if you are too tired to use them. Most everyone realizes this so I don't plan to spend any more time on the obvious. To be a champion, get in great physical condition. And now, let's cover a generally-avoided aspect of conditioning: dread.

Most athletes, even excellent ones, even champions, have a certain distaste for conditioning. Sometimes the distaste is more than that; it's fear, hate, boredom, dread, Regardless of what it is for you, don't worry about it. Don't conclude that you are not a real champion just because you don't love the idea of running sprints up and down a field in the hot summer sun. If athletes' minds could be read in the midst of particularly difficult conditioning sessions, people might be shocked at how many were entertaining the idea of quitting the team. "Is this worth it?" "Do I really want to do this?" "Why don't I just walk back to the shower room and turn in my gear?" "This must cause me more pain than it causes the others."

It's a good thing athletes are too tired to talk to each other during especially difficult conditioning sessions. If they did, the whole team would just mutiny occasionally, just walk off the field and tell the coach to shove it. I make this clear because I think athletes ought to feel comfortable with their hates, dreads, and fears. Hating conditioning doesn't make you a loser, it merely makes you just like almost every other athlete who ever strove for perfection.

So now what? There are some things you can do to minimize the pain, and there are some other realizations that may at least give you a different perspective as you struggle to prepare.

First, start sooner. Too many athletes let themselves get too far out of shape. Then when the first day of official practice begins the physical demands are pure hell. With some better planning and some advance conditioning on your own, the demands won't seem so great. In other words, even a lazy athlete can benefit from planning and considering the big picture. Why put yourself through hell? Start in advance. Work up to your ideal weight and endurance level little by little. It will take more time but it will be less painful.

Second, consider the purpose of conditioning. Some of you may increase your hatred of conditioning because the whole time you're out of breath, sore, aching, and feeling terrible physically, you're thinking the pain is unnecessary. Perhaps your season is months away. Why go so crazy so soon? Hasn't your coach ever heard of pacing? If you let yourself get angry or disgusted, or if you lose respect for your coach, the physical effort becomes much more difficult.

Have you considered the fact that conditioning may have a purpose other than just getting you in shape to perform? It does. One of the best uses of "physical punishment" (no use continuing with this conditioning charade) is for team building. *Many coaches realize that forcing you and your teammates to share pain will enable you to get closer as a team.* Shared pain, like it or not, is an effective glue for building team cohesion.

You may be aware of the lifelong friendships that develop between soldiers who have been in a war together. That is the ultimate shared pain; physical deprivation and fear for your life. These experiences overcome every sort of family or racial barrier, and unite people who normally would have many differences.

In the same way, a team may include many athletes who

are jealous of each other, competitive (of course), and irritated with each other's habits and idiosyncrasies. Athletes who must be together under intense circumstances and over a long period of time have abundant opportunities to dislike each other and engage in petty squabbles. But let them share pain together (or put them through hell, as a coach might say) and they are likely to emerge as friends. The pettiness will disappear, the jealousies will vanish. Not always, but most of the time.

Show me a team racked with petty jealousies and usually I'll show you a team that isn't working hard enough. The average athlete typically sees conditioning from a strictly personal point of view, or from a strictly physical point of view, never guessing that a coach may be sitting in a coaches' clinic hearing a lecture on how to promote team spirit through rigorous conditioning.

If you were aware of these kinds of things coaches think about, you would likely put aside your own petty complaints and focus on the job at hand. Few athletes are overjoyed at the thought of conditioning. It's tough. It's demanding. It causes pain. But everyone has to do it. You can spend your time more wisely by trying to think up ways of making it more tolerable. Concentrate on details. Envision results. Try to put your mind on other things. Focus on others. Observe things going on around you. Recall a poem. (Yes, right during the toughest part of conditioning practice.)

There is no magic I know of. You try things. You keep trying things. What works today probably won't work tomorrow. Just stay mentally active. Good conditioning pays off. Whatever you have to do to get through it, do it. At some point later you'll be happy you did (if for no other reason, just for the pride of knowing you did it).

If you ever come across a bestseller promising great physical condition without any effort, don't buy it. It's a hoax. There is no easy way. But there are better ways than others. Find your own ways. Millions of athletes would like to know. In the meantime, relax in the knowledge that all athletes are in this together. We all go through the pain of conditioning. It's the main reason we deserve the respect of people who just sit all day in hammocks and drink Kool-Aid.

20.
Confidence

"Yeah, I know that Goliath fellow is big. But how's he ever gonna reach the kid? Last I heard, Michelangelo was already taking measurements for a big statue he's doin' up in Florence..."

Confidence is what comes along after you have trained diligently and learned to perform flawlessly. A lot of people seem to think you can get confidence through some gimmick or mental technique.

"You just gotta have confidence in yourself," they say. "You can do it."

"Not if I can't do it, I can't."

If your figure skating routine includes a maneuver that causes a spill half the time in practice, then you really don't have a right to go into competition feeling confident that you can do it.

Maybe you can, maybe you'll be lucky. You can expect to be lucky about half the time and unlucky the other half, except that the added tension and pressure of competition will likely push those figures to 25 percent lucky and 75 percent unlucky. Gee, how unlucky that tension and pressure should do such a thing to a nice person like you.

You probably get my point. You can be confident that you will perform in competition about as well as you do in training, plus some for adrenalin, minus some for pressure. So there's really no reason for having any more confidence than precisely what you should have. *Your confidence level mirrors your skill level,* and that's as it should be. There's nothing much more foolish than the confident chatter of a mediocre performer going into battle against a champion.

When David went out to meet Goliath, it wouldn't have made much sense for him to assure everyone that everything was fine if he'd forgotten his rock and sling that day. But with his weapon, and in spite of the size difference, the smart money may have been on David all along. Anyone who watched him each day knock targets off fence posts at fifty yards probably had a pretty good feeling as they watched him walk out there.

You can picture the sideline whispers:

"Yeah I know that Goliath fellow is big. But how's he ever gonna reach the kid? Last I heard, Michelangelo was already taking measurements for a big statue he's doin' up in Florence. I'm tellin' you, the kid can hurl a rock so hard he can knock the head off a horse without even entering the pasture. My money's on the kid."

Hopefully through the humor you catch the compelling point about confidence and its relation to ability. You deserve to be just as confident as your ability level warrants. And you don't want to be more confident than that.

The last thing you want to see is a rock- and sling-less David walking out there telling you everything's gonna be just fine. It's not. If the ability isn't there, the confidence is completely unwarranted.

Many parents have asked me over the years, "Can you help my son? All he lacks is confidence." My reaction is always the same though I usually don't say it out loud. "No, you're wrong. Your son lacks ability."

To summarize: Don't strive for confidence, strive for ability, talent, technique. When the ability is there, the confidence will follow just the way it should.

21.
Digging Deep Down

The big moment is always now…

Sports commentators often talk about athletes who are able to dig deep down for that little bit extra. When everything is going bad, when your strength is gone, when the game is surely lost, or when you really need that last little bit, you're supposed to have the ability to dig deep down. It's a nice concept. And when you do it you have a certain sense of it. You ask yourself, "Is that what they mean? Did I dig deep down this time?"

If that's all there is to it, fine. But there's a reason I am skeptical about this phrase. I think it causes a lot of athletes to pace themselves, leaving energy and effort in reserve that needs to be used during the game, not saved. I don't think the phrase was ever intended to include pacing yourself or saving yourself.

If you want to be a real athlete, an athlete who is proud of your effort and of your will to win and so on, you need to think in terms of digging deep down constantly, not just at the end of big games. Once you get yourself to the point where you are constantly digging deep down, constantly summoning more energy, constantly demanding from yourself that little bit extra, you are the athlete you want to be.

If a commentator then comes along and thinks he or she recognized that you dug deep down at the end of some big game, fine. You'll deserve whatever credit you get. Just don't leave it down there languishing while you wait for the big moment. The big moment is always now. And the best way to be credited for the ability to dig deep down when it really matters is to cultivate the ability to dig deep down even when it doesn't.

22.
Doldrums

Rarely will you find anyone whose "mental state graph" shows just an unwavering horizontal line.

Particularly in practice.

Probably every athlete who ever caught a ball had some sense of the joy others get from sports. Adults will entertain a small child for hours by rolling a ball back and forth across the floor. There is something inherently fun in catching and throwing a ball, even when not playing a game. Of course, add competition and rules of play, and you have the excitement of the World Series, the World Cup, the Stanley Cup, the Super Bowl and so on.

But those big events are tips of icebergs. Down below the surface or behind the TV screen are all the hours of practice, of sacrifice, of effort expended to reach those points and, more often, to reach much lower points.

In this larger area below the big games are the doldrums of practice. Everyone starts off in sports with grand pictures of success and celebration; that excitement gets quickly channeled into years of energy, sweat and sacrifice in tiny gyms, on bare fields, and over cracked pavement.

Often these efforts are not fun, and when they aren't most of us suddenly wonder what we're doing wrong. Aren't sports supposed to be fun? Why am I experiencing these doldrums? Why does this seem like such a chore?

Isn't there a book somewhere entitled, "How to Make Sports

Practices Fun and Enjoyable Every Day of the Season?" No, there isn't a book like that. And if there ever is, it won't do inside what it claims on the cover. It can't. Practices, sometimes, simply are not going to be fun. Working to achieve, sometimes, simply is not going to be fun. So, what can you do when the practice doldrums hit?

First, realize that nothing strange is happening. You are experiencing what every athlete in every sport experiences often, at least those who are really serious and trying to improve.

Second, try to take your focus off yourself and put it onto your teammates. If you are feeling the doldrums, your teammates might be, too, although athletes do not always feel the same things at the same time. That's not bad. Maybe that means you can pick up a teammate when you aren't so down, and maybe that teammate can pick you up when you are.

You can try a lot of things, some may work better than others. You have to experiment. Team meetings sometimes help, vocal encouragement sometimes helps. Other times you may have to go to your coach with a suggestion for some very different activity. Sometimes you just have to suck it up and say, "Here are the doldrums, I knew they'd be coming."

Rhythmic clapping often works wonders at particular times. That must be the reason that generals used to have bands playing when the soldiers were marching into battle. The rhythms were good all by themselves. They added something. The next time your practice has deteriorated into silent doldrums try to get just five or six teammates to clap along with you. Smiles will usually appear; at the least you'll get a different sense of what you are doing.

Your doldrums may come when you are practicing alone so there may not be others nearby to help you out of your funk. Then what? Use your imagination. To the best of your ability, transport yourself into a whole different world. Imagine you are in the finals of a big event, on nationwide TV. Imagine whatever you need to imagine to transform the nature of your experience. If you are oppressed by the heat, by fatigue, by the length of time you've been out there working, or by the length of time you still have to go because of a commitment you have made, you are not using your mind well enough. You have to make a constant effort mentally to take your mind off the negatives and keep them on more positive, energizing ideas.

I'm not claiming it's always easy. But it has to be a constant effort, a constant competition with yourself to improve not just your skills but also your ability to work enthusiastically at improving your skills. Obviously, *the more energy and enthusiasm you can put into your daily efforts, the more productive your efforts will be.* Therefore, if you are truly striving for success, you can't afford to just gut through the drudgery." Sure, that sounds noble. Congratulations for your toughness. But to use your time more productively, to improve at a faster rate, you need to try to transform your experience.

Do whatever it takes. Imagine championship ceremonies, imagine beautiful women (or beautiful men), imagine you are locked in combat with a competitor just like you, play against the superstars in your mind. Most important, realize that doldrums happen to everyone and that you have to try to keep minimizing them. The worse the doldrums get, the more you have to challenge yourself to try some new approach to transforming them.

While making your best effort to transform or minimize them, *take solace in this: doldrums don't seem to have staying power.* If you charted any athlete's mental state during the off season you would find, in most cases, a very up and down, cyclical pattern. Rarely will you find anyone whose mental state graph would show an unwavering horizontal line. Doldrums seem to come and go. So, when the doldrums are at their doldriest (don't use this word on the SAT), be patient. Transform them if you can. But if you can't, just wait. Chances are they'll burn themselves out.

Why not make your own mental state graph, and start charting, daily, your mental attitude? See for yourself. When you're up, indicate why or what put you up there. When you're down, label that, too. You may learn some valuable lessons about yourself, your efforts, and about "Up-ness" and "Down-ness." (Also see "Imagination.")

23.
Dream Places

A quiet place where you can conjure up your aspirations and feel them take shape...

Every athlete can benefit from having a dream place. Almost all peoples in all times, regardless of religion or lack thereof, have had their own kinds of shrines, monuments, or hallowed grounds. Why?

These special places are imbued with hope and aspiration. You might say they embody the dreams of the people, or the best of what the people strive for. Sometimes the place is the tomb of a nation's greatest hero, the man or woman who stood up against great odds and prevailed against an enemy. Sometimes the place surrounds a work of art. In America we have dozens, maybe hundreds of national dream places. The Washington Monument, the Lincoln Memorial, the Statue of Liberty, Monticello, Mount Vernon, Martin Luther King Jr.'s tomb. These places point to greatness, to the belief in achievement, to the potential in us all. The Halls of Fame at Cooperstown, Canton, and Springfield and others have this same kind of meaning for athletes.

But all of these are *national* dream places. This section is about *personal* dream places. Your dream place. When I was growing up, mine was a dark outdoor basketball court behind an old condemned school. Weeds grew on all sides, and the court pavement was cracked in several places where grass grew through. It was hardly Madison Square Garden, but I could conjure up places like that just by standing in the dark and gazing up through the net and rim at the stars.

Quiet. Alone. A little kid just standing in the dark, looking up at the stars. Somehow it wound my goals and aspirations into the whole universe and touched me with a dash of greatness. I was aware of being under the same sky as everyone else in the world, looking up with hope for the future at the same stars Julius Caesar saw when he considered crossing the Rubicon, the same stars George Washington and Thomas Jefferson looked at when they were trying to turn a grand idea into a real nation.

Some people will read this and think this section is way out of line for a book about sports. Caesar? That's a pizza, isn't it? And what's this Rubicon thing? Is it something like anchovies? I don't want any of those. But I think dreaming is a huge part of sports; I'm surprised there isn't a whole book on it. Maybe some day there will be.

For now, make sure you have a dream place. A quiet place where you can conjure up your aspirations and feel them take shape. *It's when you feel bigger, part of the universe, that your goals and plans really get focused and your mind seems to drive you toward fulfillment.* It's a whole other dimension of awareness that makes the hard practices, the sore feet, blisters, bumps, and broken bones all okay, part of the master plan.

Most athletes will understand what I'm talking about. I am merely reminding you not to shortchange this part of your development. The inspiration and energy that come out of your dream place are what turn your efforts and techniques into championship performance. Go there often. Keep renewing your dreams.

24.
DUMJOX

Dress up in coat and tie one evening per week and carry a briefcase into the main college library to study…

Dumb jocks. Stupid athletes. If you're victimized by stereotyping and you don't like negative generalizations—if you don't like being classified as a dumb jock—make sure you aren't part of the problem.

The name came about for a reason. In huge numbers, athletes around the nation sit in classrooms where they don't want to be and wait for games they want to play. Traditionally, to perform for a highly publicized high school or college team in basketball or football or in any other sport, an athlete needs to be part of the school. He can't play unless he is in school, so guess what? He stays in school. If they make him go to class, he goes to class.

Usually, these jocks choose seats in the back of their classes and prop up their heads on their hands, slouch or sleep, depending on what is required of them. They make it clear to everyone that they are merely going through the motions of school while waiting for games. They impress neither their classmates nor teachers. But what happens, happens.

Schools could require students to make straight A's in order for them to participate on school teams, but other things need to factor in. In many cases, sports teams are lures that might get a sure dropout to give school a longer look. So sports can help to educate (at least to some extent) a lot of kids who otherwise would drop out completely.

Should athletes uninterested in school work be denied the right to play? Or should these athletes be permitted to play so the school has more time to get them interested in getting an education? There are valid points on both sides but a few things are clear. Down through the years, uninterested jock-students have helped stigmatize all athletes. Now, an athlete tends to be guilty (assumed to be an uninterested student) until proven innocent, eager, tuned in, and involved.

It's up to each athlete now to add to the stereotyped impression or to help to tear it away.

Some of you may be thinking, "What do I care about ancient history and people's impressions?" You may not care at all, but this stuff may have an impact on you anyway. If you walk into a classroom, choose a distant seat, and prop up your head, you can expect to get an even lower grade than whatever you actually deserve. Why should teachers and professors be any less human than anyone else? If I'm a teacher and I have a student who clearly indicates he is not interested in what I am teaching, he can be sure I will clearly indicate that I have no qualms about giving him a poor grade. You may also find yourself getting lower grades than you deserve simply because the teacher or professor might assume that you are happy with a minimum passing grade, which you may not be.

If you want to be given the benefit of the doubt, you have to let teachers and professors know that you care, that you aren't just going through the motions as many athletes have for so long. Don't waste your time being dismayed over a stereotype you aren't responsible for. We are all products of our ancestors and can't escape them entirely, whether we like it or not. If you attend a school where there have been generations of athletes who weren't serious students, people are going to expect you to be the same way.

But easy come, easy go, as the saying goes. If those people formed a negative opinion of you with such flimsy evidence, they can form a positive impression of you without a whole lot more evidence.

In other words, if you want to lift yourself from dumb jock status to "incredible, amazing, great person, real student" status in one day, do just one simple thing:

Talk to your teacher or professor before the first class.

Introduce yourself. Express your interest. Say you are looking forward to the class. And on the first day of class choose a seat in the front row-middle, sit up straight and tall, glue your eyes to the professor, and tune in to everything being said. By the end of the day rumors will be spreading about what an excellent student you are. You will have blown the professor's mind.

Your approach, not really so awesome, stands in stark contrast to generations of dumjox. Chances are, no athlete has ever before approached that professor in advance of the first class or sat up like that and paid that kind of attention on day one. As much as the past generations of dumjox have stacked the deck against you, you can re-stack it in your own behalf in a day, if you merely decide to approach your education like a serious student.

When working with college or prospective college athletes, I try each year to get some of them to commit themselves to one special activity. Why don't you try it? Dress up in coat and tie one evening per week and carry a briefcase into the main college library to study. Do you have any idea how word would spread about that? Imagine, especially, the impact of a 6 feet 8 inch star athlete making this once-a-week effort. Dozens of students who pay hardly any attention to sports would be calling home telling parents and friends about this guy who really takes his future and his education seriously.

"Yeah, I see him in the library all the time, carrying a briefcase and wearing a coat and tie. He says he's preparing for the future."

The distance between dumjox and incredible students isn't really that far. It's all a matter of public perception and how you choose to respond to it. Will you reinforce the negative stereotypes? Or will you recreate opinion in your own behalf?

If I were you, I would sit front and middle in every class and sit up straight if for no other reason than to practice self-discipline, muscular control, and peripheral vision. (Yeah, I'd want to be able to check out all the cute classmates on both sides, throughout the class, *while* convincing the professor that I was 100 percent focused on the course work. How's that for a challenge? Think *you* could pull it off?)

I think athletes ought to try carrying their pride with them everywhere. A lot of athletes consider themselves proud and tough on a playing field, meaning they are not easy to distract. Referees' bad calls don't dissuade them from peak performance, nor do taunting opponents. But get them in a classroom and every little thing distracts them. They whine that it's too hot, the teacher is boring, the subject matter doesn't interest them, the seats burn their butt. Where did the pride go?

Why not walk into every classroom for the rest of your life and play the part of the ideal student, even if you're not super intelligent, just the way you plan to enter basketball courts and football fields and hockey rinks—always playing the part of the ideal athlete? Why not?

Remember, there are athletes throughout the world who think it's okay to slack off when the coach isn't looking, who think it's okay to play poorly if the refs are no good, who think it's excusable to lose if the ball was slippery or the field wasn't to their liking. We know these athletes as losers. But do we think similarly of the same flimsy, hold-no-water excuses when they apply to a classroom? When the teacher isn't looking and the subject is boring and the test wasn't fair and the chairs were hard?

Championship performance, as I hope you are realizing, is a quality of mind that doesn't start at game time and end at the buzzer. It is a quality of mind that you take to the practice field and home at night and, yes, into the classroom.

25.
Education & Neck-Walk-Arounds

A quarterback is going to be sacked from all angles; he's going to be blindsided, rear-ended, overturned and pancaked...

Hey, why should you have to study geometry? You'll never need that stuff. I've heard kids say that their fathers sold insurance and never once used geometry. Or their fathers built cars and they never once were asked about ancient history.

Smugly, all sorts of stooopid kids say and think they will never again need some stooopid stuff they are supposed to learn in school so they feel justified in passing it off and not bothering to learn it. If you are ever in that kind of thinking rut, I have news for you. You will hardly ever need *any* of the things you learn in school.

So no use studying history, or geography, or science, or algebra. No one will probably ever require that you know what Vasco da Gama did, where Sri Lanka is located, why water condenses on windows in the morning, or at what point two jets traveling in opposite directions will intercept each other. You never have to know any of the *facts* you learn in school.

Or course, you never have to do pushups in a game, but they are worthwhile preparation. In case you have not begun to understand, let the following definition sink in.

Education is a series of seemingly meaningless challenges aimed at preparing you for an unknown future.

Once you accept that definition of education you will never again make a stupid comment about not needing this or that subject. The point is simple. You need to learn how to learn, how to respond to boredom, how to overcome fatigue, how to persist when things aren't fun. That's education and it's useful everywhere, for everything, for the rest of your life.

You may be right, you may not need geometry. But you do need practice learning new facts because whatever you do there will likely be new things to learn. In fact, in the world we live in, there are constantly new things to learn in just about every job. If you don't know how to learn, if you haven't practiced learning, how are you going to be able to learn what you actually do need to know when the time comes to learn that crucial stuff?

Can you imagine the following dialogue after a football coach asked his team to do neck bridges to strengthen neck muscles?

"Hey Coach, I'm not going to do this stuff."

"Why not?"

"I'll never need that. I'm a quarterback."

"What? A quarterback?"

"Yeah," the kid says. "I usually just hand the ball off and sometimes I drop back to throw passes."

Of course, anyone who knows anything about football sees this as ridiculous. A quarterback is going to be sacked from all angles; he's going to be blindsided, read-ended, overturned and pancaked. If he wants his career to last more than a couple of downs he will want to prepare every muscle in his body for hits he has never imagined. It makes perfectly obvious sense in football, but somehow dumjox and others lose sight of this wisdom when it comes to education, where the "hits" are even less predictable than in football.

To prepare yourself for the unknowable future, you really have only one choice: learn to master the things thrown in front of you now. By learning French and physics and trigonometry, things you might not ever need again, you will exercise your brain muscle and prepare it for the future. And you'll be glad you did.

26.
Eighty-Seven Percent Effort

In Japan, there must be some coaches, or at least some business tycoons, who are getting 1000 percent from their teams.

I used to run a basketball camp called the 87% Basketball Camp. Coaches would, on occasion, see a player wearing a T-shirt with that name and almost invariably their comment would be, "Hey, what's this 87 percent stuff? You gotta give 100 percent, Man."

Often they took it a step further. "You gotta give 110 percent." Do you think 110 percent is enough? Some coaches demand 150 percent, others want 200 percent.

I've heard there are now some coaches in California (a state that often leads the way in new trends) who are demanding—and getting—500 percent every time their players step onto the field to play. Makes you think that, in Japan, there must be some coaches, or at least some business tycoons, who are getting *1000 percent* from their teams. Is the guy who gives only 100 percent a loafer?

By now, you may have guessed that I don't like this unrealistic arithmetic. It's all hype. It's all garbage. No one gives everything. You can have your 1000 and 500 and 200 percents. I look for the athlete who gives an honest 87 percent, who knows it, and who is constantly trying to add 2 percent here and 2 percent there. I figure there's a certain complacency in the guy who calls himself a 100 percenter. I imagine he has quit thinking and quit actively searching for ways to do more because he apparently thinks he already does everything.

Better to have the guy who knows he doesn't give everything, and who spends his time thinking up ways to do more. "What could I add here? What could I add there? Is there some way to do this just a little bit better?"

"You give a hundred percent every time you step out onto the field, don't you?" A lot of coaches ask questions like that. I like the athlete that has a quick answer: "No, no way, never have...but I'd like to...right now I figure I'm somewhere around eighty seven, workin', struggling an' strainin' to get up to eighty nine." Ain't no athlete never got up to no eighty nine. At least not in my book. But keep at it, Man. And spend a little time on that grammar, too. That's part of it all. It's always possible to do a little better.

27.

Encouraging Your Teammates

You may have it in your head that encouraging means one specific thing, like chattering, "Way to go, you can do it, smack a home run!" every time some weak little strikeout king manages to get a foul tip...

When is it okay to encourage your teammates? I'd say anytime, always, now, tomorrow. It is always useful to encourage your teammates. And I would go a step further than that: if you fail to encourage your teammates often, you are failing to contribute to a significant aspect of team-building.

It is hard to overestimate the value of encouragement. *Many people don't show outwardly the effect encouragement has on them*—how it lifts their spirits, makes them proud, and inspires them to put out extra effort—but few people remain untouched by it. Often, in fact, the people who seem least touched or least in need of encouragement are actually those who are most affected and most in need.

The major point here is don't base your encouragement on the response you get, or lack thereof. If your encouragement is sincere and well-intentioned, it will hit its mark. It will be worthwhile. Learn to make encouragement an integral part of your game, of your everyday performance.

Are you quiet by nature? Then offer encouragement quietly. But don't think you can get away with claiming encouraging others is simply not your way. Running sprints in the hot summer sun probably isn't your way either but all athletes need to learn to do things that don't necessarily come naturally.

Of course, encouraging teammates and making noise come more easily to some than to others, just like running and hustling and putting out effort comes more easily to some than to others. But don't get the wrong idea. You may have it in your head that *encouraging* means one specific thing, like chattering "Way to go, you can do it, smack a home run" every time some weak little strikeout king manages to get a foul tip. But encouraging comes in all sorts of forms. Sometimes a loud urging in front of the whole team is best; other times it's a quiet pat on the back. At the same time, one athlete's best encouragement may be a gruff order while another athlete's best is a quiet question.

Sure it depends on the person. Sure it depends on the circumstance. And, even more surely, it depends on you. Are you actively tuning in to your teammates, weighing what kind of encouragement might be best in a given situation, in all situations, constantly, or are you rationalizing your failure by trying to convince yourself that encouragement isn't what's needed at this time from someone like you.

Encouragement is nearly always valuable though sometimes it's best to delay giving it for a moment when it would have greater impact. I don't want to confuse any athlete into thinking that every game has to sound like a public auction with constant chatter filling the air the way some infielders do at a baseball game. It's up to you to use your intelligence and perception to decide what's appropriate and what will be effective. Just keep in mind that the ongoing encouragement and support of teammates is an important ingredient in champion building and that people are never as certain of your support as you think they are.

What kind of encouragement works best? There is no perfect, every-time answer to this question but a few ideas might be useful here.

First, the better athlete you are and the better your personal example of hustle and dedication, the more influential will be your encouragement. After all, whose encouragement would mean the most to you, a classmate's or the president's? A teammate's or Shaquille O'Neal's? A weak little kid's or a big tough guy's? You get the idea: the more impressed we are with the encourager, the more meaningful is the encouragement.

The sincerity of the encouragement matters, too. A pat on the head from the president could be less influential than a long, well-written, totally tuned-in letter from a classmate or teammate. Without sincerity, words are wasted regardless of who offers them. But assuming equal sincerity and knowledge and so forth, nearly every person is touched by words of encouragement in direct proportion to his respect and admiration for the person delivering those words. It's very simple: *the more you gain the respect and admiration of your teammates, the more your words of encouragement will mean to them.*

So to encourage well, first be that dedicated, hard-working, respected athlete. Second, tune in to your teammate's thinking and needs. Did he just strike out after six months of training? Did he make the same mistake yesterday and last week? Does she respond best to turning thoughts to the future or would she rather have someone to talk to about the past?

Some people respond best to loud urging, to being reminded to get tough. Others prefer a quiet word when no one else is around. Sometimes a phone call a day later is the best thing. Sometimes a brief note in the mail is perfect even though you see that person every day. Sometimes you need shouted reminders during the game action. Sometimes a consoling "don't worry about it" after the game means more. Sometimes "we'll get 'em next time." Sometimes "That sucks!"

The better you know someone, the better able you will be to say or do the right thing at the right time. But don't be too squeamish about doing something even when you don't know a person well. When you have good intentions it is difficult to do the wrong thing. Even a depressed or disappointed athlete is likely to appreciate encouragement for what it is, later if not right now. Only a real solid jerk would stay upset with you for encouragement offered at a time that bothered him.

Encouragement is a trial and error thing. You'll make some mistakes with content and timing. That's okay. As the saying goes, mistakes of commission are better than mistakes of omission. It's better to regret having done something that failed than to regret not having tried.

Encourage your teammates. It will pay big dividends for them and for you.

28.
Excuses

In sports, there's a refreshing concreteness and finality. Someone wins, someone loses...

There are probably more excuses surrounding sports performances than there are balls and bats and gloves and rackets and helmets and nets and goals. Excuses. Nearly everyone has them but none of them are worth a frog's fat fanny.

If I were Czar of World Sports I would make every athlete sign an oath, as doctors have to do when they begin to practice their profession. It would say:

"I will never make excuses. I won't verbalize them, and I won't even think them. If one starts to roll across my mind, I will fly by supersonic jet to the Vatican and, if I'm not Roman Catholic, I will convert along the way long enough to confess to the pope that I have sinned egregiously, that I am sorry, and that I will make every effort to see that it never happens again. Furthermore, I will give all of my possessions to the poor, or to the rich (this isn't for charitable purposes, this is an oath) and I will check into my local sports psychology clinic for reprogramming and reentry into the real world."

That would do for starters. I've gotten ridiculous it would seem, but probably not ridiculous enough to silence all those millions of excuse-mongers out there. Excuses. They just have no place in sports. There's an excuse for everything. You would've but...you could've but.... Hey, we believe you. No kidding. But so what?

The best thing you can do, short of taking my oath above, is to decide you simply are done for life with making excuses. Performance is all that counts in sports, it's what makes sports so exciting. In other areas of life results are usually less clear. People can talk their way into and out of things, and half the time we aren't sure what's right and who's wrong. But sports have a refreshing concreteness and finality. Someone wins, someone loses. The losers, of course, have excuses, but fortunately, no one cares.

All teams have their records to refer to, and the records—thank every god that ever was believed in—are only numbers. Six and four. Twenty-two and five. Ninety-eight and sixty-four. Numbers, just numbers, with no place for asterisks by team records. No one asks how many of those losses you could have won. Some people always seem to want to talk about those near-wins but, once the game or season is over, few people care to listen. And, people rarely want to answer the question, "How many of those *wins* should have been *losses*?"

You see, the referee-this and the umpire-that, and the weather-this and the coach-that, and the time of day-this and the playing surface-that don't really matter in sports. What was your record? What was the score? Did you win or did you lose? My father/ coach always said: *"Let **them** have the excuses for losing. Let **us** offer reasons for winning."*

Despite what I say here and what your coach no doubt reminds you of periodically, you will likely have an excuse ready to explain away your next failure. Your coach, unfortunately, may have one as well. And you will probably think that, although you agree that excuses aren't good as a general rule, *this* case—your most recent failure—was different.

Many times I have heard coaches (even very good coaches) say, "I don't like to make excuses *but…*" and then they go on to try to convince me that the situation they have just experienced involves a very special set of circumstances. (It probably did seem really special at the time.) Athletes are even worse than coaches. Parents are even worse than athletes. But let's talk about you.

Take a few moments to consider what an excuse sounds like to winners, to excellent coaches, and to champion athletes. Do you already know what excuses sound like? "I know you can't blame referees for losses, but I mean, my gawd, that one call was just, I mean, there was no way." Sound familiar?

How often have you heard the excuse-maker go on to say, "But then again, we got those two breaks that we didn't deserve; actually, we should have lost by twice as much." In all the years I have been watching sports and talking to coaches and to athletes and parents, I have never once heard anyone claim that they really deserved to lose a close game by a lot more than they did.

I hope you get the point. It is possible for you to decide right now to can/toss/abjure/jettison all your excuses, for all time, once and for all. Why not free yourself to be a total athlete, a performer who evaluates each effort and each result with just one standard: did it get done or didn't it? Did I achieve the desired result, or didn't I?

Once you make that decision you're going to be amazed at your gain in self-pride, your gain in performance, and (the one bad thing) your disgust at hearing the zillion stupid excuses of people around you.

29.
Favored to Win

"Jump on 'em early."

Commentators often talk about how difficult it is to stay on top. Everyone is gunning for you. Everyone is nipping at your heels. Everyone wants a piece of you.

Are you in that position now? If you are, I have some advice for you. Sit back and relax for just a moment. (I know this is good advice because, if you're on top, you don't relax much. You don't get to the top by sitting in a hammock sipping tea all day.) Think about all the years you spent losing, as an also-ran, as a little kid, as an underdog. And now think about all the others who were alongside you who never made it to where you are now.

Yeah sure, others are nipping at your heels but you've been in that position yourself. Which position feels better? Do you like *hoping* that everything will click perfectly, that the upset just might happen...or do you like going into competition *knowing* what the ingredients are for success and having to just put them all together again?

Personally I'll take the knowing, and I'll enjoy it. Of course you should realize that you can't stay on top forever. The favored team won't always win, and constant replacement goes on in all sports. Big deal. So you aren't going to stay on top forever. Well, you never planned on being there forever. You planned, you worked, you struggled and strained, and you got there. You're supposedly better than your competition right now. Great. Enjoy it. Make the most of it. Thrive on it.

You can always be sure of one thing when you are playing against an underdog. Despite whatever bravado and confidence they show on the outside, they have doubt. They don't *know* yet. They hope they know, they think they know, but they know they don't know.

You see all that doubt come flying out when underdogs finally get to the top. They kept hoping and hoping but they didn't really believe it themselves until the final buzzer. It's that doubt you have to take advantage of as much as possible, for as long as you can.

One terrific thing you have going for you is that the underdogs will always fear you. Even if they begin with a big lead, they will respect your ability to come back and they will wonder, "Can we keep this up?" Often their fear will get in the way of killer instinct and they will let you back in a game that a champion would have put away.

That tentative outlook, that basic fear, will work against them and often buy you time as you try to reassert your championship form. Even when they have you by the throat, they won't know it. You will have breathing room and openings you didn't previously have when you were the underdog trying to overturn champions.

Keep your focus on their doubt if things start going bad, and remember your climb to the big time. You have earned your confidence. You've paid the price. You have what it takes.

It doesn't make sense to give in to worries about underdogs nipping at your heels. See their attempts to feel confident for what they are: attempts, hopes, wishful thinking.

And yes, you will be de-throned at some point but don't let it happen before your day has actually come. Make sure that when you do get knocked off your perch it comes at the hands of someone, some team, you truly respect and that really is better.

Before that time comes, make sure you go into each competition thinking about demonstrating what championship form is all about. Show off the ingredients and chemistry that got you favored and got you to where you are. Whatever you have achieved, whatever caused you to be favored in someone's mind, is something special;

most people don't have it. Assume your opponents don't either, or make them prove absolutely that they do.

Perhaps the most important thing to remember is a line my father used to tell his teams. (They were favored over their opponents 85 percent of the time.) *"Jump on 'em early."*

Don't let them start feeling confident. Don't give them a chance to think "these guys aren't so good" or as Rocky (Sylvester Stallone) said, "You ain't so baaad!" Any team permitted to become confident does indeed get better. If you are favored—and if they know it—then they have doubts.

Nearly every athlete talks about not caring what other people say and think; and nearly every athlete is lying. We all care. We try to put that stuff out of our minds and go about our business but everyone is influenced. If you're an underdog, you can't help but fear the over-dog. You've lost before. You know what it's like. It could happen again. Everyone who plays sports realizes this deep inside. We all know: the better the opponent, the better chance we have of losing.

The underdogs' doubts will work against them and impede top performance, particularly if you "jump on 'em early" and go for the jugular. If you spar around like a fearful boxer feeling out the other guy, you are losing the advantage of being on top. Feeling out the opponent is something the underdog has to do. It's foolish being reckless and not respecting the guy with the knockout punch so it makes sense for the underdog boxer to move carefully and try to get a feel for how that big punch gets delivered. They know that past underdogs failed to respect that punch and they had one-round knockouts, flat on their butts, to show for it.

The boxing analogy essentially applies to all sports. The underdog has to be careful, the champion should go for it. The champion doesn't care what the other team has. It's *you* that's got the championship stuff. Use it! Grab them, squeeze them, and never let them catch a breath. Don't give them time to think. Don't allow them to develop confidence. Take it right to them, right from the start. Your best chance, as the better performer, is to get 'em early. You need to go into each contest totally prepared from the start. If you go into competition hoping to play your way into form, you are assuring yourself a very brief sojourn as the favorite.

If you're on top, you have the ingredients. You have what it takes. The main focus of your pregame efforts should be to make sure you use those ingredients fully, from the opening bell/whistle/gun. If you do this, you may hold your throne even longer than you deserve to because you take advantage of doubt and tentative play, and stretch that early advantage into another victory.

Okay, you can quit relaxing now, but keep thinking. It's actually a very satisfying feeling having people nipping at your heels. The view from the top is exhilarating. Enjoy it.

30.
Fist Exchanges Beat Frowns

Many athletes seem to have picked up a sense, as they have moved up the athletic ladder, that frowning and showing anguish indicates that they are tough competitors who hate to lose...

Frowns aren't just down-turned facial muscles. They are devices that destroy teams, tear down positive atmospheres, and create ill feeling. Scientifically, frowns are supposed to use a lot of extra muscles and energy and perhaps even bring about the flow of some kinds of harmful chemicals in the body. I don't doubt it, because they bring about toxic thoughts and situations all the time.

You may find this strange but when I am coaching I prohibit frowns on my team. Frowns are simply banned. You want to frown? Put a towel over your face. Go into the locker room. Put your face under the shower. Just don't do it out here where the rest of us can see it. Frowns mess up people and teams. We don't need them.

You may think I'm overdoing it, but I don't think so. See for yourself, try an experiment. The next time you feel like frowning in some athletic situation, don't. Replace it with a fist.

Do you know what a fist exchange is? It's what good athletes do when the going gets tough, when they have just messed up, when the other team has just gone ahead or just scored again. A fist exchange. Two athletes looking each other in the eye and offering each other a fist and a "c'mon, let's go," which means

"Let's turn this around, let's refuse to accept this, let's give even more effort, let's work together and make miracles happen."

Do you know the power of a fist exchange between two athletes, when things are going bad? Have you ever felt that power? I have never seen that power generated via frowns. Frowns are intensely personal, selfish, and destructive. They don't encourage. In fact, they are signs of defeat, of anguish. Perhaps sometimes, amidst giant frustrations, they are unavoidable among competitive athletes. Perhaps. But usually they are simply bad habits, poor responses, and lost opportunities. They are what took place instead of the fist exchange that could have lifted performance out of the doldrums. I've never seen a player lifted by a teammate's frown, but I've seen hundreds lifted and encouraged by a teammate's fist, a simple yet determined gesture that reminds each other that they are athletes, that they have worked hard for this opportunity, that they have shared much, and that they have no plans to let these moments pass with a feeling of defeat.

Many athletes seem to have picked up a sense, as they have moved up the athletic ladder, that frowning and showing anguish indicates that they are tough competitors who hate to lose. But I don't think their frowns and displays of anguish indicate anything other than that they are good at frowning and displaying anguish. Do you want to show off what a tough competitor you are? Beat people. Overcome adversity. Smash through obstacles. Be encouraging when everyone around you has lost hope. Summon energy when you have a right to be exhausted. Need any more? Replace your frowns with more constructive actions. Try fist exchanges. They work wonders. They make even the bad times part of the joy of sports.

31.
Flippant Encouragement

When we went out meekly, 1-2-3, again, I'd grab my glove and head for the field urging everyone to be careful, "Let's try not to get hurt this inning; sports can be dangerous you know!"

The typical sports instruction book doesn't usually have a chapter on flippant encouragement. In fact, I've never seen this topic discussed by anyone, but I've used the concept often and I think there are times when it is both appropriate and effective. Let me set the stage, using baseball or softball for this example.

In the top of the first inning your opponent puts up seven big ones. Their dugout is going nuts. They bat around. Seems like on every pitch there's the crack of the bat and their uniforms are flying in a blur around the bases. People keep crossing the plate and giving high fives. You get the final out when the bases are loaded on a line shot hit to the warning track. The game has gone on for half and hour, it's 7–0, and you haven't even had a chance to bat yet. Finally, it's your turn.

It seems like years ago that you came to the field smacking your mitt, taking practice wings, fielding grounders or shagging flies, and yelling encouragement to your teammates, "Okay, guys, let's go get 'em. Let's put one on 'em today." It also seems like years since you yelled, after their first single, "No problem, let's get *two*," as you encouraged your team to get a double play.

But now it's 7–0, and your team goes out 1-2-3 in the first.

And 1-2-3 in the second. The opposing pitcher is throwing BBs, tiny little pellets you can barely see, and so fast you hear them buzz as they go by. Do you get the picture? We've all been in games of this sort at one time or another. Inning after inning you try for the old never-say-die attitude, you try to encourage your teammates and remind them that you can come back. But it starts to sound pretty hollow. It's one of those days. Going into the sixth inning, the other team has picked up a few more runs. They lead 12–0, and your team can't recall hitting even a solid foul ball. You're lucky they have *only* twelve.

You are getting your young butts soundly whipped. What is your reaction? How do you keep trying your best, maintaining your pride, and at least maintaining your self respect? Do you start *walking* out to the field for each new inning? Do you quit saying a word to your teammates? Do you mope around in silence just waiting for this nightmare to end?

I think this is the time for some humor, but straightforward joke telling is hardly the answer. Your teammates will be in no mood to laugh. Nevertheless, you need some change of attitude and you need to do something. You need to stay active. You can't just mope around.

To me, this situation calls for flippant encouragement. "Hey, c'mon you guys, let's get a run just for the helluvit." Or, "C'mon Jones. Get on. Let's start working on our base stealing." Or, with a guy on first, "Bunt him up, Johnson! Let's start chipping away at 'em. They're starting to crumble, I think I see some of the beginning signs!"

It's crazy. It's stupid. It's false. But it may just be the right thing at the right time. The good old college try won't do it anymore. "C'mon, guys, we can score twelve runs. You know we can." No they don't. They don't know nothin' of the sort. They distinctly feel that they cannot. *To have any chance at this point, or just to maintain self-respect, it is necessary to back off the old standbys which simply haven't done the trick this day.* In fact, in this situation, in place of an earnest "C'mon-guys-we-can-score-twelve-runs, it would be much better to offer a "mock-determined" tone just to deflect everyone's mind for a moment.

"C'mon you guys, let's double 'em this inning, let's score a million. Swing for the fences, guys. If you make contact this time, Johnson, don't even look up till you're roundin' third."

I'd yell this sort of thing with seeming seriousness. And when we went out meekly, 1-2-3, again, I'd grab my glove and head for the field urging everyone to be careful, "Let's try not to get hurt this inning; sports can be dangerous you know!" Or, on the way back, "Okay, that's a start. No one got hurt that inning. I think we're starting a roll now. I can feel it coming. They say this pitcher cracks under pressure, Williams, smack one out!"

A lot of athletes just plain won't know how to do this and won't know how to respond to it. Many coaches will disagree with me, worrying that you will step over the line and say something in some way degrading. But I personally would take the chance, and I would welcome the humor and the deflected thoughts and I think other competitors do too.

You can't win 'em all. Sometimes you can't even keep from getting your butt whipped. When that happens, I think you have to keep your sense of humor, and keep the whole affair in perspective. You have to keep trying your best physically, and you also have to keep working at the mental aspect of the game, which does *not* mean endlessly chattering hollow platitudes.

We're all human. We know when our butts are getting whipped. And there have been times when one team was getting their butts soundly whipped and then went on to win. Maybe they did that by continuing to urge each other with the same chatter until things turned around, but I don't think so. I think the big changes happen in life when someone departs from the same old thing, when someone recognizes that something different is needed and that a change of tone may be constructive. A variation from the norm is necessary.

Flippancy changes the tone, takes the pressure off, acknowledges what's going on but doesn't give up. It offers a different way of going about things and I think it's good for the team, even and especially on the occasions when the miracle does *not* happen, when you get your butts whipped thoroughly, when the game ends 17–0.

"Hey, let's win this one for Soooozie" (a girl who left one of the guys, who stood up the captain, who did a number on one of your players, a girl who would be the last one in the world you would want to do anything for). Or do it for a former coach everyone disliked, or a former player who made three errors in a past game, someone you joke about.

You get the idea. Flippancy helps you stay loose, stay up, realize that you're all in this together; you still have your self-respect. You'll be back. This nightmare will end, and you'll live to play, and win, another day.

You actually enjoy the final innings, playing with a kind of reckless abandon, with enjoyment, not because you truly believe deep inside that you can come back and win, but because you've already, during the game, put the nightmare behind you and are playing hard just for the hell of it. Maybe, just maybe a miracle will happen, and your team will come from behind to win. But even if you don't, even if the usual happens, if you get killed, you rise mentally off the ground, shrug off the doldrums, and feel good about being alive, competing, and even getting your butts whipped.

It's something that better not happen very often, but as long as it's the exception, not the norm, you can take it now and then. And a little flippancy, at those times, can keep you sane and enjoying it all.

I hope you never need this concept. But if you do, give it a try. It's the best response I know of during those times we all wish would never happen.

32.
Focusing on Yourself

*Focus your attention on what **you** can do.*

Focusing on yourself is the major theme of this book, appearing again and again in one form or another so I won't elaborate any further. I'll let this section stand simply as another reminder.

When all sorts of negative incidents, circumstances, and events are going on around you, focus your attention on what you can do to make something positive happen. One more time. All sorts of negative incidents, circumstances, and events are going to happen. So what? Focus on yourself. What can do to bring about some positives?

What can *you* do?

33.
Fun

Once you really think about it you come to realize that sport, just like business, is a transaction…

Sports are supposed to be fun. Here are some often-heard lines:

You gotta have fun.
Just go out there and have fun.
It's just not fun anymore.

If it's supposed to be so much fun, why isn't everyone laughing? There's an awful lot of talk about fun among athletes and coaches, but what is fun? Mean Joe Greene, the Hall of Fame lineman of the four-time Super Bowl champion Pittsburgh Steelers, said that coach Chuck Noll always told the team before a game to "Just go out there and have fun." The problem, said Greene, was that Noll's idea of fun was to hit heads against brick walls for three hours in the hot sun.

Obviously, with that definition of fun, a coach can easily say that he just wants his team to go out there and have fun. But what do coaches really mean when they say that? Mostly, they mean they want you to enjoy the fruits of your training efforts. There is certainly no fun in fumbling and dropping passes and missing tackles. There is nothing even remotely lighthearted about the "fun" of playing a sport poorly, in a way that entirely fails to reflect the hours of practice you have spent developing your skills.

The fun consists in showing off what you have trained hard to do. But things become very "un-fun" when the training doesn't show. The experience, instead, feels more like time wasting or stupidity.

When athletes say "It's just not fun anymore" they mean that they are failing, either individually or as a team (or both), to produce results commensurate with their training efforts. To have fun in sports, your training and your efforts and your diligence and your striving must show up in the performance of the skills for which you trained. If your performance does not reflect your training, don't expect any fun.

Once you really think about it you come to realize that sport, just like business, is a transaction. What you put in must be reflected in what comes out. Businesses themselves are tremendous fun for people who see their investments blossom into fortunes, but for those who work hard and end up with nothing, it's not fun. The same is precisely true of sport.

So, just go out there and have fun. You gotta have fun in sports. Sports ought to be fun. No joke. But keep it all in perspective. You're not supposed to be laughing to have fun. But you *are* supposed to be able to enjoy the fruits of your labors. So, work hard. Practice diligently. Overcome obstacles. Improve. Then—and only then—will the real fun of sports begin.

34.

"Getting Ahead" Time

Out there alone while the whole world seemed asleep, it was easier to roll through my mind visions of large crowds, TV cameras, and big games where the pressure was on…

There's something propelling about being up and outdoors, or in a field or on a court—some place away from home—at six in the morning. I used to think of it as "getting ahead" time. At six in the morning the streets in my little town were quiet. Often, it was still dark. But I was out there practicing and it felt good.

It felt good not because I am a morning person. I didn't like hearing the alarm ring at 5:45 any more than anyone else. But being out there did feel good. Every fake, every maneuver, every effort was infused with the notion that *other kids were still sleeping*. My competitors, the athletes I would one day face in big games, were sleeping while I was practicing. That was something I couldn't feel confident about any other time.

When you're practicing after school you have the constant awareness that everyone, all over the nation, is practicing at that same time. Each coach is giving his instructions, urging his team on, offering suggestions, yelling, encouraging, demanding, pushing. After school, anyone could be having a better day, could be working harder, could be learning something that you aren't.

But at six in the morning? You feel as though almost no one is out there doing that. The nation simply is not filled with kids who get up before school in the morning to practice and improve.

I'm not really sure I improved any of my physical skills during all those mornings but I dramatically improved my mental skills. Working hard at six made me feel deserving of getting ahead of my competition. If I was out there and they weren't, I ought to become better, right? You may be able to point out reasons this thinking is erroneous but it felt good to be working on my game when most of the world was sleeping. They were getting behind while I was darting and dashing here and there on a dark basketball court.

Three hours later while I sat in English class, the Californians might be dashing and darting on their own basketball courts. They might. But even if they were, they would only be able to equal me. They wouldn't be able to get ahead. I had already put in my time. And it was inspired time. Get ahead time.

Why was it so inspiring? Maybe because my muscles were fresh at that time, or maybe because I knew I couldn't practice more than an hour before I had to get home to shower and prepare for school. I don't know. I just remember how animated those practices were. Out there alone while the whole world seemed asleep, it was easier to roll through my mind visions of large crowds, TV cameras, and big games where the pressure was on, and everything depended on one little kid's unstoppable moves.

Zip. Run. Stop on a dime. Maybe nine cents. Burst of speed again, turn, spin. Lay it up. Slam it in. Knock it down. No. I could never slam dunk. I was too small, couldn't jump well enough. But those efforts inspired with imagination had an impact on the rest of the day. At school I saw the other kids rubbing their eyes, often complaining about how early it was. Even teachers would talk about the difficulty of getting started first thing in the morning. First thing?

I'd already been up winning titles, championships, trophies, awards. I'd been taking NBA stars to the hole, faking them out of their respective undergarments, and popping in shots that brought crowds to their feet and made future Miss Americas sigh with dreamy admiration. Needless to say, my days had a certain flavor to them, the air of championship performance, as I went from class to class, pushing pencils across papers and waiting…for the future.

35.
Getting Bigger

Bigness. It almost sounds like a bad word.

This short section has nothing to do with size. Have you ever stopped to consider how petty so many people are? And how petty you often are? Most of us are much too petty much too often.

Sometimes, when dissension seems to be racking a team and personality conflicts have surfaced, when tension is in the air and it seems as though there are many problems to deal with, just one solution is required. Everyone simply has to get bigger. *Bigger*. Less petty. Less concerned about trivial things. More aware of the big picture, of what sports and life are all about. You may be saying, especially during one of these crises, that you *are* bigger, if only those petty teammates of yours would shape up.

You may be right. But there's a solution better than hoping they suddenly choose to get bigger: *you* choose to be even bigger than you have been.

Bigness. It almost sounds like a bad word. When talking with a judge or a king, in place of Your Honor or Your Highness, it would sound funny or sarcastic. "Yes, sir, Your Bigness." So chuckle and remember, Your Bigness. *When everything around you seems to be going sour, just rise above it.* Get bigger.

Bigness is a simple matter of where you place your pride. Are you proud to be above the garbage going on around you? Or are you steeped in it, part of it? It's up to you. How big are you?

36.
Getting Organized

Being organized is an essential ingredient of productivity.

How many times have you heard someone say, "I'm not a very organized person"? A good response might be, "Why not?" Being unorganized is hardly something to be proud of. If you are unorganized, don't tell anyone. Hide it. And start doing something about it. Get organized.

Being organized doesn't mean that you necessarily make your bed every morning, hang up all your clothes every night, and never have anything on your desk. You don't have to be a neat freak to be organized. Put away your bias against organization and consider the benefits.

Reviewing for a test, for example, is much easier if you have your course materials together, your quizzes, homework assignments, notes. Of course it's going to be easier to review the important material if you have it all in one place. It's also going to take less time if you don't have to look for things you need. This is common sense but somehow neglected by many people.

Organization is useful for more than schoolwork. Phone numbers and addresses in one place, goals and plans in another, subjects to study, people who might give you a part-time or summer job, charts on your progress in weight training, running, skill development. Decide your own categories but get started getting organized.

If you can't afford filing cabinets and file folders to keep your life in order (a plastic portable model complete with a hundred file folders would cost you about $10–15) try some boxes, or big envelopes.

Being organized is an essential ingredient of productivity. If you want to maximize your time and be as effective as possible, you have to be organized. You probably know people who have to search for their car keys every time they want to drive their car. This may seem like a tiny thing but it usually carries over into many other aspects of life. Taking a five minute trip in the car often takes twenty minutes if you count the time spent searching for keys. Put the keys in the same place the moment you walk in the door, and guess what? That's where they'll be when you need them. The same goes for clothes, for pencils and paper and stamps and envelopes and anything else you need, in your daily life or from time to time.

A certain satisfaction comes from efficiency, to say nothing of the savings in time. It's hard to imagine that you are really trying to maximize your abilities if you aren't attentive to being personally organized. Almost every successful athlete is extremely busy. You have school, family responsibilities, and skill development in your sport, plus social life, possibly a job, and other individual considerations.

This whole section boils down to one simple fact. If you are really trying to be a champion— to improve in your spot and increase your physical and mental condition, and develop your skills, and get practice playing your sport, and work on your strength and agility—you have a lot to do and you simply must maximize your time. The only way to do that is by getting yourself well organized in all phases of your life. *Keep evaluating the way you do things and think about how you can do them better and more efficiently.*

So now let's go back to the beginning. Does getting organized mean you have to have a clean room? Should you make your bed? I said those things didn't necessarily matter. But give this some thought.

Once, a contingent of Japanese executives who produced machinery were all set to tour a factory; the factory owners hoped to sign a contract to supply the Japanese with parts. Before the tour began one of the Japanese executives used the restroom where he noticed a cracked window. When he came out he asked his tour guides about the crack and received a lackadaisical answer.

The Japanese executive couldn't imagine that the owners of the factory had the kind of attitude it would take to meet their exacting standards for making parts if no one had gotten around to replacing something as simple as a window. The Japanese didn't sign a contract that day. They went looking for another company, one that had the attitude of a champion, one that had pride in doing everything as well as possible.

We're all human. We all make mistakes. We can't be perfect at everything. But we can have an attitude that seeks perfection as a habit. The story is as instructive in the sports world as it was in the business world. Do you want that contract with a major company, do you want that scholarship or that championship? Better make a habit of doing everything as well as you can.

Better make that bed after all.

37.
Hoping Your Team Loses

Every player is supposed to be elated when the team wins, but there are times when your particular circumstances simply are not going to permit elation for you...

People rarely talk about this. But how many athletes do you think ever sat on a bench hoping their team would mess up, play poorly, or lose the game? There must be millions of athletes who have felt this way at one time or another. And almost all of them probably felt very guilty.

Cheerleaders yell and dance, students paint signs, mascots run around, live animals are walked onto the field, pep clubs are formed, scouts go over the opponents' plays, the coaches stay up all night, and the team practices and practices and practices. Everything is focused on one thing: winning. Just as it should be. That makes it impossible for any player, at any time, to say what he may truly be thinking: I hope we lose.

Typically, the feeling arises when you get taken out of a game for messing up. Hey, get real. If the player who replaces you does an awesome job, you won't get back in. It's very simple. It's sports. The best guy plays.

You can blame politics all you want ("He plays because the coach likes him") but politics only enter in when it's not clear who is better. When one player is clearly better than another, the better player plays. So if you get taken out and your team begins playing better than ever, you have two basic choices: you can be happy for your team and proud to be a lesser part of it; or you can hope they start losing or at least messing up, so you are needed again.

Given the choices, it's hardly surprising that many athletes will be hoping, at any given time, that their own teams don't do so well. Most athletes who have worked very hard for the opportunity to play a sport don't relish the idea of suddenly becoming a cheerleader for someone else.

When your substitute goes in, even if he's your best friend, it's extremely difficult to sit and watch and hope he's terrific. It may be possible to hope for him and to figure that you can take someone else's place. But often the situation doesn't really allow for that. If you are clearly a catcher, or clearly a point guard, or clearly a setter, or clearly a goalie, there really aren't other positions for you to slide into. When a player who plays your position replaces you, and if he does well and the team jells at just that point, there is the possibility that you may never play an important role again on your team. So you sit there hoping your team loses or messes up at least enough to get you back in there.

Shame on you. You should be happy to root, root, root for the home team, turn in your uniform, become a cheerleader, and start painting signs for the next big game. Or should you?

What *should* you do?

Obviously, it isn't easy to know. Not many of us who have worked hard at a sport want suddenly to become cheerleaders and sign painters. But don't worry about it. Take your mind off the whole issue. Your time and thoughts and emotions are best focused back on yourself, on what you must do when you get back in there.

It's not necessary to berate yourself or feel guilty for negative feelings. Nearly every athlete will have them to some extent. Just don't dwell on them. Focus on yourself and on your performance. Think about why you came out and what you have to do when you do get a chance. Think about what you can do to make your team click as never before when you get another chance to make that happen.

If you do end up sitting there the rest of the game as your

team pulls out a dramatic, amazing, come-from-behind victory, don't feel bad that you aren't quite as happy as the guys who did it, nor as happy as the sign painters, cheerleaders, and fans. Hide your unhappy face the best way you can. *Congratulate your teammates for their special accomplishments and get away from the celebrations as soon as you can.* Don't spend unhappy time in the middle of merriment. Fake it. Or go along with it. And remove yourself as soon as possible.

There isn't any easy way to deal with this. Every player is supposed to be elated when the team wins but there are times when your particular circumstances simply are not going to permit elation for you. When that time comes, identify it, be fully aware of it, go through the proper motions. Hide your disappointment, congratulate the stars, and get out of there. Get alone or with a close friend, and begin refocusing on what you have to do to get to where you want to be.

You can't be elated for others' successes at all times, but it is stupid to spend your limited time wishing for others' failure. Hope, plan, and work for your own success. Spend time on the things you have some direct control over: you.

How do you focus your thinking on your own success at a time like that? The way you always do. Plan for it. Think about it. Be specific. What needs to get done? What didn't you do? What can you do? And avoid distractions. Those negative feelings you have? Don't bother feeling guilty about them, simply treat them like all other distractions. Give them no place in your mental preparation for the future you want. That way you don't have to deny to yourself that you have those feelings. You just crowd them out with planning.

It's not as bad to occasionally hope your team messes up as it is to waste your time on those thoughts and let yourself be unprepared the next time you get your chance.

38.
Hosting Your Teammates

Your special welcome will pay off in improved play...

Before considering how this concept can work for you and your team, let's think about how a good host treats honored guests in a more typical social situation. When you visit a friend or attend a party, you knock on the door and the host comes to the door to greet you. Immediately, a good host makes you feel welcome, as though it is wonderful to see you and to have you at the party. Typically the host will take you inside, introduce you to others, and facilitate your entry among the other guests by saying good things about you and perhaps about several others, making everyone feel good and more likely to get along together. When a good host does it just right you are likely to be a better, more interesting guest, and you are likely to add more to the party. After being enthusiastically introduced, your personality is more likely to come out. You are more likely to talk to others, to communicate well, and probably help the others get greater enjoyment from the party.

A good host, then, is not helping only you by greeting you, welcoming you, introducing you, making you feel welcome, and bringing out your best. Good hosts are probably well aware that by doing all those things they will make their own party better, thus achieving their own goals. (Why have a party if you are not intent on having a good one?)

Hopefully you already begin to see the connection to sports. When a teammate walks onto the field or court whether to begin practice or to enter a game, it makes sense to make that teammate feel welcome. Imagine the reverse. The teammate gets sent into the game and the starters or the stars already in the game start rolling their eyes as though they are thinking, "Oh no, is our coach nuts? What's he putting Pee Wee in for?" What is the likelihood that that player is suddenly going to play excellently? More likely the player will feel added pressure and will mess up rather than surprise everyone.

Though an entering substitute cannot read minds, he or she can certainly see rolling eyes or feel the others' lack of enthusiasm even when they are quiet or do nothing. *If your hope is that your teammates will perform to the best of their abilities, it makes sense to welcome them into the action in the same way a good host would welcome them to a party.* Make your teammates feel as though you are happy to see them. Talk to them. Give them your sense of the game and immerse them in the action. Make them feel good and give them the impression that the whole team is happy to have them in there. Your special welcome will pay off in improved play. After all, it's your party.

It can never hurt to remind a teammate of the situation. "We're ahead by three... if we can just control the ball for two more minutes, we'll win. Make sure you hold the ball with both hands..." A reminder like that just might prevent a fumble some day. A compliment might bolster confidence. "When you get an open shot, take it."

You probably don't have to do the whole party-host thing. Often all you have to do is toss a ball to a teammate coming into the gym to begin practice, or go toward a teammate coming into a game and say, "It's great to have you in here." It's easy and it works.

39.
Humor

He was twelve, so he knew all about girls already. I didn't. I was only eleven.

Humor is a very powerful, valuable force that works wonders in a variety of circumstances. Humor helps to build and cement friendships, it is useful for deflecting criticism, sometimes it can get you out of jams. In sports, it can often make the difference between winning and losing.

During the course of any athletic season there are likely to be many ups and downs, a lot of frustrations and failures and tense situations. How you deal with those negative times will have much to do with how many positive times you experience.

It is difficult, however, to precisely define humor and particularly to explain in a book when to use it. There are times, maybe during difficult, tense practice situations, when a joke to lighten things up is just what is needed. However, at other times a funny comment may get you thrown out of practice or off the team. Furthermore, *humor welcomed by one coach may be very unwelcome to another.* So there are no absolutes, no particular jokes to memorize, no foolproof ways that I know of to contribute the humor that your team may need to get to the top. Mostly it's a process of experimenting and of learning what your coach's sense of humor is. Certainly you can't be out there on the field cracking jokes and loosening everyone up if your coach doesn't appreciate it. What you can do, rather than lament your coach's lack of humor (or the fact that he doesn't have the same kind of humor you do) is seek ways to use humor effectively, in ways that your teammates and coaches can all appreciate.

Don't bother focusing or complaining about the humor you can't use. Some humor will be inappropriate, some will be deemed so. That may be a fine subject for a psychology paper but for your purposes, all that really matters is how, in your situation, you can use humor positively and effectively. Keep one thing in mind. The humor you use will be seen as appropriate in direct proportion to (1) how hard you work in practice, (2) how good you are during the games or matches, and (3) how funny your humor is—in that order.

If you are a substitute who loafs most of the time, it is hard to imagine any coach being interested in taking time from an intense practice session to laugh at one of your jokes. Loafers have to be upbraided; it would set a bad precedent to laugh at a loafer's joke. He'd start cracking jokes constantly or at least that is what the coach would fear. On the other hand, the extremely hard worker or the star player wins some leeway for himself. Since his effort and performance aren't in question, this allow for the possibility of a break from the normal routine.

Even so, it is still up to each individual player to experiment, to think through each situation, and to offer humor when it is appropriate and withhold it when it isn't. I don't think rigid rules apply where humor is concerned. Sometimes things are funniest and most appropriate because they break the normal rules. Just be aware of the value of humor and use it when you can; good humor employed well can do very positive things for the practice atmosphere and can often reduce pressure in a big game.

I recall pitching the championship game of the Little League in our town—it seemed of enormous importance at the time—and the other team, behind by one run, had two runners on with two outs in the final inning. The catcher, my best friend, suddenly called time and ran out to the mound. Naturally, everything stopped and all of the fans (there were dozen but it seemed like thousands) had their eyes on us.

"Just think," he said, "all those people are watching us wondering what I'm saying to you and they're thinking we're discussing how to strike this guy out, but we're not. I just wanted to make sure you knew how good Leslie looks over there." He went running back to home plate and we were both smiling. He was twelve, so he knew all about girls already. I didn't. I was only eleven. Nevertheless, it was fun to have put one over on all those people, and I think it helped me to strike out the last batter.

That was only Little League. But the catcher went on to get 4.0 GPAs at Duke and to be near the top of his class at Harvard Law School. Even as a twelve year old he had a sense of how to reduce pressure, keep things in perspective, and inspire his teammates with encouragement and humor. *Staying loose, laughing sometimes, and getting breaks from the sometime drudgery of practice or the tension of important games are important at any level.*

If you ever get a chance to watch a pro game from a dugout or on the sidelines with a team, you will see that the pros use humor often and it isn't just for laughs.

40.
Hustle-CAT

"Get him!" may be all it takes to mobilize a player who otherwise would have stood there drooping...

In response to an error, Hustle-CAT is a good term to remember and a good thing to do.

In all the continuous team sports like basketball, soccer, volleyball, and hockey—and sometimes in baseball and football as well—a player will make a mistake and have the opportunity immediately either to compound the mistake or to correct it. If your error immobilizes you while you pause to demonstrate your anguish or anger, you compound your error. A muffed "kill" in volleyball isn't a point lost until you stand there frustrated and fail to make the best reaction possible to set up your defense for the opponent's attempt.

In football, although there is usually dead time between plays, in many instances—particularly on interceptions or fumbles—immediate response to the new situation would save your team thirty or forty yards, or a touchdown, in spite of the negative event.

Admittedly, a team driving for a tying touchdown late in the game will be upset if a pass is intercepted on the one yard line. If that opponent is tackled on the one, his team will be in a very precarious situation and may soon be punting the ball back to you. However, if that same player is permitted to run the ball back for a touchdown, the game is lost.

It is crucial for any player to get in the habit of immediate positive response to new situations. Sure, sometimes a late interception will lose the game regardless of where the opponent is tackled. But if you let yourself start deciding when to put out effort and when not to, you will make dozens of wrong decisions and lose lots of valuable time in the process of deciding.

The success you enjoy during your athletic career will be magnified if you simply make yourself a promise to respond immediately, then decide later if the effort was worth it or not. In other words, when an error occurs, hustle to make up for it. In mathematical terms, it looks like this:

Error = hustle.

Then it would make sense to add another point to the hustle side of the equation. C-A-T. Call A Teammate.

When a mistake is made one of the best possible responses is not merely to mobilize yourself, but to call a teammate into action. Remember, your teammates are as likely to be feeling disappointment, dejection, and immobilization as you are. They too are hoping to see the touchdown pass when the ball gets intercepted, and they may not have cultivated the habit of responding immediately to the new situation.

By calling a teammate into action the moment you make or see an error, you animate that teammate or at least have a much better chance of animating him than if you remain silent. In most sports athletes are readily influenced by the commands and urgings barked out by coaches and teammates. "Get him!" may be all it takes to mobilize a player who otherwise would have stood there drooping. One moment a player not accustomed to having the ball has made an apparently game-saving interception and the next moment he is blindsided by a furious tackler. Will he fumble the ball back to you? There are no guarantees. But he may fumble it back—the odds may even be for that happening—if (the big, perennial if) he is hit immediately and hard. And there is very little chance of a fumble if he isn't.

Another advantage of calling a teammate into action is that, if nothing else, it takes the attention off you and your mistake. Why stand there in disgust letting the world know you are guilty? At the end of the game, the only way the fans may remember that you messed up is via your gesture of disgust. Forget the gestures, blend immediately into the action and call your teammates to join you.

In basketball, when your shot is off-target, call your biggest rebounder into the play by telling him to get the ball. Yell out his name. *"Humongo! Rebound!"* By the time the ball bounces off the rim, no one—including your coach—will even remember that you shot it. Everyone will be too busy watching big Humongo's rebounding reaction. Is he trying to get himself into position to grab the ball, or is he just standing there hoping the shot goes in? If Humongo just stands there you can be sure that at halftime Humongo will take the brunt of the coach's anger. Sure, everyone misses shots, even the pros. But that's no reason giant Humongo should stand there watching the game. What's he want to be, a fan?

No doubt you get the message. Calling a teammate into action after you make a mistake is not only a good habit that promotes better results on the field, it may even spare you in the locker room.

41.
Imagination

He had Meg Ryan and Michelle Pfeiffer in the car with him. You know those Hollywood types...

The best weapon you have to keep you excited about your sport, to keep you committed to improving and striving for achievement, is your imagination.

Most every athlete has a vivid imagination. Most of us think often of what it will be like standing in the winner's circle, or on the winner's platform, or cutting down a net, being carried off a field, standing at a microphone, being interviewed on national TV. Having a vivid imagination not only helps get you through difficult practices and lonely sessions aimed at improving your skills, it also keeps you energized and on course. The better your imagination, and the more you work to improve it, the better chance you have of reaching your goals in sports.

Please note the above statement about improving imagination. Everyone has imagination, and everyone can stand to be even more imaginative. Spend time, therefore, on improving your imagination as well as your skills. *The better your imagination gets, the better your skills will get* because the more you can energize your practice sessions, the more you will get out of them.

You have to use your imagination in whatever way works best for you, but you also ought to try to get your imagination to work for you in ways it may not be doing right now. Let me give just one example.

At the end of each day, back when I was an aspiring athlete committed to out-working every possible competitor in the nation, I finally would be ready to go home and go to sleep. I had done the day's quota and put forth all the effort I could. Then it was time to kick in my imagination.

Before going, why not make one more violent fake, followed by a crossover step? One last, effort-filled attempt to perfect a maneuver I hoped some day would enable me to fake out and pass by the best defenders in the nation. So, I muster my remaining energy, make the move, score the point. And go home? Wait. Imagine, at just that moment, on my way off the now-darkened court, a classmate drove past and said "Hey, can I see that move again?" How difficult could that be? Surely I could muster the energy to show a move to a classmate. So, one more time. Make the move, score the point. Grab the ball and begin to walk off the court.

Wait. Imagine one of the girls in my class driving by. (One of the cute girls. One of the ones I always hoped would be interested in me.) "Hey, I've always admired you and the way you play and practice. Could I see that fake-and-crossover move you have?" Sure, she could see it. Would I mind waiting a minute and showing it to her mother? She was talking about me to her mother (really?) and her mother is a big fan of mine (really?) and she would like to see the way I practice in the off-season. (Really?)

So I take a few shots. And I imagine what we would talk about as we wait for her mother to show up. What other moves would I be willing to show off to this lovely girl who I never knew was even interested at all in me, until now. She's here wanting to see my moves and wanting her mother to see them, too. You get the idea. Her mother comes and goes, and she goes, and I start to go, and then the mayor comes, and the governor, and the senator, and the president.

I'm exhausted. I practiced all day. I couldn't do any more. But then a guy came, and a cute girl that I liked, and some important people and then the president of the United States was at my practice court saying he had heard about me, a little kid from a small town who no one paid much attention to, and he was interested in my shooting form and some moves he'd heard about that would one day fake out the best defenders in the nation. Turns out the president was quite a basketball fan.

After the president, Jack Nicholson came by. Everyone knows what a Lakers fan he is. I almost told him, "Hey, Jack, wait till tomorrow, I'm exhausted" but he's got that Joker smile on his face and he starts encouraging me the way he did the Chief in *One Flew Over the Cuckoo's Nest*. "Just raise 'em up, Chief. Just raise 'em up." How could I turn him down?

Oh c'mon, it's just a movie. Yeah, I started to tell him that, too. But he had Meg Ryan and Michelle Pfeiffer in the car with him. You know those Hollywood types. All the big stars hang around together all day long, right? Maybe not. But that's not important. What is important is that I'm exhausted, I want to go home, but Meg and Michelle get out of Nicholson's car. Meg and Michelle. M&M's. Not exactly plain, or peanuts, if you know what I mean.

And guess what? They want to see me make some awe-inspiring moves on a dark basketball court. They know I'm tired, they are sorry to ask, but if I can just do a few I can visit them in Hollywood, hang out with them and Jack on Venice Beach. It would soooo excite them. Can I just do a few?

Meg just loves spin dribbles. Michelle goes bonkers over little kids who can fly, stop on a dime, and fly again. "Oh that stutter step you've got," she says over and over again. She tells Meg she can't contain herself. Meg is jealous!

Crazy? Hell yes. But I think you get the picture. I went through scenarios like that nearly every summer evening when it seemed time to quit and time to go home for the day. *It's amazing how much more you can do when you make a real effort to get your imagination involved.* It was never quite like actually having Meg and Michelle there in person, but my thoughts got rather vivid and they did energize my efforts in ways I could not accomplish any longer with mere will power and commitment.

Try it. But, uh, listen. Don't use Meg and Michelle. They're mine.

42.
Imaginary Champions

You are there training your mind and body to perform to your highest possible level on the day when you find yourself up against an outstanding performer...

There used to be a commercial or, rather, a short public service video clip on TV that had a significant impact on me. The film showed a car driving down the street to a stop sign and just beside the car was an imaginary police car with a dotted line around it that ran parallel to the real car and stayed beside it like a shadow.

The narrator reminded viewers to remember the imaginary or phantom police car. "Always drive as you would drive if there were a police car directly beside you."

Most people would have to admit that their everyday driving isn't quite the same as it would be if they had a police car directly beside them at all times. And, most athletes would have to admit that their everyday practicing effort isn't quite the same as it would be if they were playing against champions in a packed arena on national TV.

This is a concept that will come up in a number of other contexts, but I want to make sure it is abundantly clear to you. *To become a champion, it is necessary to practice, to the fullest extent possible, with the idea that you are playing against champions* in big games that really matter. Often you may find yourself in practice playing against a second-teamer or a smaller, weaker player. So you let down, or you play carelessly, or you do things that work there but won't work against a star. Why waste your time? What is it you're actually practicing for? Have you lost sight of your goals, of the phantom police car, of imaginary champions?

You aren't there practicing in order to beat that little kid. You can already beat him. You are there training your mind and body to perform to your highest possible level on the day when you find yourself up against an outstanding performer. If you think of it that way, you will infuse your practice with more enthusiasm, concentration, and effort, and you will get a lot more out of it. You will actually be preparing yourself now for success when that big day comes, instead of helping prepare yourself for failure, which so many athletes unwittingly do.

It's not very hard to figure. *If you are content to do something in a slovenly way because the competition happens to be easy, you have to realize that you are not preparing for tougher competition.* Sure, you may increase your effort when you do meet that tougher competition, but what are you doing now to improve? If you fail to improve in practice, the increased effort won't be enough when crunch time comes. You can't just increase your effort to be successful in a championship game, you have to improve your skills and performance every day during the months leading up to that game.

If a star running back is preparing for a future championship game, he will be trying his best to go untouched to the goal line and not be content merely to break the tackles of the smaller, weaker players in the junior varsity's secondary. If a star center is preparing for a future championship in basketball, he won't be content to score against the second team in practice just by using his greater height, he will be thinking about the day when he will be facing a taller, stronger player and he will work on moves that will enable him to score when he doesn't have a height and strength advantage.

Keep in mind, always, that you are practicing against imaginary *champions*, and make the moves, hit the shots, swing the bat, run and fake in ways that will work against champions.

Championships are not won on the night of a big event, but years before by athletes who commit themselves daily to championship principles.

43.
Immortality

Too many fine young athletes have learned the hard way and have paid the ultimate price—with their careers and their lives.

Joe Paterno is considered one of the greatest coaches in the history of college football. He made Penn State and winning football synonymous terms. He has a lot of provocative philosophies about sports; the following is certainly one of them.

On television, he was asked why he enforced rules that the questioner found excessively strict. Paterno's answer was enlightening. First, he made it clear that he didn't like to make strict rules. It was never his intention to excessively restrict players' lives off the field. But then he added a thought. He said he felt obligated, in certain cases, to be more strict than he really wanted to be because young people have a tendency to feel immortal.

Got that? Immortal. He said that athletes, being young and being tough physically and tough-minded, have a tendency to forget their limitations. They may decide they can have a few beers and still drive their cars flawlessly. Why not? They have conditioned themselves to get past obstacles, to overcome adversity. So, what are a few beers? In other words, the very ways of thinking that help to turn them into outstanding athletes may prove to be their downfall in another realm. Despite courage and stamina and mental and physical toughness, drugs and alcohol can and do alter a person's reaction time, alter a person's awareness of reality, and alter a person's ability to respond normally and effectively. You won't think you are any different, or any less able, until it's too late....

Too many fine young athletes have learned the hard way and have paid the ultimate price—with their careers and their lives. It's not a happy topic but it's one worth paying heed to. No one is immortal. The Halls of Fame in Cooperstown, in Canton, and in Springfield—and all the others—are filled mostly with dead athletes. Everyone dies, even the greats. But at least the athletes in these places had their chance and they made the most of it. Sadder are the graveyards throughout the world filled with the bodies of dead athletes who never got their chance.

They had a few beers. They knew what they were doing. Or they *thought* they knew what they were doing. Is this a warning never to have a beer? No way. It's just a warning to keep your wits about you. Keep the whole thing, your whole life, in perspective; *don't let sports-toughness carry over into life-foolishness*. Don't let yourself be foolish. It is one thing, a very useful thing, to develop a disregard for pain, but it is pure foolishness to let that attitude spill over into areas of life where such toughness is an obstacle to success rather than an asset.

It feels good to go from being a little kid who big people just barely notice to being an athlete who big people respect and admire. The transition is so quick. When I think back on my own life it seems as though one day I was pushing little plastic cars and trucks through the dirt and just a day later I was getting applause for scoring layups and jump shots. It's heady stuff as the announcers say, and it happens so fast it's often difficult to sort it all out.

Sometimes there's a fine line between admirable and foolish. Become aware of that fine line. Be tough, be proud, be daring, but make sure you're being those things where they really are admirable.

44.

Increasing Speed and Quickness

Every athlete can improve his performance dramatically by improving his knowledge and execution.

Every young athlete seems to be interested in increasing speed and quickness. This makes sense. Speed and quickness are two of the most important ingredients in athletic success.

One big problem: it is extremely difficult for any athlete to improve dramatically in these two areas. For the most part, speed and quickness are inherited. You can jump rope a million times, run through tires, and do a thousand agility drills, but you are still not going to outrun or out-quick many athletes who have never used a jump rope and never stepped into a tire. Nevertheless, there are some things that athletes can do to compensate for a speed or quickness deficit, and few athletes pay enough attention to these.

Consider in particular, in professional sports, the number of aging or older players who manage to perform effectively in spite of not having outstanding speed or quickness. Why? What do experienced players do in order to make up for losing a step? What is so valuable about experience?

Most important, experienced players know how to do things. They pay attention to the details of their sport. They know the little things that can give them an edge over their quicker, speedier opponents.

Every sport is different but if you are playing against a quicker, faster player, you have to *concentrate on the details* of your sport and learn how to get things done effectively. In baseball, this might mean learning how to get a bigger lead off first base and learning how to recognize the pitcher's move to first. When you aren't fast enough to take off and steal second by speed alone, it makes sense to pay attention to how to get the biggest lead possible and how to make a break for second at just the right instant.

In every sport there are specific ways to do things which, when learned, can make any player much more effective. Inexperienced players should focus more attention on how to play their sports than on how to improve their speed and quickness.

Athletes should get in great physical condition. One of the best ways to outrun and out-quick your opponents is to be ready and energetic when they are tired. In nearly every game, there are times when athletes rest, pace, or loaf. The faster the tempo, the stiffer the competition, the more opportunity for the superbly conditioned, alert athlete.

Try any kind of physical improvement you can. Continue with anything you feel may be helping, and remember to give whatever you do a real chance. Don't quit after a week. Give time to whatever it is you decide to do. Just don't worry about the things you can do little or nothing to improve. Every athlete can improve his performance dramatically by improving his knowledge and execution.

Each summer I am astonished by the inability of groups of dedicated athletes to practice effectively. Although physically and verbally committed to working hard at their sports, most athletes find it extremely difficult to learn and practice new techniques effectively.

At a summer camp some years ago we spent most of a morning session teaching young basketball players the details of screening and rolling and using a two-man-game to get an easy basket. Just a few minutes later, we started to play games. One of the players got a pass and saw a teammate running toward him to set a screen. With total seriousness, the player with the ball waved his teammate away and yelled, "Not now, we're playing a game!"

That kid had made no correlation between what we were teaching and how that stuff could help him in a game. Of course, he was young and inexperienced. But his extreme example is nonetheless typical of older, more experienced players as well. They have great difficulty changing their typical way of doing things in order to add a new technique or to add precision to their habits.

If you want to get quicker and faster, concentrate on technique. *Technique is where the biggest dividends are*. While your opponents are out there doing a million rope jumps, consider staying inside and reading, or consulting a real expert and learning how to do what you do better.

I see hundreds of basketball players each summer striving to become quicker so they can beat a quicker defender backdoor for a layup against a pressure defense. All of them would achieve their goals more quickly if they learned how to set up their defenders, how to sell their fakes on the perimeter, and when to make their breaks for the basket. Ninety-nine percent of the players I observe can be guarded by very slow defenders because they give away their intentions too soon and make their breaks poorly, too far from their defenders or too close to the basket. Good technique would free them easily, but they are usually too busy trying to get a head start, too busy edging their way toward their goal, and in too much of a hurry to adequately set up their defenders, to carry out their fakes, and to cut at the right time.

Speed and quickness are great, but there is no substitute for great technique. For every player who asks me about details of technique, a hundred others ask if I knew how they can improve their quickness and speed. That ratio should be reversed. Concentrate on technique. That's where the payback is.

45.
Individual Statistics

If you find yourself looking carefully at your personal stats to the point where it is making you less a team-oriented player, do an about-face...

After a high school football game, a coach's wife told me in a restaurant that her husband was late because he was ranting and raving. His team had just won a game, 27–7 but he was upset because the other team had scored. As his wife went on talking about how angry her husband was, I got increasingly interested in what she was saying. I assumed the coach was looking ahead to tougher games the team could not win if it gave away cheap touchdowns. I hoped his ranting and raving were a result of his impatience to get back to the practice field, to explain the error to his team, and to make sure it never happened again. But I was wrong.

I found out later that the coach was the defensive coordinator and he was upset that his team did not get a shut out. He felt as though the head coach, who ran the offense, got too much credit, and therefore it was extremely important to him that his defense shut out opponents so others would realize that defense was the primary reason the team was doing so well.

His ranting and raving, it turned out, resulted from jealously and immaturity, not from a desire to prepare his team for future victories.

I said to the coach's wife that the touchdown was scored on a fumble recovery against the offense and not against the coach's defense, so he shouldn't have anything to be angry about unless he was just excessively concerned with personal stats. "Is he sort of an egomaniac?" I asked.

She didn't like that question, got upset, and left. It wasn't the right question to ask during a post-game celebration. But it was a good lesson for thinking like a champion.

Almost any time you get excessively concerned about individual statistics, you are going to come across as childish and will find yourself ranting and raving over things that do not warrant your attention. At the end of the 1996 Major League Baseball season, there was a widespread report about Cleveland Indian slugger Albert Belle staring down a teammate for not trying to score on a single. Belle was going for an RBI title and wanted to hit another run. He was, in that case, more interested in his personal stats than in his teammate running the bases prudently. As his teammate said later, "Michael Johnson (the 1996 Olympic Gold Medalist in the 200 and 400 meter dashes) could not have scored on that hit!" Nevertheless, Belle wanted his teammate to try. Winning the game for the team was not as important to Belle as winning the American League RBI crown for himself.

Belle is a great baseball player but his concern for his personal stats hasn't won him many popularity contests, or much respect, either. I suspect that Albert Belle would be a much happier human being and probably even a more productive player if he learned to put the team first and made winning games his number one priority.

If you find yourself looking carefully at your personal stats to the point where it is making you less a team-oriented player, do an about-face. Quit looking at your stats for a while. Focus on other areas of performance. Change.

Players who put team first and concentrate primarily on winning are more respected, they usually play better, and they enjoy their lives more.

Hopefully you have heard stars say, "I just come out to play each day and do the best I can, the stats will take care of themselves." That's good advice.

46.
Injuries

No injury is truly crippling unless you let it cripple your mind.

Injuries, unfortunately, are a part of sports and a part of life. If you talk with any group of pro athletes or any adults who played a sport over a period of years, nearly every one would be able to recall an injury, if not many, that put them out of some big games or caused them to miss a whole season. So there's no grand secret about injuries. If you play a sport, and if you play intensely over a period of time, it is very likely that you will get injured at some point. You can expect it. When you get an injury, try to see the big picture. Forget the woe-is-me attitude, and don't worry that your plans are suddenly ruined. Get complete information from medical experts so you know exactly what you are dealing with, and then do what they say. Often, it seems the only thing you can do is be patient and wait. I still recall the advice I got when I broke my leg in ninth grade:

In the cast, your bones are protected. The most dangerous time for you will be just after the cast comes off. Your broken bone will be healed but all the muscles around it will be weaker than ever. They will be in their most vulnerable state, just when you are chomping at the bit to get back into form. So don't rush your return to competition and don't get in games with the thought that you will take it easy. In games, your instincts will take over and you will do things suddenly, without thinking, that will put great strain on your muscles and ligaments and tendons. Then you could tear something that will take even longer to heal. Take the time you need, on your own and as soon as the cast comes off, to exercise and strengthen all those areas around the injury.

Don't get into any games until your body is prepared to go 100 percent.

I would like to add one final consideration. *Most champions became champions by developing the habit of turning liabilities into assets.* So can you. That means if you break your right arm, it's time to start using and improving your left. If you have to remain immobile then you have more time to fully develop your mind. You can always improve some part of you while some other part is healing. So think of an injury as time to work on another part of you that probably has been neglected.

No injury is truly crippling unless you let it cripple your mind. Realize that an injury can be a huge setback or it can be an opportunity for some other kind of development. Make the best of your situation and don't waste your time feeling sorry for yourself. Once you are injured you have taken a place beside thousands of other athletes who have shared your same experience. The question is will you let your injury get you discouraged, or will you make the most of the experience and turn it into an opportunity?

47.

Instructing Your Teammates

When two people work together to accomplish something that would have been more difficult or impossible individually, something special happens.

Any athlete involved in a team sport can often help his team by instructing his teammates, but this can be a delicate subject. There aren't two athletes out of a hundred who like being told what to do. It's bad enough having a coach constantly barking out commands without having teammates do the same. Nevertheless, I think this whole subject can be dealt with effectively by keeping one rule in mind.

Instruct ***before*** *a mistake is made. Not after.*

Athletes need to understand that any jerk can tell someone what to do after a play is over. The cleaning lady or a cab driver can tell us we should have been in zone coverage if man-to-man coverage resulted in a touchdown. (Hey, nothing against cleaning folks or cabbies, but they don't always do their jobs perfectly either.)

If you want to instruct in a way that is really going to help your team, you need to instruct before the bad thing happens, before the play takes place. Then the teammate you instruct will take your instruction as encouragement and as a reminder, and he will be grateful to you after the play instead of irritated.

In basketball, this opportunity—or failure—happens frequently. A star player is dribbling down the court, suddenly he stops and shoots and scores, and the defender's teammate yells: "Hey, don't let him shoot. He's killing us!" Such criticism stings. No doubt, when the dribbler approached, the defender was worried about the shot but also worried that the dribbler would race by him for an easy layup. Instruction during that worry time would have been very welcome. It would have been helpful for the defender to hear his teammate say, "Don't let him shoot. If he tries to pass you, I'll pick him up."

Huge difference. Now it's a *team* thing, not an individual thing. A teammate has offered to share responsibility directly. And you can be sure, nine times out of ten if good players are out there, the dribbler won't be permitted to stop and get off a good shot. The defender will force him to go toward the basket where another teammate is waiting to help. That kind of instruction isn't just welcome, it builds teamwork even when the play fails. Say the dribbler does manage to pass the defender, pass both defenders, and score. Usually a joint "I'm sorry" or "my fault" follows, and the two players determine not to let it happen again. A certain pact is formed on a play like that, and good things happen psychologically as a result.

Naturally, if the defensive play works and the dribbler goes by and is picked up by the helping teammate, the two players develop a sense of trust and a good feeling. Their play becomes more efficient, better. They work together to accomplish the objectives both of them recognize. Two heads are better than one. When two people work together to accomplish something that would have been more difficult, or impossible, individually, something special happens. Teamwork. Chemistry. Excellence.

"But," you're saying, you "can't always instruct before the event takes place. Sometimes it happens too fast. There isn't time." And my reply would be, "You need not always instruct." Remember, you are an athlete. That's your role. You are not the coach. So, you don't need to instruct full time, every time. You need to instruct only when instructing proves to be a good thing for an athlete to do. The coach will usually do more than enough instructing anyway. On most teams there's no shortage of instruction, there's a shortage of proper execution. Therefore, adding more instruction particularly when a teammate already feels like a failure and is angry or upset, just isn't the way to build a champion.

In the example above, had the teammate told the defender in advance not to allow the shot, but the defender allowed it anyway, the intelligence of the instruction would have rung loud and clear and nothing would have had to be added after the shot went through the rim.

If you are not smart enough to anticipate the need or not quick-thinking enough to yell the instruction in advance, my feeling is you don't have a right to say anything.

There are exceptions to nearly every rule, of course, so no use belaboring the point. You may find some intelligent way occasionally to offer instruction after the fact, but the before-or-not-at-all rule is a good one to keep in mind. Most after-the-play instruction is usually nothing more than voiced frustration or anger. It really isn't instruction at all. If you aren't able to instruct a teammate before something happens, you probably aren't the person who ought to be doing any instructing.

48.
Intangibles

The best way to get intangibles working for you is to cover all the tangibles thoroughly.

Intangibles make the difference in almost every sport, in almost every big event. The tangibles are the easy part. Both teams usually have an offensive attack and a defensive strategy. Both teams have peoples of varying sizes, strengths, speeds, and so on. Though one team may be superior in one area, a coach will usually know a style of play or plan of attack that can neutralize that strength. Everyone talks about the importance of "getting them to play our game." We need to play in such a way that our strengths will be emphasized and their strengths will be minimized.

Everyone has strengths and everyone has weaknesses. A team that seems unbeatable one week may look absolutely inept the next. Athletes are human. Even if everything were the same from one week to the next, there would still be wide variations in performance. But things are never the same. Athletes have different styles and different attitudes, there are headaches and staleness, and jealousies and outside influences. There are also the dynamics of teamwork and the interplay of personalities and all sorts of emotions that add dimensions no one can ever predict.

All of these unpredictable, mental aspects of sports are usually grouped under the name "intangibles." You can't put your finger on sudden confidence, on joint purpose, on turning points, and on rallying cries, but these things are a crucial part of sports.

How do you get the intangibles working for you? How can you make sure that your team is the team that suddenly jells? How can you make sure that the sign on the locker room wall mobilizes your team? How can you make sure that your team has the psychological edge? It seems you cannot make *sure* of any of these things. But you can influence them in your behalf. You can do something to encourage things to go your way.

Probably the most important step is to be aware of the importance of intangibles and to try to get them working for you. Open the lines of communication. Talk to your teammates. Talk to your coaches. Encourage each other. Build teamwork in the tangible ways and the intangibles will likely follow. Let me say the above in another way.

The best way to get the intangibles working for you is to cover all the tangibles thoroughly. Not just the offensive and defensive assignments, but the hustle, the encouragement, the enthusiasm, the off-the-field activities, the preseason preparation, the reading, the thinking...

Do all you can to make sure of the tangibles, and realize this: many athletes don't know the difference between tangibles and intangibles. They may claim that teamwork is an intangible, that no one knows what makes a team suddenly click. They may be right in some ultimate sense. But along the way, plenty of things can be done to encourage good teamwork. Like making sure that each athlete knows his role, is clear on his assignments, is encouraging to his teammates, is committed to winning a championship, is willing to subordinate personal goals to team goals, is willing to sacrifice in order to succeed, is willing to prepare in the off-season, is concerned about teammates. A long list of known ingredients goes into teamwork. We don't know what makes a team suddenly jell, but we sure know a lot of things that could keep one from jelling.

When you take shortcuts on the tangibles—the things we can definitely put our fingers on—the intangibles seem to go against you. You don't walk onto a field and just hope the athletes happen to get along, just like you don't walk onto a field just hoping to be in good physical condition. You work every day to build your muscle power and stamina. And you work every day to build team spirit.

From your standpoint, as an athlete, there are no intangibles. There are only tangibles. There are dozens of definite, concrete things for you to focus and improve on daily. Take care of those things and the rest will take care of itself. When you think about sports in this way, all those intangibles don't seem so elusive after all. Intangibles are usually the bad, unexpected things that happen to athletes who fail to prepare fully and who just don't care enough to dot the i's and cross the t's and take care of all the little things that are crucial to championship performance.

49.
Interviews

Imagine what you are likely to be asked, then prepare good answers to those questions…

If you are going to be a champion, interviews are going to become a part of your life. And even if you're not, job interviews, business presentations, and a modern world increasingly based on communication mean that it would be wise for you to become adept at interviewing. It's not nearly as difficult as many athletes seem to think, especially if you keep one major principle in mind: cheat.

Cheating, as you may have guessed, has a special meaning here but it really isn't much different from how most junior high school students think of it. If you know you have a test coming up, it makes sense to prepare for the questions you expect to be asked. If you know you are going to have one hundred multiple choice questions and you are hoping to get most of the answers correct, you better make sure you know about 150–200 facts. If you have an essay test coming up, it makes sense to prepare some intelligent answers in advance. Again, the process is simple: imagine what you are likely to be asked, then prepare good answers to those questions. Typically, even if you are asked different questions from the ones you have prepared, it is possible to connect the actual question to the information you are prepared to offer. That way, you are always able to give some pertinent, worthwhile information. It may not always be exactly what is asked for, but it will be close and you will appear intelligent.

Say you had a course on war. If you studied hard and prepared a super answer on the causes of the Civil War, and then you were asked about the causes of World War II, everything is not lost. Say what you can about World War II and then make a connection. "In a lot of ways, World War II was like the Civil War..." And then put down your super answer. Keep making whatever connections to World War II that you can, but if you can't make any, at least you are going to have a great answer on war. It's just that most of your answer isn't on the right war. But it is still a very good display of information if you have taken the time to prepare an intelligent, thoughtful answer. It's impressive, even though it may not warrant an A. (And it certainly is much better than leaving the page blank. You are far above a zero, even if you know nothing at all about the actual question.)

You ought to be able to realize how this kind of "cheating" works even better in interviews than on tests. On tests, a teacher or professor may take points away for not precisely answering what was asked. In an interview, there is no such deduction. The interviewer, in almost all cases, is merely trying to elicit interesting information. So, prepare interesting stuff and, regardless of the question, give them your best shot.

Let's consider a situation. You have a big game tonight, and you know a reporter may be asking you for your comments after the game. So, you prepare.

1. Try to connect your sport to some international event or to politics or science, something that makes you sound like more than just a jock. A lot of adults would be especially impressed if you could compare the game to a recent media takeover or a computer issue, or compare your teammates to local politicians angling for a lead in the latest political race.

2. Try to use some words that may not be part of your everyday slang.

3. Take the spotlight off yourself and shine it on some others. No one likes a selfish braggart. Give some credit to coaches, teammates, or to someone no one would usually think of. (Remember, there's no right answer in an interview, only interesting, intelligent stuff or dull, stupid stuff.)

Now, for the interview. You don't win, you lose. Your prepared answer was for talking about the big win. What should you say when the reporter asks what are your thoughts on losing? Just change it slightly. Go with essentially whatever you prepared, just change it around so all your ready comments apply to the other team.

"We didn't stand a chance once they found one tiny opening in our firewall, man."

You can be sure the reporter will be furiously taking down every word you say, as well as seeking you out after the next game for comments whether or not you play a good game.

If you are fortunate enough to win, consider adding a surprise name to the ingredients of your success. You might mention a former coach, a substitute who didn't get to play, or a friend, parent, or relative. Any of those people would very much appreciate seeing their names in the paper and getting recognized for contributing to your success. And what does it cost you? If you are going to be a champion, you might as well interview like one.

50.
Invitations

While playing a sport, you have a rare opportunity. You have an entrée, a free pass, to anyone…

Do you know why many of the most important people in your community, in your state, in the nation, have never attended one of your games? They never got an invitation.

It's amazing how many things never happen because of the mere lack of an invitation. You don't take your dream girl to the prom, the perfect guy doesn't show up at your party, the owner of the big local company never comes to your games. Why? No one invited them.

Invitations are powerful. This is not to claim that every time you invite someone to do something, that the person will do it. Of course not. But invitations do have a powerful impact. And they piggyback. Invite someone once and receive a no, and the force of that first invitation gets added to the power of the second one. This is hardly a secret.

We are all human. Everyone likes being wanted, needed, valued. It doesn't matter who it is. Naturally, some people are busier than others, but often the busiest people are best able to make time available for things they want to do. Most people, however important, find it difficult to reject sincere invitations, especially personal invitations and carefully targeted ones.

But why point out the power of invitations to athletes? What do invitations have to do with athletics? Plenty. If you are on a team that doesn't get as much fan support as you would like, guess whose fault it is? Yours. How many fans have you invited? How many people have you asked to come to a special event? Have you designed a program especially to appeal to certain groups of people, and have you informed and invited those people? Have you invited young people to clinics? Have you staged some special event and invited people to participate in some way?

This section is partially for explaining how to gain fan support but it extends beyond that. Invitations are important to use even if you have adequate fan support, just to spread joy, to involve others, to extend your positive influence, and make the world around you a better place. They can also help you personally.

While playing a sport you have a rare opportunity. You have an entrée, a free pass, to people in a way that is so much more difficult otherwise. The owner of the big local company, for example, is a good target if he happens to have a twelve-year-old son. Invite his son to a special clinic. Get the son interested, and you'll get the father interested. Is it wrong to impress a twelve-year-old before asking his father for a summer job or a career? I don't think so. In fact, it wouldn't hurt to write a letting explaining exactly your motives. It's a value-for-value world. You give value, you get value. If you are able to motivate a twelve-year-old, you will deserve whatever you wanted from his father, and his father will be happy to give it to you. (At least you will deserve whatever you want more than you did before you offered any value at all.)

The point is you ought to be doing things as a team, not just to increase attendance at your games but to involve your community as much as possible for the benefit of everyone—impressionable children who need positive role models, your careers, and the connections that can be made. There's no need to precisely pinpoint your motivations. There's nothing wrong with having a personal agenda and goals to achieve.

Every act can be made to look purely selfish, and I don't mind starting out that way and dealing with this issue directly. I don't think selfishness is the issue. There are a lot more errors of neglect (not paying attention to others) than there are errors of exploiting others. The business people in your community will be aware enough of the value-for-value world we live in that they will not let themselves be used anyway. If you invite them to something worthwhile, they will appreciate the value you gave them and they will be happy to give some value in return.

In business spheres this is called a win-win transaction. I win. You win. I get what I want. You get what you want. I find out what you want and give it to you, so I can get what I want from you. There's not a thing wrong with that. You give value to get value.

How much value do you have to your community? How many people have you invited to anything? How many clinics have you held? How many kids have you inspired? Most athletes are simply playing their sports, hoping to have winning teams and hoping that fan support materializes out of thin air without assistance.

It is true that fan support tends to flow to winners. And it should. Who wants to waste time watching people who haven't paid the price to perform with excellence?

If you want fan support and the benefits that come with it, then work on your sport. Become excellent. Win. But also, look around you. Find the people you want to be involved with. *Find the people who would add something to your life, and then add something to theirs.* Plan a special event. Give it some thought and time, and send out some invitations. You will likely be surprised at the reaction. Remember the line from the baseball movie *Field of Dreams?* Invite them. And they will come.

51.
Justifications

Auerbach recognized that the Celtics had, potentially, a much more devastating disadvantage to deal with. They had a ready-made justification for losing...

Excuses are little petty things that most athletes learn early to avoid. No one like excuses and most athletes know that. But justification is a whole other banana. It's bigger, grander, more complex. The very word is longer, it sounds more scholarly, more philosophical. And it is. It's a broader term. It's a concept, not a mere comment. As a result, it's potentially a lot more damaging to your quest for championship performance. A lot of players and coaches who are proud of not making excuses for their failures, nevertheless often *feel* justified when they fail. So be careful about elevating an excuse to the level of a justification. It would be good to not only eliminate excuses from your talking but also eliminate justifications from your thinking.

Consider the baseball player at the plate who takes a called second strike. The batter often takes the first strike on his own, to get a sense of how the pitcher is throwing. Or maybe the manager gives the "take sign" to make the pitcher throw a strike. Perhaps the batter swings and misses the first or second pitch. Or maybe he hits a 400 foot foul ball that just barely misses being a grand slam homer. No matter. He has a strike on him one way or another, and the umpire calls a second strike on a pitch the batter feels sure is out of the strike zone.

Typically, the batter steps out of the batter's box and he lets his displeasure show. He grumbles at the umpire and stomps around, maybe tosses some dirt, and then he steps back into the batter's box. He may take another ball or two, and some more time may pass, but then a good pitch comes sailing toward the plate and the batter swings and misses. Strike three! He's out.

Before walking back in disgust to the dugout, he glares at the umpire, still angry at him. If the umpire hadn't called that second strike, he reasons, he would not have struck out. He is sure of that. And so are many others who will have the same reaction throughout the season. If it weren't for those blind umps, they think they'd be .400 hitters.

Maybe all these strikeout victims are correct. Maybe none of them would ever strike out if umpires could see those second strikes for the balls that they really are. Maybe. But I wonder if all of these baseball players know how stupid they look game after game after game. And I wonder even more if they realize how much they are sabotaging their own batting averages by failing to learn to put that second strike behind them (completely) and take full responsibility for their time at bat *before* the third strike gets thrown.

Naturally they all think they have legitimate excuses. It is true that if the second pitch hadn't been called a strike—therefore getting the batter behind in the count instead of ahead—the batter would not have to guard the plate nor swing at pitches near the corners of the plate. Ahead in the count, a batter waits for his pitch. Behind in the count, he's more defensive. He has to swing at a pitch he'd rather not take.

So, yes, that second strike is important. But that is something a batter (and a manager) has to think about before the first strike is taken, or when the first pitch is fouled off. The big picture is, you're up there to hit and you have three chances. You know in advance that there are likely to be some close calls, there's simply no way that all of those pitches will be called in your favor.

The issue here is not sportsmanship but performance. In general terms, these baseball players need a better sense of a dictum of human nature:

Give a person a legitimate justification for giving into failure, and he will use it, and fail.

It is bad enough that the umpire's call puts the batter mentally in a hole. But what is even worse is the batter giving in to that feeling and getting in deeper. "That ump put me in the hole. How can I get a hit now?"

The legendary coach of the Boston Celtics, Red Auerbach, understood this aspect of human nature clearly, and he talked about it with the Celtic players before a championship playoff when he was president of the team but no longer its coach. I heard about this from a brief TV interview I saw with Celtic superstar Larry Bird. The questioner asked Bird if Red Auerbach said anything to the team. Bird answered that Auerbach rarely said anything to the team since he wasn't the coach any longer and he preferred not to meddle...but in this one case, Auerbach made an exception. He called the team together and asked them if they felt capable of beating their opponents. He made a point of adding "with the conditions as they are." This was especially important because the Celtics had several players out with injuries. In other words, the Celtics had a legitimate justification for losing to the Los Angeles Lakers that year; they had some key players missing from their team.

Along with this clear-cut disadvantage going into the playoffs, Auerbach recognized that the Celtics had, potentially, a much more devastating disadvantage to deal with. They had a ready-made justification for losing and Auerbach was painfully aware of that dictum, which is worth repeating: Give a person a legitimate justification for giving in to failure, and he will use it, and fail.

Auerbach called that meeting just to make sure the Celtics got it clear in their minds that justifications didn't cut it. He not only didn't want them to make excuses for any failures in the playoffs, he didn't want them to feel justified in failing. (He wasn't worried about the Celtic players acting petty and voicing excuses. He was worried about what the players would be thinking.)

He wanted the players to go on record, before the games had begun, as believing that they could and should win with exactly what they had available to do the job. It was useless to talk about the players they didn't have. That was history. What he wanted to talk about was current events. Forget the injuries, he told them. Do you or don't you feel that the necessary tools are here in this room to get the job done?

In that way, before the games, Auerbach forced the Celtic players to commit to a way of thinking conducive to winning, and he eliminated the potential justification the players had for losing.

Deprived of a back-of-the-mind justification for losing, the Celtics were forced to concentrate entirely on winning. Did they win that year? I don't remember. During the 1980s they beat the Lakers sometimes, and the Lakers beat them sometimes. But the lesson is crucial regardless. Right thinking doesn't guarantee that you will always win, but wrong thinking permits you to lose games that you otherwise would have won.

Whenever you feel yourself harboring in the back of your mind a justification—for striking out, or for doing anything other than committing fully to performing with excellence and taking full responsibility for it—root it out. Get rid of it. *If you don't eliminate your legitimate justifications for failure, they will actually contribute to eventual failure.*

I hope you understand this fully. It's a terrific lesson that too few athletes are aware of. What Red Auerbach did was masterful. He robbed the Celtics of their justification for losing. Try hard to rob yourself of any justifications you may have along the way.

52.
Kicking Some Butt

If we're fifty points better than you, then we ought to beat you by fifty...

When you play a sport, you ought to play it. Really play it. You ought to go out there with the idea of kicking some butt.

What does that mean? A lot of people seem to get bogged down in sportsmanship at times and to forget that one of the true joys of a sport is seeing two tough competitors go at it. It's not life and death. You aren't out to hurt anyone. But who gets hurt by getting kicked in the butt? When was the last time you heard that a pro player would miss the next game due to a kick in the butt? It doesn't happen. They get ankle sprains and ligament tears and cartilage rips and broken bones, but they don't miss many games because of kicks in the butt. So you're free to kick the other team's butts, literally and figuratively. Go at it. Play hard. Play harder. Play rough and tough. As long as you don't try to hurt anyone, your opponent will respect you for your toughness and your approach.

This is hardly a call for neglecting sportsmanship. It's just a reminder that you don't deserve admiration for your efforts in sports—and you won't get it—unless you are going at it with ferocity.

Be tough. Be fierce. Be aggressive. You can be a good sport without this kind of approach. But you can't be a great one.

Go out and kick some butt. And don't be afraid to run up the score. Win by a hundred if you can. Personally, I've never understood the etiquette of winning by only a respectable amount. I think when you're playing a sport you ought to pile up as many points as you possibly can. I think that's what sport is all about, and any other approach just degrades the whole experience.

Have you heard the line "What goes around comes around?" The idea is if you beat someone by a humiliating margin, someday the reverse will happen and you will get beaten by a humiliating margin. Really? Does that sound like a good warning to you? It doesn't to me. My response to that way of thinking is "Good luck. Have at it. If you can beat me by a so-called humiliating margin, that's exactly how badly I want to get beaten, and not a point less. I can't imagine any joy in getting beaten by seventeen when I know you were actually able to beat me by fifty. Where's the satisfaction in that?"

In fact, let me go a step further and make this perfectly clear. I don't respect coaches who squawk about some other coach or team running up the score.

I think true athletes want the score to reflect exactly what happened on the field.

If we're fifty points better than you, then we ought to beat you by fifty. If you're fifty points better than me, you'll be demeaning me by beating me by any less. Here's an example that will explain the wisdom of this way of thinking.

Several years ago my brother and I went on weekends to play racquetball at a local racquetball club. My brother was much better than I, and he won every time we played. So, how could we keep going to play, weekend after weekend, and keep enjoying it? I think we kept going and kept enjoying it because each of us did the other the special favor of respecting each other and the sport.

I tried very hard never to get discouraged, never to give up, and never to give away any points. I tried to make my brother work his butt off for every point he got. Even though he was clearly better, I tried very hard to give him a tough competitive experience. For his part, he paid me the respect of not giving me any points; in fact, he tried hard to get every point. He tried to shut me out in every game we played.

Why do I call that respect? Why did that enable me to enjoy the experience of playing him? Because with him trying to get every point I could be legitimately proud of each point I got. I could feel a sense of accomplishment and satisfaction. Okay, so maybe I couldn't beat him. But a 15–10 game was a real accomplishment for me. In a sense, I beat him that game. I played above my ability and he played below his. In a 15–2 game, he could feel satisfied, and I would feel defeated.

Assuming our typical game would end about 15–7, there was a kind of victory for me every time I could get 8 or more points and, conversely, a victory for my brother every time he could hold me below 7. If he had chosen, instead, to give me some points, to work hard sometimes but not others, and to let most games end up 15–12, where would any satisfaction be? Where would the spirit of competition have gone? Where would respect and satisfaction and disappointment and accomplishment have gone? How could I feel good about even beating him if I suspected he let me win or gave me ten points while playing at 50 percent effort? Do you feel good losing by just ten when you know the other team could have beaten you by forty?

I think the answers to these questions are pretty obvious when you stop to think about them and about the real meaning of sports. It is a lot more humiliating to find yourself playing against someone not doing his best than to play against a star and get your butt kicked. Yet in every league during every season, you read about coaches even in pro sports grumbling about some other coach running up the score.

Wimps! Grow up, guys. Have enough respect for yourself and for others to do them the favor of playing your best the whole time. Have enough respect for them to beat them by fifty if you can, and enable them to feel the joy of bringing the score down to 45 near the end—due to their efforts, not because you let them.

And finally, *respect yourself enough never to want a score to be respectable* as a result of early substitutions or diminished effort or outright gifts. If you're a real athlete, you want the score to reflect the actual circumstances of the contest. There's no humiliation in losing by fifty to a team that is actually sixty points better than you. In fact, there's some joy to be found in a game like that, unless they give you ten unearned. Is the concept clear enough? I don't care if we're playing checkers or Tiddly Winks, do me the favor of beating me by as much as you can and understand the respect I am giving you when I try to beat you by as much as I can. That's the only way sports are fun for me. What about you?

53.
Leadership

*You lead **only** by example? Then you lead poorly...*

Leadership is very important in any sport, and most athletes seem not to understand what it is. There's a good reason for this. I think the word itself is misleading. Most of us think of a leader as being like our kindergarten teacher. She knew just about everything, we knew just about nothing, she told us what to do, we did it. We all seem to understand the kindergarten form of leadership perfectly. The problem is, in the adult world it isn't like that at all.

Theodore White, who wrote a book every four years called *The Making of the President,* had an enlightening analogy about leadership in the front of one of his books. He compared a president (he could have been talking about any leader) to a wagon train scout in the Old West.

The scout rode ahead of the wagon train. He was the leader, but he had all sorts of limitations. Sure, if danger lurked ahead he and his horse could hide behind a rock or tree. But the wagon train? It couldn't hide. It churned up dirt and made noise that could be seen and heard miles away. It left tracks so wide, deep (and smelly) they could be followed effortlessly a month later.

In other words, the scout was the leader but in a very real sense, he was a follower. If he got too far ahead of the wagons, his information would be useless by the time the wagons arrived. If he gave an order for everyone to sprint for cover, the order would necessarily be disobeyed; wagon trains don't sprint. If he decided it would be a good idea to cross a stream and sneak through a narrow pass or to travel on the side of a hill, his decision would be ridiculous. Sure, *he* could do it, but not the train with all those slow, heavy wagons.

I hope the point of this is clear to you. There must be a large portion of follower in every leader. Doesn't do any good to bark out commands that your wagons—or teammates—aren't able to carry out. Your commands, when you offer them, have to be in tune with your teammates' thinking and their abilities. Get just a bit outside their understanding or ability, and you've lost them; your barking becomes an irritation and a hindrance to success, rather than an aid to it.

"I told them what to do, they just didn't do it."

"Big deal! If they weren't going to do it, what good was it to tell 'em?"

"Maybe they'll learn from their mistakes."

Yeah, maybe they will learn from their mistakes. And maybe they'll tune you out completely. Maybe they should. Nearly every athlete gets his share of advice, from parents, from friends, from fans, and even from enemies. If you perform in public, all sorts of strangers will feel free to offer you advice whether you want it or not.

On most teams, the head coach says enough. In addition, the assistants get in their two, four or eighty-nine cents. It's not all that necessary on most teams for the so-called captain to be out there issuing orders, too. If there's a play to call or some signal to be given, fine. That's play calling or signal giving. Let's not make a mistake here. Fans may mistake those things for leadership. But they aren't leadership. They are play calling and signal giving. Period.

So, what is leadership? Is it something the elected or appointed team captain does? I don't think so. In fact, I would emphasize this point. *Leadership is what every team member does.* It's what every team member must do on a good team. Leadership is first and foremost leading yourself, doing what needs to be done, setting a good example, doing your part.

The most effective way to lead is by example. Without the example, any commands you choose to bark out will be seen as incongruent; they will be unwanted and usually ignored. With a good example as a foundation, you can be sure you will have a powerful influence before you ever open your mouth. And when you do open your mouth, your words will have impact. They will be heard.

So, the first rule of leadership is get your own house in order. Do *your* job. Set the example. The rest is useless without this. Once you have laid the foundation, once you are doing your job and setting a good example, your leadership will be very valuable. The three ways to lead, then, the three basic things a leader does are (1) encourage, (2) instruct, and (3) involve yourself with your teammates. You encourage any time, all the time, as often as possible. You instruct carefully and intelligently *before* a mistake is made, not after. (For more detail on encouraging and instructing teammates, see the sections on "Encouraging Your Teammates" and "Instructing your Teammates.") Finally, you involve yourself in the things going on around you. You observe, you listen, you try to see things through your teammates' eyes and then respond accordingly. Realize that if you are on a team you need to consider yourself a leader. You can't sit back and assume it's not your job to lead just because you weren't elected or appointed captain.

There is such little difference between a good leader and a good follower, and their roles reverse so often, that it is crucial (if you want to play on a winning team) that each team member consider himself a leader. If you are on a team and you do *not* consider yourself a leader, you are failing to inject your talents and abilities sufficiently, and you are hurting your team. By not encouraging, not instructing and not involving yourself with your teammates, you are failing to help your team reach its potential. I don't know how to say it any more clearly. If you sit back and expect someone else to do it, a lot will never get done.

Championship teams are forged when each team member takes it upon himself to set a good example, to earn the respect of the others, to encourage the others constantly, to instruct them in order to prevent needless mistakes, and to stay involved with them so inevitable problems and distractions and personality conflicts don't get magnified and impede performance. (On most teams, they do just that.)

Can a basketball team have twelve leaders or a football team have forty-five? To be champions, every player must be a leader—not a dictator, but an example-setting, encouraging, instructing, involved team player.

You say you're just not one of those noisy types? *You lead **only** by example? Then you lead poorly*. And you are missing an important part of the intangibles that lift a team to a higher level. Leading by example is wonderful. The better you are, the better your example, and the more powerful and influential will be your leadership. But leading only by example is inadequate for athletes trying to do all they can do. There are so many times—away from the field, during practices and during game—that leadership can make a huge impact on the performance of your teammates. You just can't leave this vital area to take care of itself. You need to strive constantly to sharpen your communication, increase your encouragement, and improve your ability to tune in to and respond to the situations and personalities around you.

"Coach, I would love to lead. But they never want to do what I say."

Have you ever heard or said or felt something like that? Just remember, real leadership isn't telling people what to do and watching them do it. You don't need a leader to do that; a mere sign will suffice. Real leadership begins when the people around you are not doing what they need to be doing and probably don't want to. It's often frustrating. It takes thought and sensitivity and character and effort. Sometimes you have to listen, sometimes educate, sometimes be patient, sometimes struggle and strain. Make sure you understand this and don't bother being discouraged. Remember, true leadership typically begins when you find yourself in the muck of a discouraging situation. In fact, true leaders bring their rubber boots, wade into the muck, and stay awhile.

In the old Westerns, a dude on a white horse rode into a bad town in the morning, cleaned things up in the afternoon, and rode out at sunset (usually with the town's only gorgeous, twenty-eight-year-old virgin on the back of his saddle, totally in love). That's a nice movie but don't let it affect your notion of what leadership is all about. You'll need those boots, and some gloves, too. I think a true leader would say that leadership is more like having your hands full of packages, with an umbrella wedged between your shoulder and cheek, trying to keep everything dry while running through a pelting rain. It will take all your best efforts and will seem essentially hopeless most of the time. But the effort to be a real leader really does make a difference.

54.
Listening for FIGS

Urging you to listen in order not to miss anything is hardly the way to get you to put your hammers, anvils, and stirrups into play...

Listen carefully, boys and girls." Teachers, instructors, and other authorities might as well add, "or you won't get to hear what the nice, boring man is saying." What a warning. The precise reason you are not listening carefully is that you have no interest in what the nice, boring man is saying. But how often do you hear this sort of thing? How often do you have to put up with it yourself? In my opinion, the whole problem is one of definition. Teachers typically tell students to listen carefully to things they are not interested in. It's not a great psychology.

"If you don't listen carefully, you may miss something."

"Thank God," you're thinking. "If only we could miss it all."

If you had your choice, you'd leave the guy there talking to himself. Clearly, urging you to listen in order not to miss anything is hardly the way to get you to put your hammers, anvils, and stirrups into play. But let me suggest four reasons for listening to any speaker or teacher. The reasons start with the letters F, I, G, and S.

1. Listen to Flatter.

Flatter the speaker. He or she came to talk to you, probably with good intentions in most cases. He would like to help you.

He has something that might be good for you to learn. At least he thinks so. (Someone thinks so, otherwise he wouldn't be there.) And he might actually have something worth hearing. You will never know unless you listen. But even if he doesn't have anything of value for you, he's still a human being. He would rather be flattered than ignored. Why not flatter him by keeping your eyes on him at all times? Not yet convinced?

2. Listen to Impress.

Impress the speaker. Send him away thinking and talking about what a terrific student you are. Send him away amazed at the attention you gave him and the interest you showed. It is possible to de-press a speaker or to im-press a speaker just by the kind of attention you give. With this choice, why not choose to impress? Not yet convinced?

3. Listen to Get ahead.

Speakers, teachers—anyone—often can help you in ways you never imagine. But why would anyone want to make any special effort to help you get ahead? Maybe because you have flattered and impressed. If you have flattered and impressed someone, he is going to want to help you. If you have ignored and depressed someone, he is unlikely to do anything for you.

Why not give yourself a chance to get ahead, perhaps with a summer job or a special connection that will help you get what you want? Can some speaker do that for you? Just about anyone can help you get ahead if he has a special feeling about you. Just about anyone can make a call, knows some friends, knows about a job or a possibility.

Impressing people on your way through life is a lot like playing a game. You don't know at the beginning of the game what plays will turn out to be the big ones so you have to try to play well the whole time in order to make sure you are playing well when the really important moments occur. In the same way, you rarely know who can help you. You don't know who is talking to whom or what connections a person may have. It sure can't hurt having as many people as possible out there spreading good words about you.

4. Listen for Self-discipline.

If you think you can go through life always knowing who can help you and who can't, who you should make an effort to flatter and impress and who you can afford to ignore and depress, you're wrong. You'll never do it. Sometimes the people who seem least in a position to help you are those who can do the most. Other times people who act like they can give you the world won't actually lift a finger for you. The intelligent thing to do, if you want to get ahead, is be the best you can be at all times, which brings us to self-discipline.

You ought to *learn to listen with your eyes and body*— looking attentive and holding your body erect—as a matter of developing your own self-discipline. Do you have the guts, the muscular development, and the ability to be able to flatter and impress someone who is saying things you have no interest in? That's a skill you need to work on.

Losers can't spend even ten seconds listening attentively to someone who doesn't immediately grab them as having something useful to say. In fact, some people have such bad habits and such dismal self-discipline that they are disruptive, show discourtesy, and act stupid before the speaker even begins. They have conditioned themselves to believe that every teacher or speaker has nothing worthwhile to say to them, so they can't even begin listening.

You can teach yourself to pay attention to something that does not initially seem interesting. Intelligent people, and self-disciplined people, realize that all sorts of things of value don't show their value from the start. You may have to listen for it, watch for it, dig for it. It doesn't just grab you, you have to grab it. And to do that, you have to be able to put yourself in a position to be able to grab it.

So why do you flatter and impress a boring speaker? Maybe because he can help you get ahead. But maybe just for practice. The next time you come upon a boring speaker, you can flatter and impress sufficiently to make that person want to help you get ahead.

Don't fool yourself into thinking that you will wait till the day you meet an important person who has something valuable to say to you, and *then* listen attentively with your eyes and body posture, turning over each phrase in your mind, nodding here and there, and occasionally tilting your head to show you are thinking. If your listening skills are poor, you will never get yourself in position to hear that important person. The invitations will have gone out to others as they do all the time.

Sorry for the disparaging label, but the stupids don't even know the game is being played. They don't even know what invitations they are missing or the parties going on around them. They see no correlation between listening skills, attention spans, and the willingness to flatter and impress for no apparent reason, and getting ahead, getting invited, getting opportunities. They think the careful, flattering, impressing listener is wasting time or, possibly worse, brown-nosing. And if they asked why you were listening to that crap they wouldn't even understand the answer, "For practice."

The intelligent person who is interested in maximizing opportunities in life will begin to *see the most boring speaker as an opportunity itself.* An opportunity to practice an important skill under difficult conditions. Anyone can listen attentively to a great teacher or speaker. But how good are you at listening attentively with your posture and your eyes when the speaker or teacher is monotone and dull, and the subject contains no initial interest for you?

Good challenge. What resources can you bring to the encounter to enable you to listen attentively? How animated can you keep yourself? What can you focus on? What can you tune in to? How well developed are your neck muscles? Can you keep sitting up straight and stay alert? Can you imagine that some movie star is watching you from the other side of a one-way window to check you out for some big movie role and some huge bucks?

As the old, Super Bowl-winning Pittsburgh Steelers used to say "Whatever it takes." That's the attitude of a champion. Not how boring the speaker is, but how good your response is. When your self-discipline reaches the point where you can listen attentively under the least enjoyable circumstances—when others have dozed off—you can be sure of one thing: your mailbox will be filled with invitations. Use every listening opportunity to practice your self-discipline, and when you get to the point where people around you are marveling at your ability to seem interested in the most boring stuff, be proud.

"Gawd, how can you listen to that stuff? How can you stand that class?"

"I practiced!"

55.
Little Kids and Role Models

...way out in center field where even Babe Ruth couldn't have hit a ball, telling me to be ready, in case someone hit a long one.

Little kids are an integral part of sports, and every athlete ought to be aware of them. Every athlete was a little kid once, hanging around on the periphery of the action, wanting, hoping, trying to become part of the event by grabbing a ball as it bounced off a court or field, or by running out onto the field before the game or at halftime.

Every athlete has a story about being on that periphery. It seemed to last forever—being too small to play, being yelled at by adults for being someplace where only big kids, real athletes, were supposed to be.

It was so important to become part of the action, to get some of that attention, to grow up. And what a powerful influence those athletes had on us when we were those little kids struggling to be part of it all. I remember my father putting me way out in center field where even Babe Ruth couldn't have hit a ball, telling me to be ready, in case someone hit a long one. I would be back there yellin' and smackin' my mitt, waiting for my chance to get in the action, to retrieve a ball...in a high school baseball batting practice. I thought it was the most important thing in the whole world when one of the players, an actual big kid with a uniform, rolled a ball to me and told me, "good throw" when I heaved it back to him on five or six bounces.

Is there any need to elaborate on the concept of role models and how important they can be in a little kid's life, when every slow roller and tiny encouragement is an enormous life experience? When you think of it this way, how can any athlete pretend that his behavior and actions don't matter? How can any athlete fail to notice the little kids constantly hanging around? How can any athlete not want to add what positives he can? A word here and there, a few seconds of your time, just noticing. It can mean so much. How can you forget your own childhood?

Ask a kid to make a muscle, to do some pushups, to run over and touch a tree and run back, while you count and "check out his speed." You don't have to be a millionaire motivator on TV to know how to inspire a kid. We all know how. We just have to want to take the time.

You just need to realize that a few of your minutes, in the exalted position of athlete, can be worth hundreds of hours of teachers and principals and police in the future.

That's a lot of power. And you have it. So use it.

56.
Locker Room Walls

Let the other team try getting psyched up by this superficial ammunition, and load your guns with the real stuff...

Much is made by sports commentators about words on locker room walls.

This guy said something about that guy, some reporter quoted him in the paper, and a manager put a clipping up on the locker room wall; now team members can't wait to pound their opponent because they want revenge for what was said.

Words. Words. Words.

I've never been very impressed by this kind of talk and I've never been convinced that athletes can take words or slogans off a wall and translate them into winning plays on a field. I might be wrong. But I have two basic thoughts to convey.

First, it's not particularly bright making a bunch of negative comments about another team or other players. Why do it? Why go through your life spreading negatives at all, about anyone? Say good things when you can, speak out when you must, and the rest of the time, shut up. Don't bother with garbage in your life. Shouting matches and name calling and such things are for losers, for people with a lot of extra time, and for small-minded wanderers trying to have impact by means other than their performance. Athletes should have better things to focus on, better things to do.

Second, if a team does have a so-called rallying cry on their locker room wall, good luck to them. If they are able to trump up some comments into a battle cry that inspires them, big deal. They probably aren't a very good team. Good teams don't spend much time looking for battle cries. They develop techniques. They build team spirit. They focus on excellence. And they assume the other team is always out to get them, battle cry or no battle cry. Why should some words on a wall make a difference?

My major point is this: if you can use some words to motivate you, use them. But then consider who you are, what you are, and how you are preparing. Words on a wall should truly be tiny considerations compared with your own goals and commitment to excellence.

If you can get inspired by hearing that someone said something negative about you, then open your ears or at least your imagination. There are always people saying negative things about you. If you haven't actually heard any, then just imagine them. Don't wait around for a reporter to do your job for you. Put the words up right now.

They hate us. They want to beat us. They said we dress funny. They said we're dumb. They said we don't know what we're doing. They said we'd never win the championship and never make the pros. Plus, they said we smell bad!

Choose any words you like. And in the meantime start thinking more about sports preparation, about doing your best, about giving more effort, about achieving your goals and performing like a champion. The intrinsic beliefs that inspire champions are a lot more effective as motivators than comments coming from other teams.

Pride. Consistency. Dedication. Excellence.

Some phrases can be inspiring, particularly when they help to remind you of the self-image you want to have.

"When the going gets tough, the tough get going."

"It's not the size of the man in the fight, but the size of the fight in the man."

But think about it. The words on the wall really don't compare with what you have inside you, with what you are and want to be. I think true champions take their inspiration from stuff more significant than some comment which, maybe or maybe not, was made by an opponent (and maybe or maybe not quoted correctly by a reporter). And I suspect that off-the-wall kinds of inspiration don't do a lot of good late in a game when you're tired, having some problems, and trying to overcome various conditions in addition to beating your opponents.

Let the other team try getting psyched up by this superficial ammunition. Load *your* guns with the real stuff.

You don't want to play well tomorrow because they said you're dumb. You want to play well every day because you're proud of playing smart. You don't want to play well next week because they said you're weak. You want to play well every week because you've trained to be strong.

I'm not saying you need to take down that new, flashy, two-colored bulletin board your coach just put up in the locker room. It's nice to have articles and reminders and sports news up there if you're lucky enough to have this sort of thing. But don't lose sight of what's really important. The true words of inspiration are already up there. And they don't need a wall, thumbtacks, chalk, reporters, or anything else.

57.
Loyalty

Loyalty to friends, to teams and to nations is unwarranted when it conflicts with doing what's right.

Loyalty is a word often associated with sports. Some coaches emphasize its importance. Personally, I am skeptical about it. If you find yourself demanding or asking for loyalty, you may not be doing the things necessary to inspire it. Loyalty is often requested when it is undeserved. A person caught cheating doesn't want you to report him and claims that doing so would be disloyal. Or a person breaking a law wants you to break it, too. In those cases, if loyalty is going to be a factor at all, it is loyalty to yourself, to your integrity, and to doing the right thing.

The way loyalty gets twisted is what I'm concerned about here. Make sure you remain loyal to yourself and to the principles you believe in. Loyalty is not always admirable; loyalty to friends, to teams and to nations is unwarranted when it conflicts with doing what's right.

You have to decide for yourself what's right. I just wanted to raise a caution flag about loyalty. Mostly, when I heard the word at all, it was at a time when loyalty was not deserved. Usually when you are part of something special, there's no question about loyalty, and the word never even comes up. Of course you are loyal to a good friend, to a good coach, to a team working hard to win a championship. But there's little reason to be loyal to someone who is lying or cheating or breaking rules.

There may be fine lines involved in your particular circumstances, so I won't give a lengthy explanation. Instead, I'll close with one reminder. The most important loyalty is loyalty to the set of principles you believe in and to your own integrity.

58.
Maturity in One Hour

During practice, seek to be mature, not right. After practice you can work out the rights and wrongs, removed from the tension of competition and performance.

In the title of this short section is the answer to a very important question every athlete ought to ask and think about daily.

What is the difference between a mature athlete and an immature athlete?

Upon hearing this question and its answer, a lot of athletes assume they have heard something incorrectly. They look confused, and they need to hear it stated clearly:

The difference between an immature athlete and a mature athlete is one hour.

An immature athlete gets criticized in practice and immediately offers an explanation or an argument, or maybe just makes a face or a gesture.

A mature athlete waits an hour to respond. He may, if he then feels so inclined, do the same things an immature athlete does. The responses themselves are not really what determine your maturity level. What matters is whether or not you have learned to consider your responses. Can you wait till you've cooled down and had a chance to think and put the comments or criticisms in context? Or do you feel compelled to answer a negative the moment it comes at you?

Thousands, probably millions, of athletes around the world have all sorts of explanations and justifications for why they do what they do and why they had no choice in a particular instance. But they are still immature. They never learned the value of waiting. If you wait before you respond, then even if you choose to roll your eyes or frown or question or argue, your coach will respect your maturity and probably your ideas. But if you feel compelled to respond immediately, you will lose the respect of your teammates and your coach. You are immature.

Learn to take all the criticism or negatives and hold onto them for an hour. If, after practice, you still think something is important, you would be wise—and mature—to bring it to your coach's or teammate's attention. And you will very likely be respected for doing so if your ideas have any merit at all. The problem is that there are a lot more immature athletes than mature ones. While they argue with their coach to prove they are right about something, they don't even realize that any champion looking on would find them to be immature and wrong even if their argument seemed right.

During practice, seek to be mature, not right. After practice you can work out the rights and wrongs, removed from the tension of competition and performance.

Inexperienced and selfish athletes, and losers, often go through their whole lives never realizing that, in building a championship team, it is much more important to be mature in practice than it is to be right in an argument with the coach.

The difference between a mature and an immature athlete is one hour. It makes perfectly good sense after all, doesn't it?

59.
Mental Toughness

A lot of coaches and others like to talk about "the foxhole question."

Some people are naturally tougher mentally than others but don't let this fact dissuade you from making a special effort to improve your mental toughness. Mental toughness is one of the most important ingredients for success in sports, and it can be developed like any other skill regardless of how much of it you have now.

As you work on your physical skill and strive to train harder, longer, and more efficiently, your mental toughness will improve just as your skill level does. In other words, training diligently to improve your skill level will automatically improve your metal toughness, assuming you really are pushing yourself to improve.

It does, however, make sense to concentrate specifically on this quality itself—to think about it, to measure yourself in whatever ways you can, perhaps to give yourself a score in various areas that you define, and to be aware of wanting to increase your toughness.

Do you want responsibility under pressure? Can you push yourself past fatigue and injuries? Can you ignore petty issues and remove yourself from squabbles and other distractions? Can you keep your mind on the big picture? Can you stick to the plans you make for yourself?

If you work on these things and take pride in making progress in these areas, you can definitely improve. Although evaluating mental toughness seems a subjective concept, it becomes less so when you really think about it. For example, think for a moment about your teammates. Which of them do you consider the toughest mentally? Which of them would you trust most under pressure, in a crisis? What is it in them that you sense? Why do you trust some more than others?

A lot of coaches and others like to talk about "the foxhole question." If you were in a war, in a heated battle, and you found yourself under intense enemy pressure in a life-or-death situation, which teammate of yours would you most like to have with you in your foxhole? Obviously you'd want someone tough, intelligent, resourceful, etc. The point of asking this question in sports contexts is simply to get you thinking about those qualities. And of course, to try to get you to want to be the soldier that your teammates would choose. Are you that soldier, or athlete? If you would like to be the chosen one, usually just thinking about it will tend to make you a bit tougher, less of a complainer, more reliable.

Want to improve your mental toughness? Make a conscious effort to be the person your teammates would choose under pressure. The more you convince them, the more you will convince yourself. The biggest problem usually isn't a lack of courage or toughness or intelligence. Usually it's something more like laziness or selfishness, the tendency to complain or to think about your own problems instead of developing pride in toughness, in being a non-complainer.

Be the athlete who is actively, consistently, trying to make everyone else better and trying to make the atmosphere better—during practice, on the bus, in the locker room, and on the field—and chances are you'll amaze yourself with your own increase in mental toughness. A lot of it is focus more than actual strength.

60.
Mistake-Response Graphs

It is important to understand that your mistake-response is a habit, nothing more, nothing less.

What is your typical response after you make a mistake? In nearly every sport this can be charted or graphed in some way, if not by fans then certainly by good coaches. In sports like basketball and soccer, the impact of a mistake and a bad response can quickly result in another mistake since the action often continues in spite of the mistake. The same is often true of football, volleyball, and baseball even though these sports don't have the same kind of continuity.

In other words, in many sports, a negative response is not just an indication of a bad attitude but it actually constitutes an additional mistake in itself. For example, when a basketball player misses a shot, throws a bad pass, or gets a dribble stolen, a momentary lapse in effort results in insufficient defense and gives an additional advantage to the opponents. Not only did they benefit from your first mistake, but they continue to benefit while you are going through your lapse.

When a football player fumbles, not only can the ball be lost but failure to react quickly may allow the opposing team to run the ball for a touchdown instead of getting tackled and still, perhaps, having ninety yards to go for a score.

It should be obvious to all athletes that it is important to recover immediately from any mistake and to take the appropriate action dictated by the new situation. Hang your head later. Kick the water bucket, throw a towel, later. After the play is over, not at the time of the mistake. This is, of course, not a recommendation for head hanging, bucket kicking, or towel throwing at *any* time, but it is advice to separate these actions entirely from the initial mistake. Regardless of what you plan to do later, a good athlete will learn to respond immediately to the new situation, just as though someone else had made the mistake or just as though no mistake had been made at all.

A good athlete simply responds to what is going on. The other team has the ball and is attempting to score. Doesn't matter whether this is basketball, football, soccer, or hockey, the other team must be stopped. The fact that you just lost the puck or you just fumbled the ball is irrelevant. The only important thing is: what is the situation and what is your response?

If you think in terms of a graph, this concept will come into even clearer focus. A mediocre athlete with a bad attitude usually has a graph that looks like the one below.

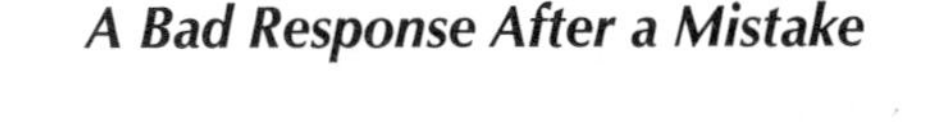

A Bad Response After a Mistake

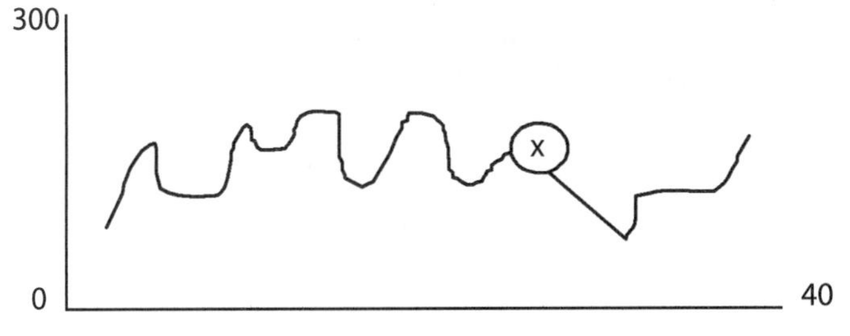

This graph measures effort (in heart beats per minute) and shows the typical ups and downs during the course of a forty minute college basketball game. The X indicates that a mistake has occurred. After the mistake, the athlete's effort obviously drooped considerably before normal activity resumed. Or, as we scientists say, "That SOB loafed!"

A good athlete learns to ignore mistakes entirely, not thinking about them until after the game is over. The time to consider mistakes is during the viewing of game films or during a game review. At the time of the actual action you can choose one of two winning responses.

1. Ignore the mistake, act as though it did not happen.
2. Hype the action. Pick it up. Expend a burst of energy to see if you can immediately reverse the mistake before the other team has had a chance to react and take advantage of it. Often, by going into fast motion, a player who makes a mistake can make up for it. The ultra-fast-motion approach is a good response to a mistake and can become just as habitual as the droop in effort of a mediocre player.

It is important to understand that your mistake response is a habit, nothing more, nothing less. If you practice a fast-motion response, that will be your habit. If you let yourself stand there hanging your head, that will be your habit. Some athletes seem to think that a show of disgust will make it clear that they care about winning and losing and that they are therefore great competitors. Don't let yourself be fooled in this way. Your desire to win and your competitiveness are not demonstrated by negative responses to mistakes. Below is the response of a winner.

A Good Response After a Mistake

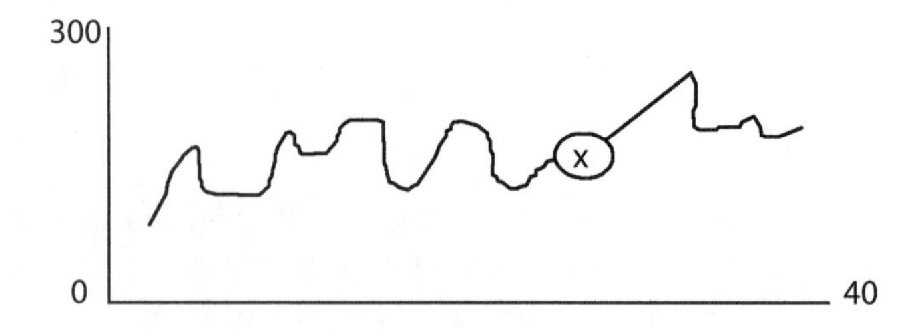

After the mistake in this game, the athlete's effort obviously increased before normal activity resumed.

Think about your response to mistakes. When happens to your energy level? It may be helpful to sit down after a game and put your post-mistake responses on paper in graph form. If your response is inadequate, you will have to draw your line downward and you will probably hate the way it looks. Most athletes, when they see themselves in black and white like this, make a definite effort to change the look of their graph.

What does your mistake-response graph look like?

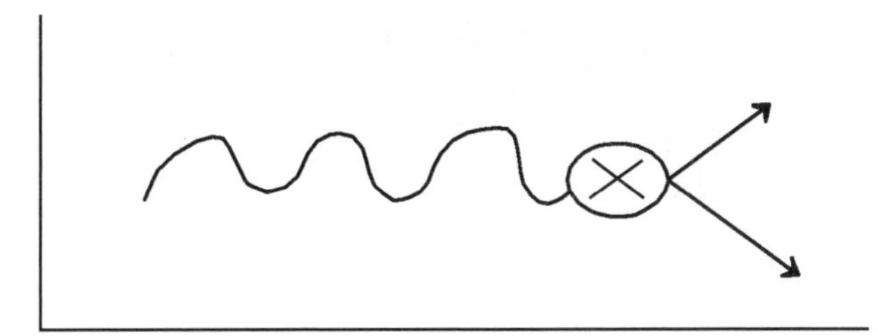

?

61.
Negative Thinking

"Lose? Oh my Gawd, you didn't say 'lose' did you? Never say lose. You gotta think positive..."

Every athlete hears about the importance of positive thinking and many have heard, or your coaches, at least, have heard of a book called *The Power of Positive Thinking*.

But I want to talk about the power of *negative* thinking. I can remember years ago walking across campus for a game and having students say good luck and so forth. Occasionally someone asked, "What do you think about the game tonight?" They asked that question particularly when they were worried themselves and usually they were seeking reassurance. They were sincere fans. They really wanted us to win. And they wanted to hear me say something like, "Ah, no sweat, piece of cake, we can take 'em, easy."

But I always disappointed them. My typical answer was something like: "I don't know. State is tough. We could lose."

"Lose? Oh my gawd, you didn't say 'lose' did you? Never say lose. You gotta think positive."

They were deeply troubled. What began as just some friendly words and encouragement on the way to the gym turned into something very different. Invariably these well-intentioned fans suddenly felt a sense of mission. They had to do something about my attitude. They had to try to pump me up. Saying "we could lose" was no way, they thought, to go into a game. They grew up in the old "think positive" school. That was okay. I understood. In fact, I found it kind of amusing. (In fact, often I reminded them that they ought to use an adverb in that phrase "positively" not "positive." Gotta have that "ly" and stay grammatically correct.) But fans were seldom amused. They were worried and almost invariably they felt obligated to encourage me and obligated to try to correct my thinking. But their efforts never altered my thinking. (Though it is nice to have fans who care.)

In my opinion, *thinking about losing is one of the best motivators there is.* I mean, don't just toss out the idea, but really think about it. Turn it over and over in your mind. How will it feel to walk off the court having lost? What glee will the other team's fans be showing off in the stands? What taunting will we have to swallow? What embarrassment? How will it feel going to class tomorrow, walking around campus, passing friends and strangers, all of whom saw the game and the failure? How will it feel knowing you let your family down, and your friends, and your coach and teammates? And yourself?

That kind of negative thinking can be incredibly energizing. It reminds you of just how much you don't want to lose. And it helps to catalyze your very best physical effort.

Think about that: your very best physical effort.

It is surprising how many athletes train and train and prepare and prepare and sleep and eat and think for success, and then go out and fail to give their very best physical effort. It's as though they are pacing themselves, waiting for overtime or an extra period. Then the match or the meet or the game is over, they have lost and they still have a lot of unspent energy. An abundance of it. In some sports, of course, you can't help it. If you are a golfer, you're going to have physical energy left after a game. But if you are a basketball player or a football player or soccer player or distance runner or hockey player (you get the idea) you'd better make sure that you're putting all of your physical energy out there, and adding in your mental energy, too.

You have no doubt read the suggestions of people who believe you can glide through the motions with a grand vision of victory dancing in your head, experiencing "flow" as it's called these days. Nothing against visions of victory or against flow, but I am making a case for considering everything, losing very much included.

When you think about losing in advance it helps you put forth your very best effort on the very first play, in the very first minute. It helps to assure that you aren't going to find yourself wishing, after a loss, that you had worked harder and given more effort. You just can't afford that.

Think about the negative consequences of not doing your best. That's a very positive way to approach a game.

62.
Nervousness

Here's that glorious nervous feeling…

Athletes are concerned about nervousness. "I get so nervous before a big game. What should I do?"

There is only one answer. Enjoy it!

If you think about nervousness as some terrible menace, you need to reevaluate completely the way you approach sports. In the proper context nervousness is seen as wonderful. It's a special feeling that athletes and other performers and entertainers get. Few others have the opportunity to experience its stimulating sensation.

When you start to feel nervous, instead of trying to deny the feeling and make it go away, invite the feeling to consume you. It may help to say to yourself, "here's that glorious nervous feeling, proof that my mind understands what's going on and has transferred the importance of it to my body." It may also help to broaden your thinking, to consider future days when nervousness will be a thing of the past for you, something you may never experience again. That is a much more terrible feeling. Instead of avoiding nervousness, roll it around in your mind.

Consider the alternatives. You aren't in any big events. Your performance doesn't much matter to you or to anyone else. Nothing really excites you. No tests, nothing to look forward to.

Consider including a hospital on your mental trip. Think about all those people who would love to trade places with you. They are nervous about walking again or about breathing freely. And you? You have an important game to play. There really isn't any comparison. Anyone in that hospital would willingly jump out of bed and trade places with a nervous athlete about to participate in a sports event.

Your nervousness should be welcomed because it indicates your state in life is a good one, that you have the freedom, the luxury, to be concerned about sports. Millions of people are thinking how lucky you are to have that body, that ability, that opportunity...and you are squandering the experience by focusing on one tiny negative, that a chemical is being secreted in your stomach making you feel queasy and on edge.

Would you rather your nerves be dull and numb? Of course not. That nervousness, that adrenalin, tells you that all systems are go and that your body is willing to do its best, even supply some extra chemicals that you don't have access to during routine training. Why are so many records broken during competition instead of during the un-pressurized atmosphere of the practice field? It's probably those extra enzymes, that adrenalin, the excitement of nervousness.

I don't know how to say anything more than what I began with. How do you deal with your nervousness? Be grateful for it. Love it. Absorb it. Invite it in. Glory in it. It ain't gonna last forever. How many old athletes have you heard say that? Believe them. And enjoy it while you can, even, especially, the nervousness. It's one of the best parts of the whole experience. You just have to realize it.

63.
New Stuff = Failure

Games are not the place to try out new stuff…

This may not seem to be a very creative title but I thought the equation just might stick in your mind and help you understand a seldom talked about sports principle.

Almost any time you meet something in a game you haven't seen before, you will mess up. In basketball, a defense you have never played against will likely confuse you and cause turnovers and missed shots and a loss. In football, a coverage you have not seen will likely cause an interception. In boxing, a fighter with an unorthodox style may well defeat a better boxer. In tennis, an unusual serve will likely result in a lot of winners. In baseball, if you have never batted against a curve ball, that first curve ball pitcher will seem to you like Cy Young throwing black holes in the night.

In other words, *if you aren't experienced enough or smart enough to anticipate what you will be facing, you will probably lose.* Even the biggest stars usually mess up when they are confronted with something new. You might say that's why it pays to have a good coach who will get you prepared for anything. True, but also that's why it pays to be a student of the game so you understand what's going on and you recognize slight variations in defenses and offenses. What seems different and new to others could then actually be quite familiar (and therefore rather easy) for you.

And speaking of slight variations, not only does new stuff used by the other team make you likely to fail, so does new stuff used by you. If you try some clever new pitch for the first time in a game, you are likely to throw it wild or watch it get knocked out of the park. If you try some new defense for the first time in a game, it is likely to fail miserably. Games are not the place to try out new stuff. Games are the place to use things you have worked on and repeated over and over again in practice. When you use a defense in a game it is only new to the fans and, hopefully, to the other team. It better not be new to you, also.

New stuff confuses and trips up even the best stars. But the reasons the best stars are the best stars is they have played long enough and studied their sport intensely enough not to get fooled very much any more. They have seen hundreds of tricks and surprises and novel offenses and strange defenses and they have learned form past failure. That's why people say there is no substitute for experience. That is also why coaches will urge you to play and play and play. Take on all comers. Go everywhere you can. Play everyone you can. Let them throw the kitchen sink at you. And learn from each new team and player and tactic.

Most veteran stars would tell you, "I can still be fooled by new tricks, I just don't see many new tricks any more." The sooner you learn your sport and all the ins and outs, the more foolproof you will be.

64.
Nodding to Your Coach

Even accepting the idea that many of your coach's comments and criticisms may be flat-out wrong, any real athlete would still want to hear them...

This suggestion seems so obvious that no book should have to include it; yet, from midget leagues to pro leagues, I've seen thousands of athletes who need to learn it.

When your coach tells you something, you should not only listen and hear what he or she says, you should look your coach in the eyes and nod to indicate that you understand.

It really doesn't matter if you agree or not, or if you like the comment/criticism or not. You nod to indicate you heard it, you understood it, you got it.

You do this for a reason beyond good will, which is something you should actively promote with your coach even if you don't particularly like him or her. You nod to make sure the coach will continue to make comments to you. If you fail to reinforce a coach's efforts to communicate with you, those communications will diminish. There is no avoiding it. Even a very demanding coach will say less to you if he or she senses that it is a chore for you to listen.

Initially, you may think that's exactly what you want—fewer coach's comments—since you don't like the things he or she says. But consider the bigger picture. Of course you are going to dislike a coach's criticism. No one likes criticism, especially when it's delivered with intensity or hostility or sarcasm as coaches' comments often are. But, you are probably smart enough to realize, at least as you sit and read a book, that criticism is inevitable, it is part of development, and you need it.

Even accepting the idea that many of your coach's comments and criticisms may be flat-out wrong, any real athlete would still want to hear them all, in order to sort them through and learn from the ones that are right.

If you have the attitude that, sure, you want to hear the intelligent criticisms, it's just all those stupid things your coach says that you don't want to hear, then you are living in a dream world. No one on the planet could tell you a hundred things and have each one come across to you as intelligent. (Even if they all were intelligent, chances are you would not recognize that intelligence.)

You really *do* want your coach to keep pointing out everything he sees. That's the only way to be sure you will keep getting the opportunity to improve. In fact, the more stupid your coach, the more you have to encourage his comments in order to come away with helpful information. If your coach offers intelligent criticisms half the time, then you only need to elicit twenty comments to get ten good suggestions. But if your coach comes up with only one useful suggestion from every ten times he opens his mouth, you need to encourage him to say one hundred things in order to get the same ten good suggestions.

Most athletes are not naturals at listening attentively to criticism. It's a skill that has to be developed just like running and jumping and skating and spiking and kicking and shooting and hitting. We picture situations where a smart coach is giving a truly insightful instruction to an aspiring Olympian who is eager and grateful to receive the exact suggestion needed to propel her training to gold medal levels. But how often does that happen? Fans and commentators think it happens more often than it does because true athletes learn to pretend it's happening even when it's not (so they continue to get the benefit of their coach's instruction). Often, as well, good coaches require athletes to act as though they're hearing great advice (so the coaches feel good about continuing to instruct).

A good coach might say, "Look, I don't care if you think my ideas are looooney, fool me. Pretend. Look me in the eye. Nod to show me you got it." That coach, depending on his style, may also add, "You are free to whisper under your breath that I am a complete nut. Just make sure no one hears it, and make sure I have the impression that you think my idea was incredibly on target and intelligent."

The problem is that you may not have a coach who has that kind of style. In fact, it is most likely that your coach will *not* spell those things out and you may find yourself being bothered by negative comments, not listening to your coach, and starting a cycle of ever-worsening relations that never needs to happen.

The inexperienced player will say, "But I've been taught to be honest about my feelings. How can I pretend a comment is intelligent when I think it's absurd?"

You do it the same way you create enthusiasm during a tough practice when you're sore and tired, with effort. That's what you do in sports. That's how you remain honest in sports. With effort. You transform situations constantly. You remain upbeat when your team is behind and things are going bad. With effort. You encourage the teammate who has just messed up and perhaps cost you the game. With effort. You make your opponents think you have plenty of energy left when they're panting. With effort. In sports, you are fooling people all the time, and it does take effort.

So, fool your coach if you must, or just listen attentively if you can. But whatever it takes, do it. Nod to your coach after each instruction. This will pay dividends in a variety of ways you probably could never imagine as a young athlete. But try it anyway just for the helluvit. And some day, attend a practice that does not involve your own team and watch all the immature athletes who fail to look their coach in the eye and fail to nod to their coach after criticisms. I believe that if you do that just once, it will be impossible for you not to agree that it makes sense to nod and be attentive, even when you don't like your coach.

65.
Non-Injuries

Applause. Admiration. Acclaim. All A's! That's all you want from fans, just like from teachers.

All injuries that are not clearly major, and even most of the major ones, should be treated by athletes as non-injuries. A non-injury is a bump, a bruise, a bang or a bonk that no one should notice but you. You might repeat this definition several times and memorize it. It has a nice ring to it, and it is worth remembering.

A bump, a bruise, a bang, a bonk that no one should notice but you.

In nearly every sport, there are Academy Award-worthy cases of what might be called prolonging-injuries-for-effect-and-for-winning-the-attention-and-sympathy-of-friends-and-family-and-fans-who-don't-know-any-better.

In basketball, this usually comes in the form of a non-injury that occurs when a player is on offense. He falls or gets hit in the eye with an elbow, and he lies there on the court supposedly too injured to sprint down to the other end on defense. Miraculously, however, when his team gets the ball back and he suddenly finds himself in position to score—medical marvel of marvels—he recovers instantly, darts on to the basket and, well-rested from having taken the previous play off, calls urgently for the ball. He no longer thinks about his injury.

No coach who plans to win tough games and championships

will tolerate these charades (or rest periods) intended more for attention than recovery.

It is true that when you fall or get hit in the eye or the arm or whatever, the incident may cause you pain. But it is also true that the pain isn't likely to be any different whether you lie on the ground or play on as if nothing has occurred. Therefore it makes no sense, from the standpoint of anyone seeking championship performance levels, to lie, sit, or stand while nursing some wound that can just as easily be ignored or nursed on the run.

If it ain't gonna cause you pain a minute from now, you don't deserve anyone's sympathy or attention. If you are so starved for attention that you need that kind of attention for pain resulting from a non-injury destined to be completely gone several minutes later, then you need a girlfriend or a boyfriend or a doctor or maybe a particularly compassionate counselor or therapist or librarian. Nothing against librarians. (I like them.) But I hope you get the picture. Sympathy elicited for momentary pain is very unbecoming to someone claiming to be a tough athlete.

If you're an athlete, you ignore those kinds of pain and you're proud that you do. You don't want sympathy and attention for bumps and bruises. You want acclaim for successful performance. Period.

Leave sympathy for the losers. Run out there, into the arena, onto the field, the court. Look at all those people. What do you want from them? Oohs and ahhs over collisions? Shrieks over hard falls? Concerned whispers? No. None of it. What do champions want? Applause. Admiration. Acclaim. All A's! That's what you want from fans, just like from teachers. All A's. At least that should be all you want if you are a serious athlete seeking to become a champion and striving constantly for ways to get a slight edge on your opponents. All of us who identify with this way of thinking know there will be bumps and bruises along the way. We expect to feel sore after hard practices, we expect a certain amount of physical contact with other players or with walls or playing surfaces.

Most of us, if we are dedicated at all, learn to overcome a certain amount of physical discomfort. That's a given. You simply cannot stop and check every scrape or ache and pain. In fact, you cannot even pause. A champion doesn't stop to check how he's feeling. He checks while playing at top speed.

On the other hand, when a little kid playing sports for recreation gets knocked to the ground unexpectedly, he will stop everything and look at his bruise. Maybe he will show it to his mother. Or wait for a coach to ask him if he's okay. That's fine for the midget leagues. But a champion...

What if you break your leg? It's okay. Your habit of playing through pain will nearly always be interrupted when your injury is a truly severe one. But that is not a problem. No one expects you—champion or otherwise—to continue playing with a broken leg.

But what any coach or good teammate does expect is that you develop the habit of playing through, and learn to ignore entirely, all minor injuries. What happens entirely too often to many good athletes is that they get an injury that involves a lot of initial pain destined to last for just a few minuets. It could be ignored but they fail to ignore it. Instead, like midget leaguers, they look at the bruise and wince, and stand still or lie on the ground while the action of the game goes on without them. The other team, finding itself with a sudden numerical advantage, scores a goal or makes some extra yards or gets an advantage that wasn't warranted.

The player, momentarily reverting back to midget league form, gets distracted long enough to give the opponent something easy. Why is this so bad? Because most big games are decided by just a few points. Would-be champions can't afford to give away points.

If you are on a football team where every player has a lapse like that just once per game, that's twenty-two times that you are going to be giving your opponent an advantage. That's no way to win championships. This is quite obvious when you think about it numerically.

My father's way, as a demanding basketball coach, was something that I have named "the one second decision." In a nutshell, his rule was this: if you ever get an injury and nurse it for a full second, it will be deemed a true injury and you are done for the game. You get a shower. You put your street clothes back on. And you watch like a fan.

Can you imagine the result of a rule like that? At first some players are angry and their parents are upset. They get hurt in the first quarter, they lie on the court, hold their bruised elbow and walk off the court while the fans applaud. And the coach ignores them the rest of the game.

"I'm okay now, Coach, I can go back in."

"No, you can't. You're hurt."

"No, I was hurt. Now I'm fine."

"No," says the coach, "we don't have that. Here, if you're injured for a second, you're injured for the game."

Players and parents—especially squeamish ones—may not have liked this way of doing things. But I know that champions understand the result before I explain it. On my father's teams, players didn't waste any time lying on courts nursing bumps and bruises, and they didn't give other teams any cheap advantages. That's a good way of doing things for any athlete on any team.

66.
Off-Season Improvement

The best way to improve is to compete ferociously against your perfectly matched competitor…

If you are striving for excellence in athletics, no doubt you already realize that you have to make at least an eleven-month commitment. It's year-round with perhaps some time off for resting and reflecting. In reality, there is no off-season (even the rest period is scheduled) but most sports still have a season when the main competition takes place. In this section we are considering the rest of the time, when the main competition is *not* taking place.

In some ways, the competitive time is probably less important than the rest of the time. Or, you might say, the competitive time is the test, the chance to demonstrate what you mastered during the off time.

During the off-season you have to budget your time wisely and have a schedule or chart of activities specifically aimed at maximizing improvement. If you aren't repeating some activity, you cannot expect to improve. If you aren't charting daily levels, times, or scores, you are not truly working to raise the level of your performance.

To raise the level of your performance, you first have to know exactly where you are. You have to measure yourself. In basketball, for example, you might shoot one hundred free throws and one hundred jump shots from the three point line.

In swimming, you time your events. In sports where measuring is not so apparent, you better be creative and find some ways to measure where you are. Any good coach can help with that; coaches always have ways of measuring. They know who is good and who is not. How do they know? That's what you need to find out, and that's what you need to measure and improve upon.

What is so important about measuring? It fine-tunes your concentration the way mere playing or practicing cannot. Think about it. The best competitor, the perfect competitor for you, is You-Yesterday. You-Yesterday has the same size, speed, and physical attributes of You-Today. You-Yesterday, assuming you did your best, has the same willpower, the same determination, the same amount of just about everything. Hooked up in battle, You-Tuesday and You-Wednesday are more equally matched than any two competitors who ever engaged in any competition. For You-Wednesday to eclipse You-Tuesday's performance level it will take very fine-tuned concentration. And of course, for You-Thursday to beat that.... You get the idea.

By measuring your performance levels and striving to improve them each day, you maximize your effort and concentration, and constantly pressure yourself to use your abilities to the fullest. Let me use a common basketball example to explain.

The player who just goes out and shoots basketball will make some shots and miss some shots. Despite his best effort to do as well as possible, his concentration while shooting around will not nearly equal his concentration when he is competing against yesterday's best effort. If yesterday a player doing his best made 412 shots out of 500, today it will be necessary to concentrate on each shot in order to beat 412.

As a result, the 367th shot today will be taken with concentration, with full awareness that there just isn't much room for error. A player who makes 412 shots out of 500 is averaging about eight out of every ten. (80 percent of 500 is 400.) Sometimes he makes nine, sometimes he makes seven, but rarely does he hit all ten and rarely does he drop as low as six. With this knowledge, and the act of measuring, the 367th shot isn't just another shot. It is a shot taken after six others in the thirty-seventh set of ten. And it is important, all by itself, to the performance level to be attained.

Let's look at that set of ten. The psychology of breaking an improvement session into small parts is important. Is the player six for six, with a chance to score a nine or ten for the set (and thus be above the 412 pace), or is he three for six, figuring to score a seven at best and in danger of getting only a five or six for this set, which would put him well off the 412 pace?

When a competitor who has high goals and diligently seeks improvement breaks down his practice sessions and measures each one, he can't help but concentrate better. He can't stand to be three for six (when he needs at least eight for ten to improve) and he will never let his seventh attempt be haphazard or careless in such a circumstance.

Reading all of these numbers in a book—500, 412, 400, 80 percent, three for six, etc.—may seem confusing at first, but any champion understands the tension created and the concentration required when a commitment to excellence and improvement is coupled with a measurement of performance.

If you want to improve in the off-season so you can reap the benefits during competition, you have to practice diligently in the off-season. Measuring and charting your performance will create game-like conditions even when you are alone.

In nearly every sport, it makes sense to monitor your strength and endurance, as well as your actual skill level. Weight lifting and running-for-time offer easy ways to measure strength and endurance, and nearly every town has people who can help you develop a program to follow. In addition, many books are available which can help you run and lift effectively.

As for skill development, that of course depends on specific sports, many of which are beyond my field of expertise. But it should be easy enough to find out what the stars in your sport can do, what they work on, and how they measure their off-season improvement. The tough part is not in finding out what to do, but in making the commitment to compete with yourself daily and to spend the time and effort necessary to do it successfully.

You are your ideal opponent. The best way to improve is to compete ferociously against your perfectly matched competitor, You-Yesterday. And there is no better way to do that than by charting and measuring. If you don't have a chart on your wall or a notebook under your bed—some way of comparing your competitive effort—you aren't practicing effectively to improve. So do it. Get a chart. Get on a program. And get ahead.

67.
Overconfidence

You don't have to be a student of sports history to realize that many lopsided scores have been reversed the second time around.

"Don't get overconfident. Make sure you don't take this team too lightly."

I always wonder about statements like those. Actually, I don't believe them. Maybe you'll understand me better if I put it this way: I don't think that I personally have ever played a game in my life in which I was overconfident. Nor do I think that any real champions ever lose as a result of overconfidence.

Sometimes you go into a game knowing that you have, on paper, the better team and you know you should win. But I think every real athlete understands that you can always lose. The record books and the newspapers are filled with detailed accounts of how some mediocre team beat a team that was "unbeatable." Only a complete fool would ignore all this evidence and go into a game thinking, "These guys could never beat us."

Athletes are not infallible. What we did yesterday we may not be able to do today. We can get hurt. We can mess up. The other team may get a new player, or a new coach, or a new purpose, or a new determination. I think the joy of sports is the awareness of uncertainty.

Do any athletes believe they can go into a game thinking they can merely dally around and still win?

I envision, as I write this section, a coach who may want to have his team read about avoiding overconfidence on the eve of a game against an opponent they beat by forty the last time around. Is he expecting me to throw a scare into his team about what could happen tomorrow? Well I think that, if you beat someone by forty last time, then kill them by eighty this time. Jump all over them. Make them hate competing against you. You *should* kill them. So, kill them.

But as for false scares, who needs them?

Surely you know you aren't a machine. Surely you know they would love to beat you this time. Surely you know there are no guarantees that things will go as well as they did last time. Surely you realize that certain conditions could arise and change the outcome.

But I wouldn't focus on those conditions. I would focus entirely on making sure that what happened last time happens again. If you're stupid enough not to realize that the tables could get turned, you deserve to lose. You don't have to be a student of sports history to realize that many lopsided scores have been reversed the second time around. *Every champion carries with him the normal athlete's fear that you can always lose.* Great hitters can smack out sharp line drives, but there's no guarantee that those drives won't be hit right at someone on a certain day. Great shooters can perform all the mechanics perfectly, but the shots may not fall on a particular night. A quarterback can put perfect touch on six consecutive passes, but they can all be dropped or, even worse, deflected into the hands of defenders and result in touchdowns for the other team.

I don't have much patience for teams that take other teams lightly. I don't understand that concept any more than I understand coaches who say, after games, "I think we took them too lightly." If you are a half-decent coach, you don't allow that kind of thinking at all. You don't even allow it in practice, against the second string JV team.

In a nutshell, there's really no place in sports for taking any opponents lightly, or heavily. Take them to lunch, or to dinner, if you have the money. That's all the "takes" there are. You don't take opponents, you compete against them. You do your very best every time. You beat them by as many as you can. You attempt to hinder their every move, and you strive to accomplish your every plan.

There's no under-confidence. There's no overconfidence. There is just focus and effort to get the job done. I hope this is clear to you. The typical definition of taking an opponent lightly entails not coming ready to play, not trying as hard as you can, not giving your very best effort. A champion simply cannot identify with that kind of approach to sport. A game is a game. A practice is a practice. At both, you come ready, you try hard, and you do the very best that you can. There really isn't any other way to become a true champion. As soon as you realize this, overconfidence will be something that *never* applies to you.

68.

Parental Involvement

(A Special Aside to Parents)

You probably won't take this advice, but at least your son or daughter will always have the opportunity to read this section and have a sense of "I told you so."

You want what's best for your son or daughter. You know how much things mean to him or her. And you are willing to fight to see that your son or daughter gets what he or she is entitled to. That's wonderful. Now let's take a look at the history of parental involvement in sports.

Parents help teams financially. Parents can help organize bake sales, auctions, and other fund raisers, so that teams get opportunities they wouldn't otherwise have. Sometimes parents can help with transportation or provide food. Parents can cheer for their sons' and daughters' teams and travel to away games to provide support. Wonderful.

Now what about coaching tips? Should parents offer coaching tips?

No.

But what if you know more than the coach?

No.

If you want to be a coach, become a coach. But stay out of trying to coach your son or daughter if you are not the coach. Even when you are correct, your help will usually, in total, be more negative than positive.

The best way you can support your son or daughter is by encouraging him or her to live the experience fully and to make the most of it. Sometimes the circumstances may be very bad. Sometimes they may be very good. Both sets of circumstances can be worthwhile learning experiences. The bad set may even turn out to be more valuable in the long run.

"Yeah, but what if my son has worked very hard for an opportunity and a stupid coach prevents him from enjoying the rewards and fulfillment he is entitled to?"

Yeah, what about that? That puts you squarely among nearly all the sports parents who ever lived. Nearly all parents think their kids aren't being used properly, aren't being given the opportunities they deserve, aren't being this or that. It is almost universal. Every coach has stories of parents—intelligent people—who walk up and say, "I don't want to be one of those typical, complaining parents. I realize that parents are biased, but..." And then they go on to relate biased stuff about their kids and almost invariably they turn into those typical complaining parents. Nearly all parents think they have something new to say, nearly all think that their son or daughter's situation is unique. Yet they rarely have something new to say and their situations are seldom unique. It's the same old stuff over and over again. "Just a little suggestion, Coach. You needed to see Johnny in the summer, or in the driveway. You just don't realize what he can do."

Even if the coach doesn't realize something crucial, big deal. It's sports. So what if the kid has given it his heart and soul and cares so much. Big deal. Hundreds, thousands, millions of kids give their hearts and souls and care so much, and so what? It's sports. Welcome to sports, young man. Or young lady. Sports are filled with failure, with coaches who don't understand, with situations that should be better.

"But it could be so good...."

Yes. And it is going to get that way if the kid works hard, endures injustices, and overcomes adversity.

If that moment arrives when you decide that, this time, this one time, you simply have to step in—when you feel you absolutely must do something to make the coach see that he is hurting your child—go ahead. Step in. Help the coach understand. Get it off your chest. Make things the way they ought to be.

And realize that you have done this for yourself. Not for your son or daughter. The best thing you can do for sons and daughters, once you have permitted them to become involved in a sport, is let them play it out. If it's too painful for you, let them quit. But don't butt in.

For every time a parent has successfully butted in, there are probably twenty thousand parents who should have kept out. You shouldn't like those odds. Of course you won't take my word for it. But try consulting some coaches. You probably won't find any that can recall a time that a parent's intrusion helped anyone, least of all the son or daughter who was the object of the effort.

As much as defeat and obstacles and fatigue are a part of sports for an athlete, frustration and the desire to butt in are a part of sports for a parent. Both athletes and parents have to learn to accept the negatives inherent in their situations. If you are a parent who is hoping for one of those grand sports experiences for your son or daughter, you are normal but your expectations are probably already skewing your son's or daughter's view of reality. Better to expect all sorts of conflicts and negatives, and allow yourself to be incredibly surprised if a miracle—a truly fine, fair, appropriate, well-coached athletic experience—occurs.

This is not intended to be cynical. Experience teaches that if you expect difficulties, it is much easier to deal with what is likely to occur than if you allow yourself to hope for an ideal situation.

If you can move or switch your son or daughter to another team for next season, consider that. It makes sense to move to a better situation whenever possible. But during a season, assuming there are no other reasonable alternatives, I think it would be better for parents to let their kids work out the problems for themselves—with your advice, of course, but not your direct involvement. You probably won't take this advice, but at least your son or daughter will always have the opportunity to read this section and have a sense of "I told you so." That's not a bad feeling for a kid to have every once in awhile.

69.
Pep Talks

The words aren't just words, they are catalysts, and the drummed up emotion can last even after the yelling stops and the lockers quit taking a pounding...

It's nice to be part of a team that has a coach who gives inspiring pep talks. You hear the encouragement and you get all excited and start hollering and you start pounding lockers and hitting each other...and then you go out to play.

Few teams can sustain the emotion raised during a pregame pep talk and use it to play harder when the game begins. But even when they do, the impact of any particular words will soon be gone, and your practice, training, and preparation will decide what happens throughout the main part of the game.

For most teams, the emotion of the pep talk probably just gets burned off as excess energy during warm up exercises. But this is not to say that pep talks are a waste of time. Rather, I would say, if your coach is good at giving pep talks, enjoy them and make the most of them. But if your coach is bad at pep talks, don't worry. It won't matter.

My father and his long-time assistant, Jack Heimbuecher, were particularly good at pep talks. They made tears come to your eyes and chills fly up your spine. I remember that clearly from when I played for them and, fortunately, I had the opportunity many years later to be in the locker room to hear them still getting championship teams ready to go into battle. What was it that made their talks so inspiring? It was good to have that later chance to find out as an adult, free of personal involvement in the games. What did they actually say that aroused all those emotions? And what good was it?

Turns out that their words, if repeated, wouldn't be especially impressive. What was impressive was their ability to put the game into perspective and to paint the big picture. They did that by reminding their players of the importance of the event, of the people who cared, of the efforts already expended to get the opportunity, of the high opinion others had of them, and finally of what a special time of life it was to be competing…

Such words don't seem like much on a page.

"Fellows, you know how hard we've worked. You know what we've been through. And now is our chance. The bleachers are filled out there. Hundreds of people out there believe in you…and you better make up your minds right now not to leave anything in here, boys. Don't cheat yourselves or all those people out there by coming back in here with an ounce of energy left in your bodies. Leave it out there, boys, leave it out there."

Nothing all that special about those words. But I cry as I recall and write them. A lot of you understand. Simple words like these can stir your soul as they wind through your self-image and your determination and your dreams and the years of practice you've put in. Particularly when they are spoken with heartfelt sincerity.

The words aren't just words, they are catalysts, and the drummed up emotion can last even after the yelling stops and the lockers quit taking a pounding. What is important isn't so much what is said but what those words remind you of: who you are, what you are, what life is all about. And these kinds of ideas will stick with you for hours, even late in a tight game, when you are tired and things aren't going well. Maybe especially then….

It never hurts to be reminded of the big picture, of the special opportunity you have to be young and healthy enough to be playing a sport, to be competing in front of people who care, to recall the effort you have expended in practice and in off-season preparation, and to think about the family, friends, and people who think highly of you.

If you don't have a coach who gives pep talks and who helps to remind you of all that you and sports are about, don't sit around grumbling about the lack. Give yourself the pep talk. It doesn't have to come in neon light, with fireworks, or with stirring, Hollywood-style excitement; it doesn't have to come accompanied by locker pounding and screaming teammates. Just remind yourself what it's all about, where you've been, how far you've come, what you've put into it, where you're going, who you are.

The greatest pep talks in the world are the ones that stir something within you, not just during pre-game or halftime but throughout the whole game and through practice, through training, through the off-season, every day.

How are *your* pep talks?

70.
Perfectionism

Nearly all teams, and nearly all groups of people involved in any important enterprise, have tension created by the varying degrees of perfectionism among the members.

Some have it, some don't. Some want it, some don't. Perfectionists want to do everything just right. And the trouble is, they want everyone else to do everything just right also because they realize that what other people do matters.

Whether you are making a movie, running a school, selling a product, or playing on an athletic team, one person can't make the enterprise successful. Success requires the efforts of many people. Knowing this, the perfectionist can't help but care what others are doing and—this is the bad part—usually can't help but find fault with others.

In other words, a perfectionist isn't likely to be very popular. He probably won't be voted captain and probably won't be voted Most Valuable Player unless he is clearly the best. The perfectionist's very determination to do things perfectly may be a detriment to building teamwork and to getting others to do their best.

There are two simple points to this section.

1. If you are a perfectionist by nature, realize it and try to tone down your negative impact on others as much as possible. Or

at least try to compensate for your negative impact by praising and complimenting those around you whenever you can.

2. If you are not a perfectionist by nature you are probably irritated if there is one on your team, or if your coach is one. You, too, ought to realize your situation and tone down your irritation. A perfectionist is going to find fault with the things you do. Not necessarily with you, but with the things you do. That's all there is to it. Try not to take it so personally.

Nearly all teams, and nearly all groups of people involved in any important enterprise, contain tension created by the varying degrees of perfectionism among the members. This tension causes elation when something special is accomplished but also causes stress when things don't go well.

Is there a way to even out the variations in perfectionism? Probably not. Just be aware of the problem, do your best to live with it, and try to shape it as much as you can. Maybe you can be a middle man. Get the fault-finder to cool it a bit while you encourage the lazy player to fire up.

For a final exercise, jot down the names of the players on your team and rate them on a 1–10 perfectionism scale. The guy who wants to get away with everything and doesn't really care how well anything is done gets a one, while the ten goes to the person who is never satisfied, wants everything done just right.

You think it's bad having a perfectionist coach? Wait till you see the frustration of a perfectionist player who has a slovenly coach.

Often, just by giving your team members ratings and being aware of this issue, you will be able to deal more effectively with managing the tension and the problems that inevitably surface on any team. Your 9's and 10's will want to put some effort into diffusing those problems, not merely pointing them out and enlarging them.

71.
Playing Handcuffed

It would make sense for you to think about this now, in advance, so when your time comes you don't have to quit or rant and rave or act like coach is a nut or the world has come to an end.

Playing handcuffed is something I have heard so often, in so many sports, that I think every athlete should think about this concept, expect it, plan for it, and be able to avoid thinking about it when your handcuffs come.

Do you understand already what I am referring to? In basketball, a big gun will complain that the coach won't let him play his game. He wants to dribble to the basket or put up a long shot, but the coach makes him pass and set a screen. Is it the coach's fault that he doesn't make the winning basket, or the player's?

To give a runner a chance to steal a base, a heavy hitter in baseball may be asked to take some pitches which may lead to a strike out instead of a home run. If it does, is it the coach's fault (making the hitter take some strikes) or the hitter's fault for missing the third strike?

Sometimes a homerun hitter may be asked to lay down a sacrifice bunt. "How can I hit a home run if Coach is going to make me bunt?"

Quarterbacks in football often want to throw long passes or try some razzle-dazzle but the coach may call for off-tackle bursts. Or the coach may choose to punt instead of going for a first down.

In hockey, a coach may choose to play conservatively, keep everyone packed in around the goal, and not let his best scorer bust out or take any chances.

Even if you are highly skilled in your sport and you are the best performer on your team, there will undoubtedly be times when your coach requires you to do things that aren't conducive to you becoming the hero or even getting a chance to use your abilities at all. It would make sense for you to think about this now, in advance, so when your time comes you don't have to quit or rant and rave or act like your coach is a nut or the world has come to an end. In nearly every sport, among the world's very best athletes, this handcuffing has occurred. *Nearly every athlete who has achieved high levels of proficiency has, at some time, felt handcuffed.*

"I could've won the game, but the coach wouldn't let me."

When this happens to you, be patient. Be understanding. Be quiet. You aren't always going to agree with your coach. And your ability isn't always going to be used in the way your parents or you would use it. Sometimes, maybe you will be right. Your way would have been better. Other times, though you may be reluctant to admit it, your coach may have done what was best for the team.

It's not really important who is right and wrong. In sports, many decisions have no clear cut right or wrong. Should you play zone or man-to-man? Should the coach pinch hit for the pitcher? Should we go for the 4th-and-2 or punt the ball? Even the individual golfer has those same kinds of decisions. Play it safe or try to hit the ball over the water? If the ball goes over the water and you score an eagle, you're a god. If the ball goes in the water and you lose the tournament by one stroke, you're an idiot.

But we all know that post-game commentary is a lot easier than during-the-game decisions. When you find yourself in a situation where you aren't being permitted to use your skills to the fullest, challenge yourself to see how well you can perform handcuffed instead of going into a funk over those handcuffs. It happens to the best, and it's likely to happen to you. Remember, coaches' handcuffs are as much a part of the obstacles to overcome as are referees' calls, bad weather, injuries and any other conditions that athletes have to learn to take in stride.

Handcuffed? Congratulations. You have joined some very elite ranks. Make the best of it.

72.
Playing Hard

Considering the discrepancy between what athletes perceive and what demanding coaches know, it is necessary to realize that playing hard is a skill...

The first question good coaches ask in just about every sport, after they have established that a particular player has talent, is "Does he play hard?"

How hard do *you* play?

People who aren't champion competitors don't even understand the issue here. The typical fan thinks that everyone is out there doing his best or, occasionally, that they're all loafing. The fan rarely makes the distinction that a demanding coach makes immediately.

Consider an example from Prep Stars, a summer basketball camp for high school stars which I directed for more than a dozen years. Nearly every player—there are 250–350 in each session—is there to show off skills to college basketball coaches who may have scholarships to offer. Each player is warned by letter, usually a couple of months in advance, that the physical demands will be great and that it would be advisable to come to camp in excellent physical condition. The warnings are hardly necessary. Typically, the athletes look upon camp as an opportunity to demonstrate what they can do and they don't take the opportunity lightly. They work hard to get in excellent condition far in advance of their participation, and they come prepared mentally to go all-out.

I have gone into detail with this explanation to emphasize the importance of the point I am about to make. Although they are nearly all high school stars, very motivated, and in excellent physical condition, it is always possible to pick out one or two who play obviously harder than all the others. This seems really strange to me. Naturally, some athletes will be taller than others. Some will be stronger than others. Some will dribble better, shoot better, jump better, run better than others. But why should there be a difference in how hard they try?

Consider a hundred meter dash. Some of the competitors are tall, some short, some strong, some weak, some heavy, some light. But it is extremely difficult to notice, in a short race, that any of the competitors aren't trying as hard as they possibly can. Some may have prepared more diligently, trained longer and harder, but I'm not talking about training and preparation here. I'm talking strictly about effort during the performance.

It would seem that well-conditioned, motivated performers would all exhibit the same hard work in sports like football, basketball, soccer, hockey, and so forth. But they don't. A good coach can watch for just a short time and then say, "*That* kid really works at the game."

It's a nice compliment for the hard worker. But it's a real slam on the others. What are they doing? Why are they allowing all those hours of preparation to be wasted or at least not maximized? Why don't they work as hard?

If you asked two hundred of the athletes at Prep Stars why they were not singled out as a kid who plays hard, they would be stumped, shocked, and probably argumentative. They hustle all the time, they would assure you. And they would be convinced, sincere, and persuasive. Their parents, if you talked to them, would be almost universally overwhelmed at how much effort their sons put out and they would be shocked, upset, and probably disbelieving that some coach failed to notice their kid.

Considering the discrepancy between what athletes perceive and what demanding coaches know, it is necessary to realize that playing hard is a skill just like throwing, catching, spiking, skating, hitting, etc. You have to work on your ability to work hard. It sounds almost redundant, but it's true. And it's crucial.

You are sitting there right now, reading this book, wanting sincerely to be a better athlete and convinced that you are doing all sorts of things to accomplish this. Most of all, you are probably convinced that you work extremely hard when you play your sport. But chances are, you don't. I think back over all of the athletes I have accused of not working hard enough, and I think of all their blank faces and their failure to understand what I meant. It makes me realize that you, sitting there reading this book, will be thinking that this criticism is one that doesn't apply to you. But it almost surely does.

Now let's try to do something about it. Make yourself one promise: Instead of telling yourself how hard you work, spend time thinking up ways in which you could work harder. Are there times during the games when you could inject more energy? Are there situations where you have thought that extraordinary effort is not necessary, but maybe it really is?

No use arguing with me about your effort. Maybe you *are* that one kid out of three hundred stars who can be identified as the hardest worker. If you are, I congratulate you and I know that you will understand, better than all of the others, the words I am about to use to finish this section:

You aren't doing enough.

73.
Politics

You are not very likely to become a sports star without accepting some compromises along the way…

By politics I mean the aspects of sports that relates to favoritism, to advantages gained off the court or field, and finally to life itself and all the peripheral considerations not directly related to athletic skills.

What comes first to my mind are the many athletes who complain about not making a team and the lame excuses they offer as explanations. "The coach kept his son" or "the principal's son made it" or "he only picks the guys he likes."

My first comment to complaints like this would be, "Are these one-man teams?" Maybe you *are* better than the coach's son. But what about the other spots on the team? Did the coach have twelve sons? As former Marquette basketball coach Al McGuire once said, "That's my boy, that's my own flesh and blood. If you want to play, you have to beat out someone else!"

Coach McGuire said that somewhat tongue-in-cheek but with a whole lot of seriousness as well. The essence of it is true; the coach's son and the principal's son and the guy the coach likes do indeed have a better than average chance of making the team. It makes sense, in any endeavor, to work with people you care about, people who matter to you in some special way, and people you enjoy. Rant and rave about this all day long if you want to but this is life, and you may as well get used to it.

In fact, start factoring it in to your pre-season preparation.

If the coach plays the guys he likes, then you would be wise, instead of complaining, to find out what the coach likes and give him that. If the coach plays favorites (all coaches do) then find out what the coach favors and do that. Be one of the coach's favorites. It usually isn't very hard to do. Most coaches favor athletes who put in long hours in the off-season, who work hard in practice, who are punctual, conscientious, good students, tuned in...need I go on? It's usually not much of a secret what a coach favors. Most coaches will be quick to tell you.

So, say your coach doesn't like earrings, and you love to wear an earring. Your coach may not be justified in cutting athletes who wear earrings and you may possibly have a court case you can win. That's a decision you have to make. But if you want to play, the short way is to take off your earring for that coach and do what he wants a good player to do.

Is that compromising your standards? Is that selling out? Being a wimp? Only you can decide how important earrings are to you. No doubt there are some cases where holding your ground would be justified even if it meant being cut from the team. But the majority of the time, your stubbornness just means that you aren't willing to pay the price.

You have undoubtedly heard that cliché many times, paying the price. That may mean working hard in the off-season and it may mean giving up eating certain things or spending leisure hours in a hammock or taking off an earring. It means different things at different times in different sports with different coaches in different situations.

But don't fool yourself. *You are not very likely to become a sports star without accepting some compromises along the way.* If you have to give up an earring to please a narrow-minded coach, I would advise you to do it, give it up, be the best player on the team and the best in the whole league and then, from a position of stardom, talk to the coach about perhaps changing the earring policy.

Let's consider politics from an opposite angle. Some athletes will say, "I don't want to make the team because of my dad, or by going to the coach's summer camp, or by having my parents take the coach out to dinner."

Obviously there are different degrees of politics, and some things you are willing to do, some things you may not be willing to do. But just make sure you think carefully about these issues before you come to a decision. If your dad can help you get on the team, if I were you I'd feel free to accept the help. In your particular situation, it may be necessary. (Of course, we all wish everything was based strictly on merit but we don't live in Utopia, we live on Earth.) Some compromises may very well be necessary. And ultimately, it's not really important how you get on a team, it's what you do after you are on it. So if you need a boost from a father or a friend or from whomever can give one to you, take it.

If your coach wants his players to attend his summer camp, you better make plans to attend. If your coach seems to be influenced by parents who take him out to dinner, I would not only beg my parents to take him out to dinner, I would try to do something extra to make sure it was the best dinner he had. Call his mother or his wife. Find out what are his favorite foods…you get the idea.

Sports are no different from the rest of life. Consider the days ahead when you will be looking for a good job or career. Do you know the best place to start? It's calling the people who know and like you. Those are the people who will best be able to help you. Is that politics? Is that bad? It may be. But it is life, and you may as well get used to it.

"Oh he made the team because he goes in the coach's office every day after school and brown-noses the coach and talks to him."

Brown-nosing? If that's your idea of brown-nosing, you better get on the phone and call Sherwin-Williams or Crayola and start painting your nose. As a coach, I want athletes who want to communicate with me, who are willing to come in and talk, who want to organize things and find out what I want and how I want things done. Players who do those things are not brown-nosers, they are team-members. A lot of what you may think of as brown-nosing is what a good coach calls "interest."

When I hear athletes talk about sports I am constantly surprised by the many who have what I call a "midget-league mentality." Everyone is entitled to play, the coach has to be kind and understanding at all times, the practices have to be fun, and everyone gets a trophy at the end. The real sports world isn't like that. More toughness is required, more sacrifice involved, more compromise, more bad things, less good things. Politics is a part of sports just as politics is a part of life. Get used to it. And get involved. Get politics to work for you, instead of standing on the sidelines complaining about how it is working against you.

74.
Positive Places

People who have positive places to go to, and established routines to follow, can get so much more accomplished.

Presumably, an ideal home would be a place with a mother and father, a dog and a cat, several TV's, a DVD player, an aquarium, a brother and sister, a study room, each kid with his own bedroom, own computer, own desk...

And that would just be for starters. The father would be home each day by 5:00 but able to get off work three or four times per week to visit the school, attend afternoon games, or take the whole loving family out on a surprise picnic right after school on a warm fall day by the side of a stream with the sun beaming down. Everyone would excitedly talk together yet listen curiously to each other.

Get real. A third of families don't have a mother and father. Dogs and cats get in fights. The parent can't get off work but has to take two jobs just to pay the bills. Or the parents have a pile of money but can't stand each other. There are personality clashes, alcohol, problems...

No one ever promised you that your life would be problem-free. And hardly anyone's life is. Some people live in incredibly difficult circumstances. Others have seemingly wonderful circumstances, but you can't always be sure that what you see on the surface is what is really happening underneath.

Anyway, why talk about all of this? What does all this have to do with being a champion or with "positive places?" Everything. And I think it's important to put all of this in context, to make sure there's no impression that creating positive places in your life is necessarily easy.

Creating positive places in your life is often *not* easy. But it's something you have to strive to do, even if the only positive place you can create is the space between your ears. That space is the most important. But once you've taken care of that space (which is what this book attempts to help you do) you have to try to make some other places as manageable, as positive, as perfect as possible for yourself.

Forget your problems and the obstacles. Most likely there will be some. Or many. Just focus on what you can do. How can you create a good study place? How can you create a good athletic training place? How can you create a good reflecting place? Some people have all three already and they don't use them. They don't even know what an advantage they have. So don't bother yourself with what others have or don't have. Concentrate on getting three places you need, and commit yourself to making the most of them.

Positive Place #1: an athletic training place

Do you have a place where you can go to work on your skills? Preferably a place where you can work uninterrupted, without distractions. For some it is a weight room, some a basketball court, some an empty field. Many people take an available training place for granted. Their neighborhood is saturated with courts and fields and facilities. For others, jogging would have to be through dangerous city streets, the only basketball court is jammed day and night with people, and there aren't any weight rooms around except those that cost a lot of money to join.

Whatever your situation, try to makes sure you have a place you can go that is conducive to working diligently to improve. It's not that you have to necessarily have the place all to yourself. But it should be an atmosphere where you can learn the joy of uninterrupted effort.

Do you know the joy of uninterrupted effort? Of a daily routine of piling up repetitions and concentrating on techniques? Some athletes have all the facilities but haven't learned to think of the process as containing any joy. Others would love to repeat drills but can't find a good place.

Find a place. Establish a routine. Change it as often as you need to in order to find a pattern that suits you. But keep working till you find it.

People who have positive places to go to and established routines to follow can get so much more accomplished. They can build on their strengths and piggyback their efforts and propel their improvement. Plus, they are more likely to feel good about themselves in the process. As an athlete you need a place to go and a routine to follow. Work to develop your place and routine. And don't worry if there's no immediate joy. Your job—finding the joy—may be just as difficult as someone else's job—finding a place. That's okay. We didn't start out saying there was one ideal situation anyway. Everyone's different. But everyone can benefit from the self-discipline of place-and-routine.

Positive Place #2: a study place

You probably have the idea already so there's no reason for me to go into the same amount of detail. One kid has his own quiet room, a big desk, a nice lamp, baseball bookends, banners on the wall, calendars, charts, graphs, a revolving globe, a telescope aimed out a window, a computer, a cabinet filled with education software, self-study courses, a laser printer...but he can't stand going into that room to study.

Another kid lives with eight people in two rooms. He likes learning, but there's never peace and quiet. There's barely space to breathe. There's not one book in the house. A pencil or a piece of paper is hard to locate so when the phone rings, no one can take a message.

Everyone's got different conditions. What matters is your ability to create adequate conditions for yourself. What are adequate conditions? *Conditions you can thrive in.* It doesn't do any good to have all those globes and telescopes and computers if you don't use them to your advantage.

As a student you need to work to create a place where you can go to study, and where you can develop a sense of joy about the process. Uninterrupted. You sit down, you open a book, you seek information. For some that sounds interesting all by itself. For others it's pure hell already. Just the idea of sitting down with a book causes a restless feeling.

You can change your conditions and you can change your response to your conditions. You just have to realize that learning to sit down and grapple with ideas in books can be enjoyable, even for people who don't right now consider it as such. It's all a matter of training and of finding a place where you have a chance to succeed with that training.

Few people like running sprints the first time someone takes them out on a hot August day, makes them sprint again and again, and prevents them from resting as long as they'd like between sprints. You have to learn to enjoy physical conditioning. It's not easy. In fact, it may very well never be your idea of great fun. But you can improve your enjoyment of it which you'll have to do if you are attempting to perform like a champion.

The same applies to book-learning. You can't get away with saying, "I just don't like books. I hate sitting down with a book. That's just the way I am." My reply is "Garbage. That's *not* just the way you *am*. That's just the way you happen to be at this particular time." You don't like what you haven't been trained to like. You haven't been properly exposed to books so you think that means you just don't like books. If you think like that, your very thinking process may be erroneous.

There may not be anyone around to help you, but you can help yourself. Go to a quiet place and think and weigh and consider and contemplate. You may have to roll this concept over and over in your head until it makes sense:

It is possible for you to increase your enjoyment of things you think you don't like.

You have to be willing to open your mind up to this possibility. And you may already have guessed a way to do this. But are you accustomed to going to a quiet place to think and weigh and consider? If you're not, that's something that you need to work on. It will help you to become a champion.

Positive Place #3: a quiet place of reflection

For you to make the most of your life, you have to realize you're an individual, even if the people around you still treat you like a kid. You are in charge of your life and your destiny. You can blame your conditions and problems all you want, but thousands of people overcame conditions worse than yours and they could overcome your conditions right now. So can you. But you have to realize at the outset that no one is claiming it will be easy.

If you want to take charge of your life and start seeing things clearly, see how you want to spend your life, and figure out ways to maximize your time on this planet, you need to have a place to get away from it all so you can think and reflect. You don't have to sit at the top of a lighthouse at Cape Sounion on the tip of southern Greece in order to get away from it all. A library in any major city might do the job fine. A closet in your own house may work, too. It's not really the place that matters, it's the state of mind you get when you go there. It's a sense of perspective that you want. And then what?

It's not so much that you want to think energetically as much as to just sit there and be aware of life, of yourself, of your surroundings, and of the part you are playing in the film of your life (which is unreeling every day whether you think of it like that or not).

What are you proud of? What would you like to change? What can you change? What must you accept and make the best of? How can you get added help? Where can you get a boost? Who might be able to help you? At least once a week you ought to be disappearing into some quiet place and giving yourself a chance to get away from everything long enough so that the events around you can just sink in, and so that some new possibilities can float through.

Reflection is something nearly all champions do, in all fields, in all nations, in all times. But a lot of people, especially busy young students and athletes, have never even been told that this is an important ingredient of success at champion levels. In the rush to learn to read and spell and write and add and catch a ball and run and avoid drugs, sometimes important things get left out.

Don't leave this place out. Or the other two. Find your three positive places and learn to enjoy the processes that occur in each of them. Experiment. Try. And try again. Trust your own power to change and improve yourself, and keep at it. Call for tiny improvements, not miracles.

Remember the famous line: All great journeys begin with a single step. So take some steps. Create your places. And let yourself flourish in them.

75.
Prayer, God and Beliefs

Athletes in general seem to perform better when they take their minds off themselves…

A lot of athletes pray before competing, and a lot of athletes thank God after they are finished. Many of the athletes who pray become champions, and of course, many of the athletes who lose to these champions have also prayed and lost. So what does it all mean? Should you pray? Does it help?

I cannot pretend to be an expert on religion or prayer but I am going to offer a suggestion, based on observations and some personal experience, which may be helpful to you. I don't think it is possible to claim that one prayer is better than another or that athletes who pray are necessarily better or more successful than athletes who don't pray. There are many examples to fit every religious or non-religious belief.

One thing, however, seems clear to me. Athletes in general seem to perform better when they take their minds off themselves and commit themselves to something beyond themselves. Some athletes claim they are putting their performance in the hands of God, some dedicate a game to a parent or a sick friend, still others set their sights on money or fame or some far off goal.

All athletes seem to benefit from attaching themselves to something larger than themselves.

Therefore, I think it makes sense for any athlete to do this in some way. It seems to help athletes get more easily into that "flow" stage where they seem to run on automatic, reacting effortlessly and intelligently, and doing their best without hindering their performance with excessive analysis or second-guessing.

Some people will claim that my observation is a gross oversimplification, that prayer is actually much more powerful. Perhaps they are right. But considering the number of religions, the variety of beliefs, and the available evidence, I think it would be presumptuous of me to go any further than to urge you to be true to your beliefs, to get beyond yourself, and to be willing to give your very best effort in pursuit of your goals.

76.
PRIDE: Where is Yours?

There is no correlation between how much an athlete wants to win and how he acts after a loss…

Where do you place your pride?

There may not be a question more important to an athlete than this one. Most athletes, and most people, are able to follow through on the things they are truly proud of. For example, nearly everyone who is proud of having a new article of clothing will make a significant effort to keep it clean and looking nice. That new sweater will not get tossed on the floor the way an old, torn t-shirt will. And its owner will probably use better posture and have greater confidence when wearing it. It's a simple matter of pride. Where there is pride, there is nearly always special treatment and success.

People who are proud of their handwriting, to use another example, are typically much more careful about spelling, margins, and punctuation, than people who will tell you readily that they write sloppily.

This isn't much more than stating the obvious: you do better at the things you take pride in. Knowing this, the question, "Where do you place your pride?" comes again to center stage, particularly for athletes. Why does one athlete shake his opponent's hand graciously after a tough defeat while another stomps and mutters and throws things?

Do you think the stomper wanted to win more? Maybe, but maybe not. There is no correlation between how much an athlete wants to win and how he acts after a loss. There is, however, a correlation between how an athlete acts after a game and what kind of behavior that athlete is proud of exhibiting.

Painful defeat or not, the athlete who is proud of being gracious in defeat will be gracious in defeat, and the athlete who believes that stomping and throwing things will mark him as a special competitor will stomp and throw things.

You can call it temper or poor losing or bad attitude or fierce determination but all those labels miss the point. Tens of thousands of hot heads become gracious the moment their sense of pride is redirected by a good coach. Once that happens, nobody needs to say a word about their tempers or controlling their tempers. Temper becomes a non-issue. Pride simply takes over.

Where do you place *your* pride?

If you think it is cool to point out bad conditions or to say things like "No one could win in a rat hole like this" then no doubt you will point out bad conditions and probably lose when you play in rat holes. But if your pride is being a champion—practicing like a champion, playing like a champion, winning and losing like a champion—you will become a champion. When you get to a rat hole, your natural response will be, "Here's a chance to show we can win anywhere, even in this rat hole. Here's a chance to show off the great stuff we are made of." The champion looks forward to playing in the rat hole, to show off in the finest way available to an athlete. The champion uses the power of his pride to great advantage. It lets him fire up and go for it at precisely the time when others get discouraged and give up.

The importance of this concept cannot be overstated. What you are proud of will get done. But when your pride is misdirected, something misdirected will get done. If you think kicking and throwing things shows you are a terrific competitor who hates to lose, and if you are proud of being a terrific competitor who hates to lose, then you have no choice but to kick and throw things when you lose. Your pride requires it. Your problem is in your thinking and in where you are placing your pride.

Take time to examine yourself and to examine what you are truly proud of. Consider what changes you might want to make. An athlete who is proud of never complaining never complains. To that athlete, not complaining is easy because he's proud of it. An athlete who is proud of playing hard plays hard even when he has a headache or an upset stomach. And it's relatively easy. Because he's proud of it.

Once you get proud of something, doing the thing does get easy. Which is why the athlete who is proud of "not taking no crap from no one" has an easy time walking out of practice and quitting a team when a coach yells at him. He ain't takin' no crap, so quitting is easy. If, instead, that same athlete were proud of his persistence and dedication, he would take all sorts of crap from his coach and never even think of walking out or quitting. In fact, at the end of a practice in which he had weathered all sorts of criticism, he could say to the coach: "Thanks for the help, Coach." And mean it.

Do you get irritated every time a defender makes contact with you? Do taunts bother you while you are playing? Do referees' or umpires' bad calls bother you? Does the lighting or the weather or the playing surface bother you? Take a look at your pride. Where is it? Where could it be? When you decide to put your pride in performing and behaving every day like a true champion, all of these peripheral considerations become unimportant.

The potential power of this very book lies not in the cleverness or intelligence of the writing, but in *you*. This book simply defines championship performance. Once you realize what championship performance is, you can adopt it at once, overnight if not sooner, and suddenly respond to all sorts of so-called negatives like a champion.

It is a simple matter of where you place your pride. Why not place your pride in championship performance in every aspect of your life? Saying, "you can do it," isn't even necessary. If you place your pride in performing like a champion, you won't be able to avoid it. Your pride will do it for you.

77.

Psychological Preparation

Don't think that if you just had a great pep talk or some other psychological gimmick, you would suddenly be able to perform a miracle...

How do you prepare yourself mentally for a big game, big match, or big event of any kind? Athletes have a variety of ways of preparing. Some need quiet just before game time, some like to chatter and release excess energy. What you need or prefer depends on your personality, but one crucial aspect of preparation should not depend on anything but intelligence.

Thousands of athletes, even good ones, sabotage their own psychological preparation by entertaining destructive thoughts that, to borrow a phrase, "would never hold up in court." For example, if they usually play on Saturdays and suddenly play a game on a Monday, and play poorly, they may get the idea in their minds that "We just don't play well on Mondays."

Typically these kinds of ideas, that often have a powerful influence on performance, seem absolutely plausible to the athletes harboring them. Yet sometimes the idea is based on only one or two cases. There is no rational reason that one or two cases should be given any special belief but somehow those cases stick in your mind.

"I just don't play well under that kind of lighting." "I just never play well on that kind of surface." "I don't know what it is, but I just can't seem to get started when I play in the morning." "I always give my best effort but somehow I just don't seem to get the same results when it's raining." "I just don't play well when my father comes to watch."

All of these statements—these beliefs—and many more like them crop up in the conversation and, worse, in the psychological preparation of athletes. The results can be very negative because if you are convinced you have a reason to perform poorly there is a much better chance that you will in fact perform poorly.

What you need to realize is that a team of scientists, or a decent attorney, would laugh at your reasoning and make your way of thinking look very stupid even if you have seven or eight cases to base your idea on and not just one or two. Can you imagine the line of questioning?

"You say you play poorly when your father watches, right? When did you first notice this? Are you certain that your father's presence was the reason you played poorly that first time? Are you aware that millions of athletes throughout the world are able to perform well in their father's presence and could most likely do so in your father's presence? Are you aware that several thousand athletes around the world once attributed their poor performance to things like their father but then discovered that they were simply victimized by stupid thinking patterns? Do you think you could play well if your father watched on TV? What if he merely watched a tape of your game a day later? What if he watched for a few minutes, then left, then came back and kept watching intermittently? Do you think you would ever "feel" him being there, only to find out later that he actually was out getting a hotdog? Do you think you would be free to perform well if your father wore a mask to your games? What about if he wore some big ears and a big red rubber nose? What if he kept his back to the action the whole time or sat far away in the last row or up on a distant hill? What if he watched through a telescope from an adjacent building?"

The line of questioning could become hilarious, bizarre, crazy, ridiculous, and all it would do is make you look really stupid because such mystical thinking represents a giant step into the supernatural. You might as well just claim that little green men from Mars are making you play poorly. It will make about the same degree of sense.

You may choose to play poorly when your father is watching because of something destructive in your relationship, but you have to realize that your performance is a choice you are making, and not something that must automatically happen.

The best choice you can make is to take all the circumstances into consideration and then make a simple statement to yourself.

"Under these circumstances there are athletes in the world who could perform well. I choose to be one of those athletes." Period.

Perhaps you now understand what I think about psychological preparation for sporting events. In a sense, the best preparation is no preparation. Your preparation is what you have been doing all year long—practicing, repeating, repeating, practicing. You work diligently to perfect your skills. If you have the necessary skills, you go out and use them. There isn't any grand plan necessary once you have the skills. You simply go out and show off. That's what you have been trained to do.

That means the only real consideration is that you don't sabotage your skills with some type of negative thinking. "You can do it, you can do it." Of course you can do it. That's what you've trained yourself to be able to do. If you can't do it in rehearsal, don't fool yourself. Don't think that if you just have a great pep talk or some other psychological gimmick, you will suddenly be able to perform a miracle during the actual performance.

In other words, proper mental preparation is not much more than making sure you aren't giving in or being victimized by negative or stupid ways of thinking. Let me give an example and elaborate.

A surprising number of basketball players are victimized by a variety of shooting superstitions. "If I shoot well in practice the day before the game, I don't shoot well in the game." Or, "If I shoot well in warm ups before the game, I won't shoot well during the actual game itself." Conversely, "If I'm missing in warm ups, I usually hit during the game."

Thought patterns like these actually encourage some basketball players to hope they are missing the day before a big game or to hope they are missing a high percentage of shots in the warm ups or, even worse, to shoot haphazardly and perhaps to try to miss in warm ups so they'll perform at their best in the game.

What a bunch of wasted thought and misdirected focus. These same players should be focusing all their attention on grooving their shot, on getting it just right, the day before, the minute before, the game. Their thinking should be as follows.

If they're shooting well the day before the game or in the warm ups before the game, they should think, "Great, I'm in the groove, on a roll, ready to explode during the game." If they're shooting poorly before the game, they should think, "I've practiced hard, I'm an excellent shooter, but my shots aren't falling right now. The law of averages indicates I will soon start making everything."

Regardless of the circumstances you have a right to assume you will demonstrate your ability during the game, so prepare yourself to do just that. Good shooters have a right to assume they will shoot well. Any other assumption is counterproductive and may actually keep you from performing up to the level your ability merits.

Turn every event, every circumstance, every condition in your favor. That does not assure that you will perform to the very best of your ability in every game you ever play in. What it does do is assure that you will play as well as possible given your ability level and the fact that you are human.

Get rid of stupid thinking patterns. If they won't hold up in court, discard them. Make sure your thinking is "right." Prepare yourself to perform well in all circumstances, and then do it. Don't look for supernatural explanations if you fail. *Sometimes, failure is simply the very best you could have done under the circumstances.* Learn what you can then get up, brush off your pants, and move on. There are always other games to play and new challenges ahead.

78.

Quitters Never Win?

They couldn't recognize the difference between quitting with a sense of giving up and quitting with a passion to do better...

The actual line goes, "A winner never quits, a quitter never wins." That's old time locker room stuff and worth thinking about in limited circumstances.

First, for all you scholars who smashed the Scholastic Aptitude Test, you know that "always" and "never" should be viewed as red flags, warning signs.

Never? Most lines that include never are wrong, just like this one. Let me make it clear: Winners sometimes quit. Quitters sometimes win. In fact, let's go a step further. Winners are sometimes smart to quit. Those who have quit on occasion are sometimes terrific winners.

Let's use Troy Aikman as an example. Troy went from high school to the University of Oklahoma to play quarterback on the Sooners football team. Things didn't go as well as he hoped they would so he transferred to UCLA. No doubt there were many people in Oklahoma who said, "Troy's a quitter." Or, "If you can't stand the heat, get out of the kitchen." So Troy met some adversity and didn't have the guts to take it like a man and push through it. Right? No, wrong.

Troy Aikman transferred to UCLA because he believed his talents would be better developed and demonstrated there. To Oklahoma Sooners fanatics, Aikman may have seemed like a quitter and many called him one. Many, no doubt, claimed with great assurance that he would never amount to anything, but they were wrong. Aikman when on to star at UCLA and to become the NFL's number one draft choice when his college career was over. When he signed to play football for the Dallas Cowboys, he became set for life financially.

Aikman went on to become one of the NFL's best quarterbacks. He won Super Bowls under two different coaches (including Barry Switzer who had been his coach at Oklahoma). Was he a quitter? Do you think he cared that some fanatics claimed he would never amount to anything? The important thing to learn from this example is that Aikman didn't quit on himself. When he quit Oklahoma, it was with the intention of bettering himself. His goal—to become a great football player—hadn't changed one bit.

Aikman was true to his goals and true to himself. He didn't consider himself a quitter at all. He was, in fact, a constant seeker and striver, continuously looking for ways to do even better. And if that meant transferring from one school to another, so be it. People could say what they wanted. It was their problem if they couldn't recognize the difference between quitting with a sense of giving up and quitting with a passion to do better.

In my opinion, Aikman didn't quit. Quitting is when you get behind in a game, get discouraged, and stop hustling. You may still be on the team but you quit trying to do the best you can. Or you aren't playing in the games as much as you think you deserve to play, so you quit doing the best you can to improve in practice. You say to yourself, "What's the use? The coach doesn't play me anyway." Your effort diminishes. You become a player with a bad attitude. You quit trying to do your best. That is real quitting. You are still going through the motions but no longer giving it your best.

Transferring your efforts is different from quitting. It is intelligently changing from a possible dead end to a new doorway. I recall a father telling me once how his son hated playing on a basketball team—he was riding the bench all season getting no playing time at all—but, the father said, "He went out for the team and I told him 'Once you start something, you have to finish it. No kid of mine is going to be a quitter.'"

He said it with self-assurance as if it were wise advice. He thought I would agree, but I think my answer surprised him.

"Why make your kid stay involved in something that isn't worthwhile for him? Seems like a stupid use of his time. Seems to me he would be a lot better off if he put his effort into something else where he could be more enthusiastic and probably enjoy greater success."

The guy looked at me like I was a heretic. How could I say such a thing? How could I think such a thing?

But hey, it's a big world out there. Why be an also-ran at one thing when you might be a star at something else? If baseball turns out not to be the sport for you maybe you should try hockey, or tennis, or squash. Many activities, not just sports, offer a person satisfaction and fulfillment. If one particular sport or activity is failing to do that, get out of it. Get into something else. Nothing wrong with that.

Just make sure you don't stop what you're doing at the first sign of an obstacle. Here is where the title of this section, and that opening line, have real meaning.

If you get the idea that when the first problem arises the intelligent thing to do is quit, then you've missed the point entirely. You don't quit until you've tried and tried and tried again, and then thought about things, and tried again. You don't quit a team after a game or two fail to go as you had hoped. You don't switch to a different activity each day, failing to stick to anything.

You have to have some pride in your persistence, and a realistic expectation about obstacles—that they are inevitable and that you can overcome them—before you can put yourself and your decisions properly in focus. If you continually transfer your skills and efforts from one thing to another, you may not be a quitter but you will be a dabbler and that is just as bad.

So, think about it. If you have tried hard, if you have persisted and worked and if—during this time while you are still working hard to succeed—you see a better opportunity for yourself, a better place to put your efforts, then make a change. Re-channel your efforts, but don't just quit out of frustration.

Whatever you do, do it to the best of your ability and keep trying to do that until a better opportunity presents itself. If no better opportunity presents itself, keep at what you're doing. If a better opportunity comes along, then feel free to transfer your efforts.

If some people call you a quitter, don't worry about them. Tell them you're a "transferer." They won't understand what you mean but that won't matter. Just make sure you're seeking excellence.

79.
Reading

At least try to become a curious, frequent browser…

Seems as though adults are always telling young people to read, stay in school, etc. "It's valuable later in life," they say. Or, "it's something to fall back on." I'd like to make a different case or two.

First, education is good because it's easier to go through life smart than stupid.

Second, reading can be worthwhile now, in your sport. That's what I want to dwell on in this section.

When I was about thirteen or fourteen years old, I read an article by Tommy Heinsohn, a Boston Celtic basketball player. He explained, very briefly, a maneuver that sometimes enabled him to strip or steal a rebound from another player. I read the article carefully and immediately tried the thing on the court the next day. And it worked! I was surprised, and of course delighted.

I recall telling my older brother about the maneuver and he acted skeptical until I used it on him not long afterward and got a steal. Instead of being mad, he yelled "Heinsohn" at me, as if to say, "Don't take credit for that steal, that one was Heinsohn's!"

I'm not going to go on and on except to say that I used that same maneuver to get steals literally hundreds of times in my playing career, counting practice and pickup games, and I honestly don't think I would have gotten any of those steals had it not been for Heinsohn and that article I read. I never heard anyone else talk about that maneuver nor do I ever remember anyone ever trying it on me (although few had opportunities since I didn't get many rebounds). But the point is, I learned something from reading that helped me in my sport the next day and throughout my career.

A lot of people would claim there are better reasons for reading than getting some extra steals occasionally in a sport, and they are probably right. Many things you learn from reading can save you time and money and foolish mistakes. But for now, while reading a sports book, you can forget all those bigger than life reasons and just see if you can find something that will actually help you today or tomorrow or next week in your sport. There are worse things to do with your time. And don't stop here. If you never become a truly avid reader, at least try to become a curious, frequent browser. There are gems out there—strips and steals and game-winning tips—in books. Look for them.

80.
Referees and Umpires

In the worst-case scenario, playing with blind cheaters who hate you, your best course of action is to stay focused on yourself.

They're blind. They walk with Seeing Eye dogs. They can't even find their way to an eye doctor, let alone see the chart.

You can think whatever you want to think about the vision of the persons in charge of officiating your games. And you wouldn't have to stop with eyes. They cheat. Their sons and daughters play for the other team. Their best friends are the other team's coaches. They are getting paid by the other team. They all gamble heavily on games—all against your team. You can think whatever you want to think about referees. It's okay. In fact, let's make it more emphatic:

They are all blind. They all cheat. They all hate you.

Now we can begin. Let's start with a whole new title, now that we have this beginning fully established. Let's just call it...

"Now What?"

In arguing with a referee you only waste your time and you usually look stupid, too. By focusing on a referee's calls you only distract yourself from performing as well as possible under the circumstances. Since you already know what you know, why waste time? Why look stupid? Why take your focus off yourself and your objectives?

Do you understand this? In the worst-case scenario, playing with blind cheaters who hate you, your best course of action is to stay focused on yourself. In this case it is ridiculous to spend time arguing with someone who can't see and who is happy to be able to cheat you.

But what if the referee is only partially blind, only occasionally cheats, and only sometimes dislikes you? Does this change anything? Maybe so. Under these circumstances, it may pay big dividends to try to affect the referee's behavior.

How do you influence a referee?

1. Help the referee see better.

Be sharp and precise. Execute everything perfectly or as well as you possibly can. The more precise your execution, the more difficult it is to miss what has happened. (Even a referee wanting to cheat would do so only on murky, unclear plays, not ones that were obvious to everyone.)

2. Reduce the number of plays that will require a referee's decision.

If a line call is going to be crucial (in tennis, for example) don't hit the ball on the line. Make it easy for the referee. Or make it nearly impossible for the referee to make a call against you. Keep the ball a foot inside the lines and add some pace. There are other ways to score points than by hitting balls within an inch of the lines. In other words, limit the referee's opportunities. Don't get in those hazy areas where the referee's judgment is involved. If you're playing football, don't even come close to a late hit. Snap the ball quickly so there's no opportunity for motion or for illegal procedure. Don't give your own players time to juke or look as though there was some movement on the line.

In basketball, in baseball, in hockey, soccer, volleyball, don't give the referee or umpire an opportunity to get involved. And if you do, then consider it your fault. You gave him the opportunity to see the play poorly. You relied on him to give you a break when you should have relied on yourself and not needed a break.

If a call can go either way, in a world of blindness and

cheating, the call will go against you. So you have to be extra precise, extra sharp. Don't let plays get to the point where they can go either way.

3. Help the referee like you more.

If the referee likes you, or at least doesn't dislike you, you will more likely get the close calls, or at least the referee won't have the tendency to manufacture calls against you.

If a ball rolls out of bounds, run and get it and hand it to the referee. If the referee is overweight he will particularly appreciate this effort in his behalf.

Shake the umpires' and referees' hands when they walk into your arena, and introduce yourself. Wish them luck. Ask them about their profession, how they got into it, how they like it. Ask them if there is anything you can do for them. Tell them before the game to let you know if any of your teammates are giving them any trouble so you can handle it. Let them know that you have come to play your sport, not to try to help them call the game. There's hardly a referee or umpire in the world who doesn't appreciate that.

Do what a good sales person does when there's a glut in the market and the buyer has many options. Sell on friendship. Get the referee to like you.

4. Be business-like at all times.

Don't roll your eyes at calls, or glare or look aghast or confused or unbelieving when something goes against you. Put on your "all-business" face and keep it on. Full time. Overtime.

5. Realize that everything looks different from a different angle.

Surely you've seen enough instant replays to realize this. When an obvious call goes against you, repeat to yourself, if it helps, some innocuous line like "Gee, that must have looked entirely different from his angle."

You have, in my opinion, only two real options when it comes to umpires and referees. They are: (1) You can ignore them entirely, or (2) you can actively work to influence them positively.

If you choose to influence them positively then you have to be consistent. You can't assume they will be impressed by a player who congratulates them for their favorable calls and then yells at them for the unfavorable ones. On the contrary, to influence them favorably you probably need to be entirely quiet when they make calls in your favor, and act approving—or at least give no reaction—when the calls go against you. This will of course be impressive because almost no athletes do it.

If you feel compelled to comment on referees' decisions and compelled to show your reactions and displeasure, you are on the wrong side of athletics. You should quit playing sports and become a referee. Then you will be in a much more effective position to make calls and to make them stick. As a player, making calls that stick is impossible. So why waste your time?

On May 9, 1996, the Utah Jazz lost a big NBA playoff game to the San Antonio Spurs. During that game, the Spurs shot twenty-nine free throws while the Jazz shot only five. A lot of people (Utah fans) squawked about the disparity in fouls and blamed the referees. Reporters asked Utah's star, Karl Malone, what he thought. (Malone, by the way, is a certified superstar. He played on the original Dream Team in Barcelona and on the second Dream Team in Atlanta as well.) The comments of this man, who was one of the top ten basketball players in the world throughout the 1990s, follow:

"I never talk about the officiating; I'm not going to start now. It's just the way it happened. We didn't do what we needed to do down the stretch."

He didn't focus on the referees. He focused on himself, his team, and on what he and his team failed to do. If only all pro athletes would talk—and act—like that, maybe you would get the message. The fact that all pros do not talk like that doesn't make them right. It is just plain stupid to focus your attention on referees before, during, or after a game.

One of the grandest goals of my life is to have an impact on the way athletes respond to umpires' and referees' calls all over the world. Personally, *my pleasure at watching almost every sporting event is marred by how incredibly mis-focused most of the athletes are*. If you want to make calls, become a referee. If you want to play, play. It seems so simple yet hundreds, thousands, millions of athletes around the world spend their time focusing partially on their playing and partially on the calls the referees make. I consider them very stupid. Or do they understand but simply lack self-discipline?

What about you?

81.

Renewal

People who can renew themselves—quickly and fully and consistently— are going to be more successful in life just as they will be more successful in sports.

Goodie and Ruff were two college guys who started out in the real world as insurance salesmen. Ruff said he just hated meeting new prospects. He always had the feeling that they were thinking, "Oh no, not another insurance salesman." Meanwhile, Goodie believed he had a terrific product and that he performed a very valuable service for his clients. When he was rejected he said that he became more confident. Company statistics showed that one of every three competent attempts was destined to succeed, so he knew his chances improved with each rejection. Two consecutive rejections simply meant he was extremely likely to succeed with that third prospect. And what if that third said no? Then Goodie was even more enthusiastic. Almost certainly, he would get two or maybe even three consecutive prospects who would buy.

It isn't difficult to see the enormous difference in the thinking of these two young insurance salesmen—and the effect their thinking had on the way each one greeted his next prospect. Do you see a parallel with the way athletes react after disappointments?

You take a called third strike with runners on, two outs in the eighth. How do you get yourself excited about running out to left field and maybe making a big catch that could ignite a rally in the ninth?

You fumble the kickoff and the other team recovers and scores a touchdown and you're back there again, awaiting another kickoff just seconds later...

You team just lost six in a row...

You just blew a layup on a 3-on-1 break...

You kicked a back to your goalie not noticing an opponent nearby...

You failed to score on a power play and the seconds are ticking away...

Failure plays a big part in sports and life. The very best stars in all sports experience many failures every day. That is the given. It's the "now what?" that really matters. What happens after the failures? What ideas, what attitude do you take with you to the next opportunity?

What can you do to make sure that your thinking encourages rather than discourages renewal?

First, I think it is helpful to understand the connection between your way of thinking and your ability to renew yourself.

Second, it is helpful to realize that the ability to renew yourself is a skill that can be developed, just as surely as skills like shooting, hitting, throwing, and kicking.

Renewal is a crucial skill in sports. The need for it comes up often: after a bad play, after a big loss, after a losing streak, after an injury. How quickly can you put the past behind you and muster the courage and enthusiasm for what is ahead? It's not so hard for an undefeated team that gets upset and has to bounce back and show what it is really made of. But what about the highly regarded team that loses its opener, and the next game, then three more?

Sometimes renewal has to come after all the traditional pep talks and clichés and deep breaths have been used up. "Hey, we can bounce back!" is a fine idea after the first loss. But after six straight losses? Will anyone listen?

There are no precise blueprints. You say whatever seems to make sense at the time. You tell yourself you can do it. And if you've used up every cliché and encouraging idea you know and still the losing streak is going on, I think you just focus on renewal the best you can, in the same way that you focus on other fundamentals of your sport.

You can never get too good at renewing yourself. It is a skill that will serve you well for the rest of your life. After a business setback, after an argument with your spouse, after an illness, after a sleepless night. Unfortunately, you'll probably have plenty of chances for renewal.

"Hey, things can't get any worse than this," some might say after a series of setbacks. (The hell they can't) Renewing yourself is something you have to keep trying, regardless of how many times you've been knocked down.

I don't have all the answers about renewal. I just know that people who can renew themselves—quickly and fully and consistently—are going to be more successful in life just as they will be more successful in sports. Sports just gives you so many opportunities, every day, in every game, to practice and to get good at renewing yourself. Make the most of it. Be proud of your ability. Try to isolate every incident of your life, every play of every game (and every drill in practice), and infuse them with enthusiasm, regardless of what has taken place before.

The pride of renewal ought to influence the way you wake up, the way you walk into the locker room each day, the way you answer questions in a classroom, the way you greet each person you see. Renewal. Enthusiasm. Joyous expectation. Are these an obvious part of the way you attack each new opportunity? Do they energize each incident of your life?

If it helps you to recall some percentages, the way Goodie did with insurance, do it. Do whatever it takes to make yourself into the most successful renewer the world has ever known. Or get as close to that distinction as you can. Make your success as a renewer a conscious part of your everyday sports preparation and development.

Can you really look in the mirror right now and say, "You are one awesome, terrific renewer. Hardly anything can drag you down or detract from your next performance?" If you can make that claim, congratulations. If you can't, get after it. That's a claim worth fighting for.

82.
Reputation

Make a player make a play, don't let his reputation do it.

I am not referring to your own reputation—keep it sparkling clean and so forth—but to the reputation of others.

This factor has a lot more to do with sports performance than most athletes will ever admit. I recall playing in a game against a player whose reputation for toughness was well established. He had not begun the game guarding me but in the second half they switched him onto me. And his reputation beat me.

I hate having to explain this (no, I actually hate having to recall it) but it may help some athletes avoid what did me in. I knew the guy's reputation and it had an impact on me. Two times in a row I dribbled down the court facing him. I saw that look of determination on his face and his clenched fists. I made fakes, got wide open, and then rushed my shots and missed both. Actually, I was much quicker than he was and he should have been easy for me to score on. He hadn't guarded me earlier because his coach knew he wasn't quick enough. But I had assumed that they were more concerned with one of my teammates so they put their best defender on him. When I turned out to be the player doing most of the damage on that particular night, it seemed natural that they would switch their star onto me. In a way, you could say I was up for the challenge. I was eager to outplay him. My adrenalin pumped and I made sharp moves, but I rushed my shots because I expected a player with his reputation to be closer to me than he was.

When I realized, after the second miss, that I could move him where I wanted to—and take my time—it was too late. The coach took him off me and replaced him with someone quicker. They had put him on me for a change, just to present a new look. And it worked.

My point to you is this: their maneuver would not have worked if I had used my head properly. If I had simply ignored his reputation and gone about my business, I would have scored or at least would not have rushed my shot. After that, although it took a loss to learn, I tried always to remember to make a player make a play, don't let his reputation do it.

Naturally, if you confront a star for the first time, you can't just do things slowly and comfortably and wait till he annihilates you to say, "Gee, now I understand why folks say he is good." But you can't allow yourself to play less than your best just because someone else is good. Put your best out there. Respect another's reputation but don't fear it, and don't let it mess you up. Make good plays mess you up if anything is going to. Never let a mere reputation do the job.

83.
Reversing Negative Atmospheres

Divide and conquer…

When working with losing teams I have noticed a familiar pattern. If you talk to the team members individually, you hear the same story over and over again: *they* are lazy, *they* are selfish, *they* don't have spirit, *they* don't really want to win.

Individually, each player will be quick to tell you that he would like to be on a team that works together. Most players will back up that idea with reference to some past team they played on when they played together and worked hard and won—proof that they aren't at fault for the current problem.

Few athletes, deep inside, take the blame for bad times in sports. Few believe they are lazy or selfish and, even if they are, they nearly always think their reactions are only in response to laziness and selfishness that occurred before they contributed theirs.

For most athletes, I have already said enough to make the point. Why is it that so many athletes on losing teams don't feel personally at fault for the myriad problems that inevitably arise? Or, an even better question, what can you do about a negative situation? It's no use assigning blame. No one will believe you anyway.

The best way to reverse the negative atmosphere surrounding a losing team is, first, not to succumb to those typical patterns of thinking—they are doing this and they are doing that. *Forget what* ***they*** *are doing, and focus on what* ***you*** *can do.*

You can change individuals one on one or, with a friend, two on one. Talk to them. Give them a chance, individually, to reaffirm their own willingness and commitment to play hard and for the team.

One very encouraging aspect about losing team members who blame each other for laziness and selfishness is they are never organized. No one got them together and said, "Hey, let's all be lazy and selfish." Lazy people don't get together very often, and selfish people don't agree too much. In other words, though it may seem temporarily as though it is you—the good guy—against all those others (bad guys), actually it is you against a collection of individuals who also don't like the atmosphere and who would like it changed. A deck that seems initially stacked against you is in reality often aligned perfectly to help you win.

Divide and conquer. Grab those teammates one by one and go after them. Find out what kind of team they want to be on and then hold them to their own standards. Often, a whole new attitude can be developed off to the side in private conversations, but not when every individual sits back quietly and blames the problems on others.

84.
Rhythmic Clapping

When a group of athletes claps in rhythm during warm ups or during drills, the impact is energizing, the atmosphere becomes charged, and the whole experience can change.

Rhythm, and sometimes even music, was considered so important an ingredient to individual courage and performance that military experts since ancient times attached drummers or whole bands to their regiments. Seems strange when you think about it, especially logistically. It's hard enough to feed and clothe all the soldiers. As a military leader you don't want the burden of carrying any more supplies than are absolutely necessary. Yet they carried not just extra food and supplies for a corps of musicians, but the instruments, too.

Why would a tough-minded general permit a band to go along unless he deemed it extremely beneficial? If you had to march off to war, it was worthwhile to hear those drums beating in a constant rhythm. The effect wasn't just disciplining, it was inspirational.

Most major teams in college and even in many high schools have pep bands associated with them. Once intended largely to inspire the athletes, these bands have become part of a total entertainment package for the fans. In the transition, most athletes have lost touch with the potential of rhythm for improving performance.

While many teams play music during warm-ups or in the locker room, their practice sessions are often quiet or punctuated only with occasional chatter and encouragement. There's a good reason. Noise, chatter, and encouragement, like rhythmic clapping, use up energy; athletes in training are conscious of not wanting to waste any.

Nevertheless, the effort expended by teammates encouraging each other and to get a team "making music" together is well worth it. When a group of athletes claps in rhythm during warm ups or during drills, the impact is energizing, the atmosphere becomes charged, and the whole experience can change. What may have been drudgery or doldrums can quickly become enjoyable.

Why do so many teams avoid this opportunity to transform their practice atmosphere? Mostly it's simply ignorance. The athletes just don't realize the benefits obtained from the sense of group cohesion that can build from something as small as periodic, rhythmic clapping.

In many team situations, where this kind of thing doesn't happen spontaneously or arise from the team leaders, the coach would be wise to require it and to make the team practice it. I have always told the players that I have coached, "A quiet gym is a losing gym."

You may not believe that, but I do. If a drill or play is not run with noise and enthusiasm, then it is not being done as well as possible and you are shortchanging your improvement. In my opinion, it's that simple. Athletes who don't contribute consistently to the spirit of the team in practice are helping to pave the way to later losses.

Do you plan to contribute to team spirit every day in practice and to try to get your teammates to do so as well?

No doubt there will be some players who, urged to participate, will roll their eyes and rebel—initially. Just as there have been, no doubt, soldiers who initially thought that the men carrying drums and bugles would better serve the force by carrying extra weapons. But they must have been wrong. Robert E. Lee, Genghis Khan, Napoleon, Caesar...many of the greatest fighters in the history of war, men who were not afraid to do things their own way, nevertheless continued to use rhythm-makers because they saw an advantage to it. You would do well to follow their example. There is synergy in the collective use of rhythm—you get back more energy than you give out. If you are on a team that fails to take advantage of this, do something about it. Get one, then two, then all of your teammates to go along with you, or at least get as many as you can.

The *ef*-fort *will* pay *off*.
The *ef*-fort *will* pay *off*.
The *ef*-fort *will* pay *off*.
The *ef*-fort *will* pay *off*.
Anyone prefer iambic pentameter?

85.
S.C.H.A.P.E.

If you fail to develop an every-day-every-play habit of precision, you just are not paving your way to championship performance…

An outstanding English teacher I once had—Myrtle Trembley for those of you scoring at home—would start the school year making her students assemble a notebook. Thirty-six stacks of individual pages, one page on each desk, would be laid out. The students, musical chairs style, would march around and around the room and up and down each aisle, picking a sheet of paper off each desk and adding it to their stack.

These were ancient days before automatic collators were attached to every copy machine but I suspect that even it if had been possible for Ms. Trembley to collate the material effortlessly herself, she may nevertheless have required the students to march around the room and do it. The effort and the ritual gave the notebook special meaning even though at the time people were cracking jokes (quietly) and carrying on, hardly treating this opening day march as a religious experience.

But to this day, I recall Ms. Trembley's pet peeves in that notebook.

1. Reason *is* because…(no "because" is needed).
2. Him and I…(he hit him, he hit me, so him and me, never him and I).

3. Different from (not different than).
4. If it was up to me (No! Conditional phrases require the subjective *were,* not was).

There were dozens more. When I hear someone speaking I often hear those Trembley grammatical no-no's and they scream out at me.

So what's the point? When I coach or teach basketball, the athletes often are surprised or miffed or annoyed that it takes so long for me to allow them on the court. They have to, figuratively, march around and around and up and down and hear my pet peeves, the big basketball no-no's, before they get a chance to actually touch a ball.

The no-no's, or the Krooshal Konsiderashunz, apply to every sport; and I don't think any athlete should play any sport without bringing these crucial considerations with him to the field or court. I call it making sure you are in SCHAPE to play. S.C.H.A.P.E. spells out six important ingredients.

Spirit.
Communication.
Hustle
Attitude.
Precision.
Enhancement.

Until I get a group of athletes to understand these, I figure the shooting, dribbling, passing, and defense can wait. See how many of these ingredients you bring to the field when you play or practice your sport.

Spirit

Spirit is noise. Do you make noise while you are practicing and playing? How about when you're standing in line or off to the side? You can't say, "I have spirit, I'm just quiet by nature." Can you imagine what it would be like to play a big game if the crowd stayed completely silent after each good play? The crowd could say, "We have spirit, we just choose to remain quiet." The whole game would be eerie because there's no such thing as quiet spirit.

To demonstrate spirit, you have to make noise with your mouth and your hands. You yell and you clap. You yell and you clap. And you keep yelling and keep clapping. You know what? It is not easy. It takes a lot of energy and few—very few—athletes are willing to keep it up. But spirit is wonderful for a team. It requires some athletes to be willing to use up a lot of energy for the good of the team. In practice. When it isn't fun.

Just about every athlete has spirit near the end of a big game when your team has just pulled ahead and the crowd is going wild. But how is your spirit during the last hour of a long, hard practice where the coach is irritated, your feet hurt, and you just aren't playing very well?

Spirit. Most athletes claim they have it and most would get a D or F if they were being secretly evaluated for spirit during a hard practice. Think about it. You know what good spirit is. (And end of game, come-from-behind celebration.) How often does *your* spirit approach that kind of display of noise and enthusiasm in practice? Do you think it's impossible to have that kind of spirit in practice? Yes, it probably is. But the closer you can come to it, the more successful your team is going to be.

If you push and urge yourself during every minute of practice to be more vocal, to fill the air with noise, you will be on the way to developing the kind of spirit that leads to championship performance. Most athletes, in practice, would get a D or F for spirit.

Communication

On the court or on the field, communication during sports competition requires the same ingredients that permit effective communication in an office or at a party. Make sure you use the ingredients consistently in practice and in games.

1. Use names.

People like to hear their names, and names are like spotlights. They focus attention on the person to whom you are talking. If you want a command to be heard at all, especially on a noisy field or court, you will be a lot more successful if you precede your commands with your teammates' names. Get their attention, then tell them what you want them to hear.

2. Make eye contact.

You wouldn't ask someone for a date while looking up in the air (at least you shouldn't) and you can't expect to get teammates to make key adjustments during quick, tense action if your communication is scattered and lacking in intensity. Naturally there are times when you cannot look all your teammates in the eye while telling them something but usually you can, and certainly you should make eye contact as often as possible. Communication always has the potential to be misunderstood or wrongly interpreted. Good eye contact definitely minimizes that potential.

3. Offer relevant information.

This seems like mere common sense but most athletes don't bother communicating at all during competition and they thereby ignore a very useful contributor to championship performance. The more often you remind your teammates of the things they should be concentrating on—both in practice and in games—the better they are going to perform.

Although you may understand this (and you probably do it during big games) few athletes make an effort to communicate effectively during practice when the foundation of championship performance is laid. Do you go into each practice drill or scrimmage aware of precisely why you are doing whatever it is you are doing? Are you constantly aware of the points of emphasis that your coach is hoping you review during that activity? A champion must be aware of what needs to get done in order to maximize that time. It is not enough to do something well yourself. If you are part of a team, you need to talk constantly to your teammates, keep them reminded of what they are doing, and keep their concentration and focus on the moment. Names, eye contact, and useful information will help accomplish this, minute by minute, day after day in practice.

Hustle

This one doesn't need much explanation except to say that it is something you have to measure every day on the practice field, not just during big games. Many athletes think they can turn hustle on and off. "Don't worry," they'll say as they loaf in practice the day before a big game, "I'll hustle tomorrow night, Baby, that's the big one!"

They believe what they're saying. But no great coaches do. Does that tell you anything? It tells me that the hustle-habit is not something you turn off and on. You think you can. But just by coincidence, the guy not in the habit of hustling constantly will let down sometime in the big game and some other player with a hustling habit will get the best of him.

If you plan to out-hustle people in games, you better plan on out-hustling them in practice, day after day, in-season and off-season. Hustling is a skill just like hitting a target or slicing a drop shot. You make it a part-time thing and it will desert you when you need it most. Every champion understands this.

Treat every practice, every play, in such a way that fans and observers would think you're in a hurry.

Attitude

Most everyone understands this one even if it's a bit difficult to put it precisely into words. You gotta play and practice with an attitude. You can't just go through the motions. Everything about your approach to what you are doing has to say "This matters, this is important, I care, and hey, want to see intensity at work?"

Amen. When you are out there on the practice field, is it clear to everyone looking on that you are intensely going about something you consider very important? It's easy during a big game. But most athletes look different when you catch them during a practice session and the coach is turned the other way.

Precision

It takes extra effort to be precise. That's why so many athletes fail at it. It seems easier to cut off a few steps, to take a shortcut. Run down, touch the line and come back? Hey, why not miss the line by a few feet and get back even faster?

Cutting corners becomes a habit that leads quickly to slovenly play. Athletes never seem to think there's a correlation between how precisely they do something in practice and how well they will do it in a big game. But again, every great coach would argue with them. Cliché or no cliché, the way you practice really is the way you will play in the games. Many athletes have a hard time believing what every great coach takes absolutely for granted. Anything less than precise, purposeful effort on the practice field will translate into foot shuffles on the field. Traveling violations, stepping on an out-of-bounds line, illegal procedure, balk. Every sport has its murky areas where lack of precision spells the difference between wining and losing. If you fail to develop an every-day-every-play habit of precision, you just are not paving your way to championship performance.

Enhancement

After all the instructions are given, throughout the criticism and encouragement, the winning and losing, a final question keeps popping into the championship equation for me. Are you out there every day actively trying to enhance what is going on? Making a drill run more smoothly? Trying to turn seven repetitions per minute into eight? Encouraging your teammates who are tired or in a slump? Trying to get your big slow guy to get some zip into his game? Trying to help the reserves feel more a part of the action? Trying to make the practice atmosphere more positive?

One of the best ways to improve drills or scrimmages is to make them into games. Often, all by yourself, you can start counting out loud and drawing your teammates into a competition with another group or into an effort to do something a certain number of consecutive times. This will focus their concentration and keep them from going through the motions or from thinking about distractions or negatives.

Typical athletes, even very talented ones, spend a great deal of their time justifying bad stuff or nursing semi-injuries, or trying to hoard energy or hoping to get by with something, or asking what time practice is over or how many more sprints they have to do. It's all natural enough, human and everything. But it does not lead to championship performance. If you want to be the team at the top, the team proud of special accomplishment at the end of the season, you can't be among all the time-wasters, non-focusers and average folks during the season. Champions spend their time trying to enhance what they are doing, what their teams are doing, and the atmospheres of their lives and those around them. Not many athletes do that. But then, not many athletes are champions.

86.
Seat Selections

Where would you choose to sit if you knew the teacher would be handing out a few hundred dollar bills during the course of the class?

Few people, particularly athletes, give much thought to choosing a seat when walking into a classroom or meeting room or auditorium for the first time. But the seat you pick says a lot about you and the person you have decided to be, whether you realize it or not.

Choosing a seat in a classroom is a lot like choosing how you enter a game when called off the bench by your coach. Those who choose to get up slowly and unenthusiastically may say that how you enter a game is meaningless, that what matters is how you perform once in it. Yes. And no.

Few coaches will look upon your method of going from the bench to the game as unimportant. While you may be technically correct that it really doesn't matter since it has no impact on actual performance, you may be very foolish to think that it doesn't matter if it upsets your coach. The way you choose to enter a game usually does have a large impact on your coach.

Whether it affects performance or not, most coaches think it does. Most coaches will say, "If you can't jump up and sprint enthusiastically into the game, don't bother at all." Many coaches will call a kid back who fails to respond immediately and with energy. "Never mind. I'll get someone who wants to play."

"But Coach, I want to play."

"Well, you didn't show it."

Most athletes understand this kind of player-coach exchange and they understand that, regardless of whether it matters or not, sometimes you have to do things the coach's way in order to get more of your way. That's how life is. It's called give and take, compromise, or "everyone's different." Name it what you like. If a coach calls you from the bench, and if you want to play, you better leave your lawyer at home along with your arguments. Do it his way. Jump up. Look excited.

"Hey," you're saying, "what does all this have to do with seat selection?" Everything. When you walk into any class or room and choose a seat in the back, you may be thinking—harmlessly enough, in *your* mind—that sitting in the back doesn't say anything about you. You will listen. You will do the work. It's the grade you get that matters, not the seat you choose. Hey, your name begins with a Z, you've always been last alphabetically, you're just accustomed to sitting in the back. It's no reflection on your degree of interest in the class. Oh, really?

Where would you choose to sit if you knew the teacher would be handing out a few hundred dollar bills during the course of the class? Where would you choose to sit if your favorite actor or actress were teaching the class?

You may choose to stick to your argument. Go ahead. Walk lackadaisically into games. Choose back row seats. Maybe it won't have an impact. Maybe. You may also, however, want to use some common sense as well. Coaches do tell players to sit back down for not responding "properly" to their commands; teachers and professors and speakers do consider seat selection important.

If you choose a back seat, it says to most people that you expect to be less than enthusiastic, that you certainly aren't concerned about hearing every word. Your attitude is not one that fears missing something. You are perfectly willing to miss several things. You are more interested in what you can get away with, or with being able to slip out unnoticed, or with being able to talk now and then without being heard, or with being able to do other things without being seen.

What? None of that is true? You want to hear and see

everything you possibly can? You plan to participate fully? You plan to concentrate on everything that goes on? No way. If those are your plans you would choose a front seat or one very near the front. Argue if you like, but you lose. The seat you choose says a lot about you and your degree of interest.

Most of you will probably be forced to admit that you haven't yet made the decision to involve yourself thoroughly in the material and in the proceedings of your classrooms. You are more worried about possibly being bored or being able to hide or being able to go mostly unnoticed, than you are about being involved, not missing anything, and impressing the teacher or professor.

Your approach to the class from the back row is somewhat lackadaisical regardless of what you claim. When it comes time to give you a B or a C (since nearly all students are borderline, except straight A students or totally flunking students), you can pretty much expect the lower grade if you sit in the back and the higher grade if you sit in the front. You can also expect to get a better recommendation when you choose the involvement that comes from sitting front-and-center, or as close to that as possible.

Beyond the discussion about where you can or can't sit and what impact it should or shouldn't have, the real question is "what have you decided to be?" Are you hoping to get by or are you trying to do a little bit extra? The difference between the "get-by" person and the "bit-extra" person shows up in all sorts of ways that the get-by person never dreams of. Seat selection is just one tip off. Actually, by itself, it is indeed a minor matter. But it doesn't usually appear by itself; it turns typically into a true reflection of what you have decided to be.

Some readers are still arguing. You say you got *assigned* to a back row seat. Sure you did. And tell me that you listen attentively each day with your head leaning forward and that, from time to time, you actually get up and walk toward the front a bit to aid your understanding. And when a closer seat is available due to an absence, you quietly take that seat and make an active effort to stay as close as possible to the action. Sure you do.

Maybe you do. It's up to you.

87.
Self-Discipline

Champions also become delighted when they realize that once they confront laziness, boredom, and drudgery, those things aren't as powerful as they seem...

Self-discipline is one ingredient that every champion must have. Whole books can be written about the subject but this section will be just a few short paragraphs.

Self-discipline is something you need to practice the way you practice a skill like shooting a basketball or hitting a baseball or throwing a football. The more you practice self-discipline, the easier it becomes and the prouder you become of it. Can you wake yourself up early to practice a skill? Can you make a schedule of training and follow it? Can you sit in a classroom, pay attention, and realize that it doesn't necessarily have to be fun?

Pushups aren't necessarily fun, nor is weight lifting, nor is listening to a speech. But what you are doing at any particular time doesn't matter as much as the way you think about yourself during that time.

Champions become proud of their ability to control themselves; they are proud of their ability to overcome laziness and boredom and drudgery.

Champions also become delighted when they realize that once they confront laziness, boredom, and drudgery, those things aren't as powerful as they seem. All those negative forces give way to the athlete who is proud of his self-discipline.

If you are already proud of your self-discipline, you understand this and you are undoubtedly working constantly to increase your ability to carry out your own goals and dreams. If you are not proud of your self-discipline, or if you think yours needs improvement, you are rather typical. Just relax and realize that you can improve you self-discipline, little by little, with practice. And when you do, there is real pride and joy at the end of that rainbow. Go for the gold.

88.
Setbacks

Everything can look so sweet, and then somehow the rug can be pulled from under you…

In sports, as in life, perhaps the most important lesson you need to learn is how to deal effectively with setbacks.

Setbacks are inevitable.

Setbacks are potentially devastating.

But setbacks can make you stronger.

I remember a man named Gower Champion who spent years putting together a play called *42nd Street*; it finally made it to Broadway but he died on opening night. A couple of American sprinters who had trained for four years missed their Olympic race because some track officials had written down the wrong time. Greg Norman, one of the best golfers of all time, had a six stroke lead going into the final round of his sixteenth attempt at winning the Masters. He had broken the course record earlier in the week but on the final Sunday he dropped eleven strokes to Nick Faldo and lost his dream by five strokes.

People talk about sports defeats as tragedies, and often they are. Millions of people around the world remember the pain on the face of Mary Decker Slaney, one of America's big track stars in the 1980s. Mary had prepared herself by training rigorously for many years and she found herself in the biggest race of her life and a favorite going for the Olympic Gold when she tripped on the foot of another runner, fell on the track, and lay there in tears as her gold medal hopes ran off in the distance.

Even more tragic perhaps, are those athletes who trained equally hard but sustained injuries before we ever even heard of them. At least we know Mary, we saw her and felt pain for her. What about the dozens (hundreds, thousands,) who got hurt before their careers even got going?

The point is, *in sports the unexpected will happen.* Everything can look sweet and then somehow the rug can be pulled from under you. Bizarre incidents during competition, auto accidents, pulled muscles, broken bones, family problems. It is impossible to list the variety of setbacks that have interrupted or ruined careers. High hopes built and sustained over years of diligent training can be dashed in a frivolous instant.

When that tragedy comes to you, when your best friend betrays you or your mother dies or your spinal cord cracks—whatever is capable of throwing you for the most devastating loop you can imagine—you can surmount it. If you are still alive, able to think, and able to breathe, you can surmount your circumstances.

I am not trying to pretend that I personally have surmounted huge obstacles. My mother died of cancer and I have had some very big disappointments in sports, but I am not claiming to be a bastion of toughness. I am just saying that many people, athletes among them, have demonstrated the ability to overcome the most debilitating obstacles both personally and physically. There is no reason to think that you can't do the same.

Perhaps most important for most of you is to realize that the setbacks you are encountering are small in comparison to what they could be. In other words, see the setbacks you are encountering for exactly what they are. Don't allow yourself to blow them out of proportion. Don't give in to throwing your hands up in despair and saying, "Things have to get better; how could they get any worse?" Some athletes will jump to conclusions like this when they have sprained their ankle before a big game during their sophomore year in high school—and they will be playing again next week.

In other words, try to get a sense of perspective. Things could very well get worse regardless of what has happened to you. But it's up to you to do everything you can to make things better, to surmount the setbacks, to learn from them what you can, and then to go on.

Pace around, yell into the sky, punch your fist into a pillow (not a wall), cry, write down your anger with a thick marker across a big piece of poster board. Get it out, get it down. See it clearly for what it is. And then sit back and say, "This is it. This is that setback, that knockout punch, that loop, that impossible event that happens to so many, and now it's happened to me."

Suck it up, absorb it, invite it in. You are a little creature walking briefly across the face of the planet. You weren't on the planet a hundred years ago; you won't be on it a hundred years from how. You have a brief time to buzz, not unlike a fly that somehow gets trapped indoors and finds itself flying back and forth against a window it will never pass through.

You have your opportunity. There were never any guarantees.

An editor told me this section is too heavy for a sports book, too philosophical, too far outside the reach of sports. But I don't think so. Sports, I think, are life itself. The lessons of sports are often as powerful and as intense as anything you will ever feel. I don't think the heaviness is out of line. Most people who play sports, the ones who really work at it, are intense, very intense, and will understand.

I wrote this section, in fact, at a time of intense personal disappointment. Something I counted on didn't happen; someone I chose to believe in let me down. Suddenly it is easy to remember the big losses, the broken legs, a coach I didn't like at all...the negatives I've encountered through sports. They fit on the same page with my mother's death. And they happen to everyone.

Take it in. Take your setback in. Grasp it. Don't try to avoid thinking about it. Let it play itself out for all it's worth. You're bigger than it is.

Sometimes we forget that. We start defining things in terms of trophies and TV commercials and recognition banquets, and we no longer see the big picture, the view standing above the globe, the little creatures moving around on the planet rising here, falling there, once at the top, soon at the bottom.

Bo Jackson played three sports, then suddenly—as a result of a hip injury—no sport. Joe Montana's career almost got cut short but he made a miraculous comeback and ended up in the Pro Football Hall of Fame. Auto accidents have cut down some stars, so have plane crashes and freak injuries of all sorts. Some careers never began. Few careers are everything they could have been. What about your career? What about your pride? What about you as a human being?

Just do the best you can. Make your decisions, give yourself fully. See what happens. It's the best you can do.

89.
Shortchanging Yourself

Five hours of preparation for every minute of performance...

You will spend many hours in preparation for reaching your goals. Most athletes run and stretch and lift weights and practice, practice, practice, month after month in anticipation of the opportunity to play in some games, some matches, some contests that seem forever in the future.

And then the future comes. And so do some parties, some offers, some temptations, some distractions. All of these comings are inevitable and I'm certainly not saying they are all bad. Looking back, I am not disappointed in myself for the parties I enjoyed, the offers I accepted, the temptations I accepted and resisted.

Everyone is different. It is easy for a coach to throw some blanket rule on everyone. None of this, none of that, none of nothing. It's the safe way for a coach. But I'm not sure it's the best way. Nevertheless, ultimately, what you decide to do or not do is up to you, regardless of whether there are rules governing your possible actions. I have just one reminder that I think every athlete should consider each time one of these temptations, distractions, or opportunities comes along.

Be true to yourself.

Remember how precious few are the minutes of actual game performance.

For every hour you put in on the practice field, in training and condition, in weight lifting, in sleeping more and eating right, in reading and studying your sport, you will be lucky to get a minute back in actual performance or playing time.

Let's take one quick example to highlight this point. A big-time college football player plays in eleven or twelve football games per season. A game clock ticks for an hour but that includes huddles, getting back into the huddle, waiting at the line for the play to start, etc. That stuff takes up most of the game but let's just call it half to go on with this point. That means the game itself, the performance time, is at most thirty minutes. Since very few football players play both offense and defense, most starting players play only half the actual time, or fifteen minutes.

Fifteen minutes a game, for twelve games. Easy math. Three hours. Did I make that clear enough? May I write it in gaudy, flashing neon and zap your hand right off the page? *Three hours* a season.

Do we even need to start adding up the time spent in preparation? Daily practice, two or three hours a day. Spring football practice. Weight training all summer. Sprints up and down the field in August when the temperature may be ninety degrees or more.

Using a very conservative three hours per day for three hundred days, you get 900 hours of preparation—for three hours of playing time. Easy math again. Three hundred hours of preparation for every hour of performance. Five *hours* of preparation for every *minute* of performance. *Five minutes for every second.*

When you think of the mathematics of preparation and performance, it makes you a lot less likely to take any opponent lightly, to take any game lightly, to do anything but your very best in every second of every game. And it certainly ought to make you think twice or three hundred times about doing anything that has even a chance to detract from your performance.

Forget the opponent, think of yourself. Think of the time you put in for the opportunity at hand. Will you stay up late the night before a game? Will you stay out partying? Will you let a headache keep you from playing? You just can't shortchange yourself like that. Doing less than your best when your time to perform finally comes turns out to be little more than incredible narrow-minded. Why do all that preparing if you aren't going to put it all on the line when you finally get a chance to show off?

If you stop to think about the math, you will play like a madman—excuse me, a mad person—every time they roll out the rock and turn on the cameras.

90.
Slumps

Remind yourself that sports, like the economy and life itself, are cyclical. If you are experiencing bad times then better times are inevitably in your future...

Slumps are inevitable. There are no sports in which an athlete can constantly perform at the peak of his talents. No sports permit an athlete to improve performance daily or even to remain at the best previous level.

What this means, simply, is that there will always be ups and downs. Sports and human beings are made that way. You will experience some slumps during your athletic career. When you do it should be possible for you to say (and think), "This is one of those inevitable slumps. No big deal."

Your interest should stay focused on minimizing your slump as much as possible. To do that, review the basics of your sport. Sharpen your focus. Concentrate on one or some of the little things you should be able to do in your sleep, and make sure you do those things with added precision. Go back over previous performances when you excelled and play those back fully in your mind. Review the ingredients of those successes and enjoy recalling the emotions you felt.

Remind yourself that sports, like the economy and life itself, are cyclical. If you are experiencing bad times then better times are inevitably in your future—assuming you haven't given up or quit trying your best.

Take a break. Talk with another athlete. Talk with a coach. Find someone new to talk to or read a book about a person who overcame adversity.

The world is filled with people who have overcome seemingly hopeless situations. Check into their lives and learn what they faced before you start going crazy over a backhand suddenly going wide or a shot currently off the mark.

Go back to the basics, revitalize yourself mentally—keep revitalizing yourself as long as it takes—and await the joy of the breakout.

Slumps end. But negative attitudes, foolish behaviors, head shaking, hair pulling, and despairing expressions of exasperation prolong slumps. Quit all the shenanigans if you've let yourself fall into a negative pattern of behavior. Quit apologizing. Quit walking around shaking your head, quit saying you don't know what's wrong. Of course you know. You're in a slump.

Go back to doing what Santa's elves do when it's getting near Christmas and they suddenly realize they've procrastinated all summer and fall. They quit chattering, quit gesturing, mostly they even quit thinking. They roll up their sleeves and go to work. They fill all their time with simple, solid, constructive activity.

Hey, it works. If you haven't been to the North Pole, don't doubt. That's the way they get it done, year after year.

91.
Sports in Perspective

Someday you may have to think about doing more for sport than just giving your best on the practice field and in games.

One of my greatest goals in life now that I no longer compete physically is to bring about major changes in the National Collegiate Athletic Association (NCAA) which I call the National Conspiracy Against Athletes. Rather than go into a lot of detail (I wrote a book about this called *Rip-Off U*), I want to make a few general points that I think are important for every athlete to think about.

Martin Luther King, Jr. wrote, in his famous letter from the Birmingham jail in 1963:

"Human progress never rolls in on wheels of inevitability; it comes through the tireless efforts of men...."

It must be remembered that millionaire athletes in the NBA and NFL and in Major League Baseball and the National Hockey League and in other sports did not happen by chance. In all of those leagues, the owners tried to give them as little money as possible. It took strife and sometimes boycotts of games and player strikes in order for athletes to realize the benefits that they now get from those sports.

Along the way, some athletes who were particularly outspoken lost their jobs and their opportunity to play. Black athletes (many young athletes never think about this) weren't even allowed to play in the major sports leagues and in many major universities in the 1950s and 1960s. In other words, there is no reason to assume that team owners and league administrators are any different from the way they were so long in the past. They will do what is best for themselves and their associates and they will claim to be doing everything they can for athletes.

Universities are not doing at all what they could do for athletes. Some of the large universities make a lot of money from football and basketball players, and they get a lot of publicity from athletics. But they systematically deprive athletes of the opportunity to receive the financial benefits that should be associated with playing a very popular sport at a high level of competition such that millions of TV viewers tune in to the events. This is wrong and immoral, and it will change in the future. But when? We have to go back to Martin Luther King's words to understand.

Someday you may have to think about doing more for sport than just giving your best on the practice field and in games. You may have to stand up for your friends and for future generations of athletes the way past athletes have done. You may have to consider boycotts and strikes, not because you want to be a rabble-rouser but because American history makes it clear that often it is impossible to bring about change—especially change in well-established, rich bureaucracies with long traditions—without taking these kinds of steps.

The day will come when athletes playing at universities across the nation will enjoy wonderful financial benefits as a result of running camps, speaking at clinics, doing commercials, wearing certain brands of sportswear, appearing on TV shows, and writing articles. This will be true for athletes in soccer and lacrosse and wrestling as well as in basketball and football. And there will be women in all sports throughout the nation enjoying the same kind of financial benefits as men. There will be Olympic hopefuls who will not have to turn down sponsorship money in order to stay eligible, and there will be athletes who will choose to stay in school while being able to secure scholarships for little brothers and sisters and a better life for their families.

Universities, diverse places as they are, have chosen to do more than merely educate students. They have chosen to participate in the very lucrative sports entertainment industry.

They have built ever-larger stadiums, upgraded and fine-tuned the national recruitment of athletes, signed multi-million dollar TV contracts, and they have paid millions of dollars for coaches to coach and not to coach (buying out their contracts). They have purposefully and knowingly used their sports programs as public relations juggernauts. A school like Georgetown University, once nearly all-white and very academic, went out and hired a black basketball star as a coach and got teams of all-black basketball players to play in Georgetown uniforms. The success has been fantastic. Awareness of the school, and contributions and applications to it, have soared over the years since John Thompson built the Georgetown program.

There is nothing wrong with universities making these kinds of choices. But there is something very wrong with educational institutions making rules specifically preventing human beings from benefiting financially from their national popularity.

Is it so hard to imagine a world in which talented, popular college athletes are able to run their own camps, make money for appearing in TV commercials, and fly their parents to big games?

Old-fashioned administrators may pay lip service to tradition, to the value of amateurism and to the purity of playing for school spirit, for the joy of competition, and for educational and social benefits. But the major universities have chosen to go far beyond that tradition with their sports/entertainment, TV-driven industry, and it is immoral to prohibit their athletes from enjoying the benefits of that industry.

Someday you may have to stand up for yourself and for your family and friends, and for athletes who will follow you. Hopefully you will spend the time necessary to think about these issues and put sports in perspective so that some authority figure's wagging finger will not dissuade you from seeking what is right. If you do something of this nature someday, some critics will call you greedy or ignorant or some other unflattering name. And you will find yourself alongside King and Christ and Jackie Robinson and every other person who ever stood up to immoral authorities in defense of principles and morality and justice.

I think all athletes have to realize that the concept of champion entails more than just running and jumping and throwing and catching and kicking and hitting. I don't expect every athlete to agree with me and with all of my ideas, but I do think every athlete should be wise enough to give his sport and his participation—at any level—a lot of thought, and to place the whole endeavor in perspective with the larger world around him. To do so doesn't always permit you to agree or to take positions popular with everyone around you. But champions understand that kind of sacrifice.

92.
Stupid Coaches

When you start to define the needs of a whole team of individuals and just what it takes to respond to those needs, you begin to realize what is not initially apparent: flawless, minute-by-minutes coaching is impossible.

If you play on a team in a competitive situation where there is real intensity—where people really care if you win or lose—then chances are there will be many occasions during the course of your season when your coaches seem stupid. I feel it is essential to point this out because I have been struck by how many athletes feel this and think they are the only ones who do.

There are good reasons for this. If you are in an intense, competitive situation, everything matters which mean everything that happens will be carefully scrutinized by you and by the coaches. You will often be on edge. They will often be on edge. They will necessarily be picky, seemingly petty, fault-finding, and often displeased. You will be ultra-sensitive. Because you care. Because you're trying very hard. Because everything matters.

In this setting the opportunity for conflict isn't just large, it's humongous.

In other words, if you have a coach who seems invariably intelligent, understanding, wise, etc., you are an exception. Not that every athlete thinks his coach is stupid overall. But *nearly every athlete is likely to think his coach does stupid things from time to time,* or even quite often.

No one can do the right thing at just the right time and be sufficiently perceptive and appropriately responsive to a whole diverse group of individuals at all times. This is simply too much to ask a coach or a coaching staff to do. Think about it. If given the opportunity, you wouldn't even be able to be the perfect coach for just yourself. There are times when you would be too easy on yourself, stopping practice before you truly pushed yourself to your limits. There would also be times when you would push yourself too much, or get too down on yourself for certain failures.

Coaching is not easy, especially when it takes place in an intense environment where the hope for success requires that tiny advantages be found. In this environment, *nearly every action a coach takes will be unsatisfactory for one of the members of the team*. The practices, for example, are always either too easy or too hard for the reserves. Either the reserves aren't getting adequate opportunity to perform in practice so they won't be really ready to perform well in games, or they are being forced to work very hard in practice in which case they may consider the effort excessive since they rarely get a chance to play in the games.

One player needs a tough approach. Another needs a more sensitive approach. Generally. But at times even these two reverse roles. There are times when the overly sensitive player needs a kick in the butt anyway. And there are times when the tough guy uncharacteristically needs a pat on the back. When you start to define the needs of a whole team of individuals and just what it takes to respond to those needs, you begin to realize what is not initially apparent: flawless minute-by-minute coaching is impossible.

Take the very best coaches in the world and at any given time, or at least often, they will be doing things that seem stupid from some player's point of view.

Look each year at the teams that win championships. Is every player on those teams in love with the coach? No. Not even on championship teams. Now think for a moment about losing teams. Teams that have renewed themselves over and over again, pulled out motivational tapes, attended seminars, taken days off, practiced extra hard—in short, tried everything—but still they lost more games than the won. Do you think the players on those teams think the coaches did everything just right? No way, Buster. Ain't ever gonna happen. Not if it matters. Not if the environment is competitive. Not if people care. Not if the coaches and team members are intense.

I hope it is obvious what this means. To me it means that regardless of who you are and who your coach is there will be times, perhaps many times, when your coach does things you think are stupid. When those times arise it would be wise, purely from a selfish point of view, for you to acknowledge that stupidity for about one or two seconds, maximum. Then go on about the business at hand as though whatever it is that is going on is intelligent, your favorite thing, a joy.

To many of you this very advice confirms the point of this section. This is *stupid* advice. How can you think about stupid stuff and put it out of your mind in just two seconds and then go on and actually pretend—in an intense, competitive environment—that the thing is intelligent and a joy? Good question. It isn't easy, is it? It's merely what an athlete should do if he is trying to get the most out of life, the most out of athletics, the most out of himself.

Why do anything different? Why dwell on inevitable negatives? Doing that is much more stupid than any error a coach makes.

Naturally there are limits to everything. If a coach asked you to do something that could seriously injure you, that's a different story. I'm not saying you should blindly follow everything any coach says. That's why I have you two seconds—just long enough to consider whether or not something is truly repugnant and will still matter to you two months later.

If it's not going to seem like a big thing two months later, it ain't a big thing now. You're just making it into a bigger thing than it really is. Forget it. Just do it. Don't bother putting labels on the things a coach does. "Let's see, that was intelligent, that was okay, that wasn't good but it wasn't all that bad, that was stupid, that was really stupid..."

Labeling shouldn't be part of your focus. You should not allow time for it. First, your performance is likely to suffer and second, you may be surprised at what you discover later.

The world is filled with athletes who once hated things their coach did but who now respect the coach for those very things. Did you get the full force of that? There are not merely a few guys somewhere who have changed their ideas about certain past events. There are thousands, probably hundreds of thousands, maybe millions.

You're young. You have your perspective. You have your ideas. You have your intelligence. No one is saying you don't. But things do change. Your ideas will change. What you thought was intelligent ten years ago you probably don't consider intelligent now and what you consider intelligent now is not necessarily what you will think is intelligent ten years from now.

What now may seem like boring repetition of no value may later by respected as discipline and ***the*** *ingredient that helped you become a winner.*

I don't mean this to be a defense of all coaches. I mean it to be a resounding call to arms to athletes. Don't allow yourself to sabotage your own careers and opportunities because of your feelings about your coach, however negative. While you are competing, withhold your judgments and learn to make the best of all circumstances. Learn to focus fully on how you can turn all circumstances to your advantage. Don't waste one second thinking about how stupid your coach is. He may indeed be stupid but you are only adding a second dose of stupidity by wasting time dwelling on it.

Nearly every coach is sometimes stupid, sometimes smart, to varying degrees. But what about athletes? What about you? What's stopping you from being always intelligent? Why must you be stupid every time your coach is? Think about it.

93.
Superstitions

You can get the job done regardless of what order you put on your clothes...

Many athletes are superstitious. Many star athletes are superstitious. So I am not going to knock superstitions, except to say one thing: Make sure you don't let them become stupid thinking.

The Lucky Baseball Bat (I think that was the title) was a book I read when I was in elementary school. In the book, a Little Leaguer came to believe that his hitting ability was dependent on a particular, lucky baseball bat. Predictably, things came to a head when the kid forgot the lucky bat, or lost it, or it broke—I can't remember. But the lesson, of course, what that it was the kid, not the bat, that was getting the hits; the bat didn't really matter. It mattered as long as the kid thought it mattered, but it was quite possible for the kid to grab a broom handle or the head of a shovel and smack out a hit if he had the right attitude.

That's the gist of what I have to say about superstitions. If you want to wear the same underwear to every game, fine. Just wash them in between. If you like going through some crazy routine like always putting on one sock, then your uniform, then the other sock and then your shoes, fine. Have fun. Just make sure all this is secondary to your basic toughness and that, if necessary, you can get the job done regardless of what order you put on your clothes, regardless of what bat you use, regardless of what routine you did or did not do.

Wade Boggs, one of the greatest hitters in the history of baseball, was legendary for his pre-game chicken-eating routines and requirements. Good, Wade. But make no mistake. If Wade needed a hit to save his life, or to save someone in his family—or just to win a game—you better believe he could do it with a belly full of Jell-O just after waking up.

Typically, great players like Boggs use routines and superstitions to establish a pattern of preparation and to fine-tune their concentration. By getting meticulous about details they tune out family and business and personal problems, and concentrate fully on the task at hand. This is a very useful way of deflecting all of the distractions that athletes are threatened by. Once you understand this, you realize how these seemingly strange routines and thought patterns are constructive, not destructive at all. The problem is, aspiring athletes may not consider this or understand it. They may see only the routine and the requirements and the superstition involved; instead of enhancing their concentration and pre-event preparation, they sabotage it, as did the worried little kid who broke (or lost) his lucky bat.

If your superstitions are working for you, pile them on. Add others. But be objective. When your superstitions start having a negative impact on your performance, and when you find yourself thinking you can't do something because some irrelevant pattern of behavior has been altered, it is time to reevaluate your thinking and revamp your routines. *Your superstitions must work for you, not against you.*

94.
Taunting

Why use a lot of time and effort just to distract a mediocre player?

What about taunting your opponent? Pointing in their faces, gesturing toward the scoreboard when you're ahead, ridiculing their efforts, trying to get in their heads?

Why not? Especially when they started out saying things to you. Isn't it okay then? Well, you can decide for yourself. It's not the worst thing in the world, for sure. But it's not the best. And why be anything but the best? There's an old saying:

When you roll around in the muck with a pig, two things happen. 1) You both get dirty, and 2) the pig enjoys it.

Just because they taunt, does that mean you want to taunt? Just because they are jerks, does that mean you want to be jerks? In my opinion, the definition of the ideal athlete clearly does not include taunting. If you think of an ideal athlete being watched by fans, being watched by TV cameras, being watched by impressionable little kids, you know that taunting is not an indispensable part of the picture.

Does it do any good? Maybe, at times. There may be a player somewhere who gets particularly bothered by taunting, who then blows up and incurs a fifteen yard unsportsmanlike conduct penalty, or starts whacking easy forehands out of bounds. I won't argue the point. If you claim that taunting occasionally leads to poorer performance in some mediocre athletes, I can't be sure you're not right. There may be cases where taunting does actually help your team.

But as a coach, I don't like my players doing it—for a reason I have already expressed. There is so much to do and think about in a game, so much concentration required, so many ways to have a positive impact on your team (so many ways to have a positive impact on players we know) that I don't really think it makes much sense to spend time exploring the psyches of opponents (who we don't know) just for the possibility that we may stumble onto something that negatively affects their performance.

Some players may be able to maintain their own concentration while taunting an opponent but can they focus on motivating, encouraging, and instructing their teammates while taunting an opponent? I doubt it. It's probably better not to use up effort on unknown potential benefits of taunting when we know the substantial benefits to be gained by focusing on your self, on your performance and on that of your teammates. I like the simplicity of total focus every game, on us, as opposed to trying to psyche out, game by game, each opponent's weaknesses and trying to find who is affected by taunting and who isn't.

Remember the idea of imaginary champions—of performing as if you are playing against stars? On that basis, taunting is wasted time. Taunting doesn't bother champions. It doesn't bother you, does it? A champion isn't affected by what some jabberer is saying. A champion has a job to do, a mission, and a focus. While the other guy is talking the champion is planning, setting up a play, taking advantage of the other guy's misplaced attention. A champion has too much pride to let himself be bothered by mere talk. After all that training and preparation, all that time and effort, can he afford to let himself get sidetracked by talk? I don't think so. My hopes and dreams and goals were always a lot more powerful than that, and I assume yours are, too.

So it's back to the old standby: why use a lot of time and effort just to distract a mediocre player? You should be able to beat mediocre players anyway. Meanwhile, if the player thinks like a champion the effort is certainly wasted and may detract from your own performance.

I think the "focus-on-your-team, don't-waste-your-time" explanation is the best commentary on the subject of taunting, but some other points could be made. Let's wrap this up with these other considerations.

Taunting won't win you many friends. You can take the hard-line attitude that you don't walk out onto a field to win popularity contests, but you don't walk onto fields to turn off potential followers either. Probably it's best to remember that, although your opponents seem like the enemy on game day, in truth those same athletes are potentially your best friends in the future. Once you're in college, for example, the fact that you played in the same area in high school gives you a sense of a common past and a real foundation for a friendship. If you find yourself playing in Europe some day, as I did once and as many athletes do, merely being from the same country becomes a point of shared experience and the basis for a friendship. Why would you want to jeopardize that kind of future opportunity for taunts of dubious value?

Also, for every mediocre player negatively affected by taunting, there are probably several who respond positively to it and perform better. Instead of taunting, let them continue to play poorly, don't give them some extra rallying point or some reason to hate you and increase their energy level. In other words, let sleeping dogs lie. I would advise against taunting both from a future friendship standpoint and from a strategic standpoint.

Aside from all that, it just flat-out isn't very becoming. It's not the way to impress your girlfriend's parents or the way to impress the owner of the local business looking for a fine young man or woman to fill a well-paying position for the summer.

Taunting, for you better students, reminds me a lot of nationalism. Flag-waving and loving your country can be wonderful, or seem wonderful in a narrow context. If you're standing among a group of Americans on a street corner during a Fourth of July parade in a small town, there's probably nothing wrong with waving a flag and shouting that America is the best nation in the world. But you'd look—and *be*—a bit stupid doing the same thing on a street corner in Oslo or Stockholm. The Norwegians and Swedes wouldn't be so sure about your ideas and they would be quick to point out all sorts of ways in which their countries are superior.

You could argue, but what would be the point? If a group of French tourists came by, heard the argument, and agreed with you (which by the way would never happen), would that make you right? Would that satisfy you?

It may seem as though I'm getting far off the track, but I think the point may be useful to some athletes. *Taunting sometimes seems cool in a narrow-minded sense, but never very cool when looking at the big picture.* Taunting may occasionally get you a slight advantage, but often it will affect you negatively. Personally, I don't like those odds. If there's a way to act which yields more dividends over time, why not take that route?

Why not make a decision right now to leave taunting to others? Why not decide to present yourself, constantly, as a hard-working, fully concentrating athlete focused entirely on your performance and that of your teammates? Then you don't have to worry who might be watching, or what someone may conclude from your actions, or whether or not you are doing the best possible stuff during that particular game.

Not many athletes can look back on their careers and say that taunting got them where they are or that taunting got them tremendous advantages along the way. But plenty of athletes owe their present status to the fact that they performed well and impressed people along the way with a consistent focus on effort, execution, hustle, and sportsmanship. Why not take the easy way out on this one?

95.

Team Jokes

You ought to monitor the things being said in your locker room and on the bus and practice field, and make sure that the positives far outweigh the negatives…

They usually start out innocently.

Probably every sports team in the world has some team jokes—things that get repeated in the locker room, on the bus going to and from games, and before and after practice. It is natural for people to comment on each other's habits, ideas, ways of dressing, peculiar characteristics, and so on. And it is also natural for humor to be added to the comments. In this regard, I want to offer just one word of warning.

On many teams, comments that begin as good-natured humor often turn sarcastic or cutting over time, and they have negative impacts on team morale that often go far beyond what was initially intended. Usually athletes just lapse into these jokes or repeated comments. Often they don't mean any real harm, but harm is done nevertheless—especially when a team is losing.

For this reason it is wise to be very careful about team jokes. At the beginning of the season or while winning, there rarely seems to be a potential for problems. When the season is fresh or the team is successful, few comments are likely to be taken too seriously or too negatively. Freshness and success have a wonderful way of keeping things upbeat for the most part. Conversely, staleness and defeat have a treacherous way of undermining team spirit and friendship.

Banter about a teammate's big ears or funny walk or crooked smile may be funny when your team is on a roll, but those same comments can often cause hostility and real dissension when things take a turn for the worse.

Knowing the dangers, you ought to monitor the things being said in your locker room and on the bus and practice field, and make sure that the positives far outweigh the negatives. Don't let the negatives sneak up on you. Don't wait until the damage gets done. Make sure the player that everyone loves to pick on gets a break—often—and be vigilant about the impact of whatever gets laughs.

How many times have you heard someone say, "I didn't know it was bothering her," "I didn't mean it that way," or "We were only kidding?"

If you are conscious of keeping your team's comments good-natured and humorous, you will probably have an enjoyable team experience. But if you get careless and let your guard drop, you may find that the comments that began in innocent fun have ended up being the source of irritation and dissension that can destroy your team.

96.

Teammates You Don't Like

Remember that self-interest is a terrific motivator and that all sorts of enemies throughout history have learned to work together when it was in their self-interest to do so.

Not a fun subject.

Whenever a sports book talks about teamwork and team play or being part of a team, it stresses the importance of getting along and working together and enjoying the tremendous satisfaction that comes from achieving goals jointly with other team members. It's all true. It's wonderful—when it happens.

But probably more often, athletes find themselves on teams where the cohesion is not wonderful, the team members are not all friends, and some of the athletes just plain don't like each other at all. Then what?

It is easy to say "work together, do your best" and all the typical platitudes, but those may not work. Then what can you do? A lot of things, but first let's take another pass over those platitudes. Remember that nearly always you can do more to help any situation. Before you conclude that you just don't like someone or that he just doesn't like you, make sure you have exhausted a variety of possible avenues leading to friendship, make sure you keep seeking new avenues even after you have tried many of them, and make sure *you* remain open to change. At least maintain the awareness that *solutions to your problem probably exist* and that there are people out there, smarter than you, who would know what to do in your situation.

With that said, and with your openness and willingness intact (because it really would be worthwhile to change the ill feeling into friendships if you can), how do you manage to keep playing with teammates you don't like?

Primarily, concentrate on the reassuring, predictable nature of selfishness. Selfishness, if nothing else, does make people rather predictable. Even though someone may dislike you, you should be able to figure that person out at least to the extent that you recognize what he wants or seems to value. You wish he wanted to be friends with you, you wish he wanted to make compromises, you wish he wanted to be part of a smoothly functioning team, but your wishes don't matter. He may not share your wishes. But what is his agenda? What does *he* want? Does he want to be the highest scorer? Does he want all the recognition?

Remember that self-interest is a terrific motivator and that all sorts of enemies throughout history have learned to work together when it was in their self-interest to do so. There are thousands of examples of Arabs and Jews, of blacks and whites, of police and criminals—groups for a long time at odds and with enmity having deep historical roots—who have learned to work together and alter their negative feelings for each other, particularly after each helped the other get what was selfishly desired.

So you don't like some teammates or they don't like you? Assuming you have tried all of the obvious things (talking, calling in a mutually respected mediator, making some offers) your best course of action is twofold.

First, focus on yourself, on doing your best, on being the best you can be, and simply absorb the adverse feelings around you as part of your athletic challenge to overcome all negatives including referees, bad weather, opposing fans, tough opponents, and unfriendly teammates.

Never forget that the real joy of sports and of athletic achievement comes from beating the odds and overcoming adversity. Anyone can win championships with the best team, the best coach, the best equipment, the best of this and that. But there is special joy in winning in the face of whatever negative circumstances present themselves—with a bad team, a bad coach, bad equipment, bad conditions. If hostile teammates become a part of the equation, consider them part of the challenge.

Like any champion you must continue to try to turn the negative circumstances to your advantage. Your team has to work to improve, your coach has to learn from mistakes (and you have to help him), you have to stitch up that bad equipment and pray for rain or sun or whatever conditions you need.

Second, try to have a positive influence on those teammates with whom you don't get along. Keep their selfish interests in mind and mesh with them in whatever ways you can. If a teammate wants all the recognition for himself, give him all the recognition you can. What do you care about recognition? If he wants all the points, help him to get them. Or to get more of them.

Even if he is just plain jealous of you, no doubt there is something behind that. Somehow he may have the notion that your success diminishes his. Or he may have some other notion that makes no sense at all. Naturally you can't always get at whatever is bothering someone. You can't understand everyone. But you can keep trying to understand, or at least try to make things better. Things do change. Attitudes that once seemed carved in stone are often different a year later.

Third, it may help to lower your goals initially. Instead of trying to go from hate to love, try seeing if there are any smaller areas you can change for the better. Make little things better. They may just lead to bigger things.

Fourth, make the relationships with the players who do get along even better. Focus on them and make those relationships all they can be.

Fifth, make your relationship with your coach even better. Remember that there are so many aspects involved with the idea of *team* that it is always possible to make aspects of it better. Don't let yourself get so bogged down in the bad that you quit enjoying the good or quit doing your best to make the many changeable things better.

Sixth, never quit trying. Never conclude that the situation is just plain hopeless. Things change. People change. There is always a possibility, no matter how bad things seem. Keep trying.

Never lapse into the feeling that you've done everything you can possibly do. You haven't. And never lapse into the feeling that you are entitled to a bad attitude under the circumstances you are confronting. You aren't.

Stay focused on what you have to do. And stay aware and active and open to what's going on around you. Keep trying. You have some teammates you don't like or that don't like you? So what? Just about everyone does. The important question is, what are you doing about it and what is your attitude?

97.
Thank You's

Finding time or making time to get in a thank you during the action of a game was a thing for Girl Scouts, not tough athletes.

A section entitled "Thank You's" in a book on sports? You betcha. Thank you's are never out of place, especially not in sports. Probably the best example I can offer comes from Dean Smith, the basketball coach whose name is synonymous with winning basketball throughout the world. In 1976 he coached the U.S. Olympic team to a gold medal win.

Dean Smith began on-court thank you's back in the 1960s as a young coach just getting started at the University of North Carolina. Smith required that his players thank each other after each basket, right smack dab during the game while the action was going on. The player who received a pass and scored had to point to the player who passed the ball. The pointing and the meeting of eyes said, "Thank you, I am sharing this applause with you. I couldn't have done it without you."

Today this pointing to say thank you occurs all over the world. People in more than a hundred countries saw the benefits firsthand in the 1976 Olympics when Smith's players not only blitzed their way to the gold medal but looked like they were having fun doing it. Pointing was a big part of it. Obviously they experienced joy from sharing acclaim and they shared it play by play during the games, not just at post-game interviews. The thank you's seemed to add to the team's momentum. The sharing of success spurred them on to ever greater achievement.

More than the pointing contributed, but that was certainly an important part of the team's spirit. The rest of the world didn't miss the significance of it. They adopted it as nearly every American team from pros to midgets, has done.

Today so many players in so many sports are in the habit of thanking each other that it seems natural. Coaches in all sports search for ways of increasing team spirit, and gratitude expressed on-the-spot has become widely recognized for having real value. It's now hard to imagine that Smith could have been ridiculed for introducing the pointed finger thank you, but he was. I saw it when I played at Duke, the biggest rival of Smith's North Carolina team. People from Duke ridiculed Smith routinely because, at the time, Smith hadn't yet won hundreds of games, he didn't have a huge arena named after him, and he hadn't amassed decades of twenty-win seasons, two national championships, and the gold medal. The idea was new. And it wasn't macho.

It was considered a showy, useless display. "Don't waste time thanking him," a determined old coach would yell at his players, "he knows you're happy. Play the game Concentrate on what you're doing."

Finding time or making time to get in a thank you during the action of a game was a thing for Girl Scouts, not tough athletes. But that was then. This is now. Now people have seen the benefits. Now every coach, even the tough ones, emphasize that there is time to point. No, there isn't time to waste, time to look around, time to take a break. But there is time to find that passer and point at him and meet his eyes on the way to doing whatever you have to do next.

Now for lesson two. If thank you's were effective and important enough to change a whole way of thinking among coaches all over the world, doesn't it make sense that thank you's may be effective and important in a lot of different ways?

What about thank you notes? How many thank you letters have you mailed in the past month? Are you unaware of the power of a written thank you? I recall being at a local hall of fame banquet during which an inductee had a few minutes to summarize for the audience the highlights of his life. He took half his time talking about a note, one tiny handwritten note framed and hanging on his wall for the past thirty years. Just a couple of short sentences. It was a thank you note from someone. I can't even remember who sent it to him, I just remember how proud of it he was, what an important part of his life it was, and how little time it took the sender to produce it.

Do you have access to a stamp, a piece of paper, an envelope, and a pen? If so, what is your excuse? Why are you failing to exert the tremendous power you have at your disposal?

Are you interested in being named to some all-star team, in being selected for some sort of award, in getting a good job? Don't underestimate the power of a few words of thanks here and there—to a reporter who does a story on you, to a photographer who takes your picture, to the newspaper that best covers your activities (or to one that never does, but could), to an opposing coach, to a special fan, to a teacher, teammate, or administrator.

There's a good reason that thank you's can take you such a long way. First, everyone likes getting them. Second, almost no one offers them. Sure we all mumble our thanks when given something directly but how many people sit down and think about a former teacher or coach who has had a real impact? How many ever thank a fan? How many take the time to jot that special person a brief note of appreciation? Not many. Not many at all. Therefore, if you ever want to distinguish yourself and take a giant step in someone's mind—in just a few minutes—send out a thank you note, one that is entirely unexpected, a big surprise.

The ripples from that note will likely go far beyond what you could imagine. You can be sure that your effort will not be kept secret. The word will travel. People will talk about what a fine young man or woman you are. And what did you do to deserve such acclaim? You did two things.1) You took a few minutes of your time, and (2) you did something almost no one else ever does. When you think about this clearly and realize how much good you can do for yourself with just a few minutes' effort now and then, you begin to realize that this is something you ought to do even if you're nothing more than a selfish jerk out to use people and get whatever you can.

Should I be nervous about giving such a powerful tool to selfish jerks? No. This tool has been around forever, its power undiminished. It is always there, waiting to be used by anyone. The jerks don't take the time to do something that might not bring immediate results. That leaves the tool in the hands of those willing to take a broader, more long-term view of things.

What about you? *Any reason you don't want a whole lot of people spreading around what a great person you are?* Any reason you're not putting this book down right now and heading for an envelope and pen? You can probably even borrow a stamp. Give it a try.

98.
This is Me!

Crack the court, soil the air, hang some gloom, deflate the ball. But you will still see me. Because this is me...

This is me? This is I? Both pronouns should be nominative, shouldn't they? Actually, neither one sounds great grammatically but the concept is good and it seems to me that, although it is incorrect grammar, *this is me* rests better on the brain.

This is me. This—what I am doing right now—is me as a writer. When answering the phone, *this is me* as a phone-talker. When playing a sport *this is me* as an athlete. When sitting in a classroom *this is me* as a student.

Regardless of what you are doing, *you* are doing it. No one else. Good or bad, it's you. I always try to picture myself, throughout the day, whatever I am doing, as though I am being watched. What do they see? This is me. And of course the question always lurking is, what *me* are they seeing? Am I proud of what they are seeing? Did I create that picture or did I let someone else influence what they see?

Hopefully you realize that the way you choose to play a sport is entirely your choice. It doesn't depend on how good your coach is or how well your team plays or how nice the field looks or how well the umpires are calling the game. Those are pictures of coaches, teams, fields, and umpires. They aren't you. Your part is strictly up to you. Although you may lose a game, there are still tremendous efforts and dismal performances within those losses. The pictures of you can be very different within the same surroundings.

The same applies, of course, to a classroom. So many students are guilty of the following response to a typical question.

"What did you get in Algebra?"

"You should have seen the teacher."

"Didn't ask about the teacher. What did *you* get?"

"That teacher was so boring. No one could do well in there."

"No one? That's very doubtful. But how well did *you* do?"

It's amazing how many poor students blame their D's and F's on their teachers. There are always possible excuses and outside factors in anything you do. But the question doesn't change with the circumstances. The question always remains. "What was *your* approach?" What *me* did you present?

Your approach is everything. You can't always win. *You will hardly ever have ideal conditions*. You can bet on making mistakes. Often the breaks won't go your way. Frequently the circumstances will work against you. But the one consistent factor is—or can be—you and your approach to whatever it is you are doing.

Therefore, it makes sense, while others are seeking excuses, to let one phrase roll through your mind any time you are doing anything: *This is me*. Am I proud of what I am showing them. It can be a phrase that promotes pride, particularly under adverse circumstances. *This is me*. Watch me. Look closely. You won't see any change. Nothing here but championship performance. Crack the court, soil the air, hang some gloom, deflate the ball. But you will still see *me*. Because *this is me*. What you see is what you get, over and over, rain or shine. Solid, determined, alert, poised.

A lot of you have already learned to try hard on defense even if you just messed up on offense. A lot of you have already learned to work hard in practice the day after a tough loss. Because you have a picture of yourself. You have become proud of the athlete you are; you are someone who tries hard all the time. Someone who gives his best. Someone who exemplifies the word "champion."

The athlete who seeks to become a true champion isn't sidetracked by negative conditions and events. The more you pile them on, the more the champion shows off.

It is surprising how many athletes learn to develop this kind of personal pride in their approach to a sport, yet fail to show similar pride in a classroom. Slumping posture, averted eyes, haphazard notes, sloppy homework. The disparity should bother you if you are seeking to see yourself as a champion. How do you explain the pride in *me* in one sphere but the complete lack of it in another? You're the same person in one place as the other. In other words, try to take your pride with you everywhere you go, in everything you do. Because that's you. *This is me!*

99.
Three Plays

You grow up thinking that great means awesome and that dismal means terrible, and then you find out that these words mean 68–65 in overtime.

Legendary Green Bay Packer football coach Vince Lombardy once said that *nearly every football game is decided in only three plays*. The problem, he said, was that you didn't know in advance which three plays those were going to be. Therefore, your only way to be prepared to do well on those three plays was to be prepared to do well on every play during the whole game. How true.

It's astonishing to think about how little difference there is between great teams and mediocre teams. A so-called great team may be described with terms like invincible, incredible, awesome, powerful, perhaps the best of all time.

The best of all time? Maybe. And yet that team, even if it went undefeated, usually had some close games against mediocre teams that had disappointing, or even dismal seasons…teams that newspaper reporters said just couldn't do it under pressure, who just didn't have what it takes, who lacked speed or strength or leadership or a coach or dedication.

Do you know what the all-time great team did against this kind of collection of dismal, disappointing patsies? Killed 'em all, right? Wrong. Won by five, won by seven, won by three, won by ten, won by one. *One?*

Did I hear you say one? All Time U beat Dismal City Prep by *one*? It happens all the time. Great teams edge out mediocre teams. Great teams build their greatness by barely outscoring teams that are said to be "no good at all."

What does it all mean? Three plays. Game after game the great teams execute just three, and sometimes only one or two, key plays better than their opponents. Not much difference, is there?

You grow up thinking that great means awesome and that dismal means terrible, and then you find out that these words often mean 68–65 in overtime. In this concept is contained the essence of sports, the importance of preparation, the cruciality of the little things, of thoroughness, of the seemingly crazy intensity of coaches.

There is so little difference between good teams and bad teams, between winners and losers that if you want to be a champion you have to develop a special view of sports. You have to have a special understanding of seemingly endless repetition in practice, of pep talks that get old after awhile, of a coach's irrational rage or apparently obsessive attention to details.

Can you imagine for a moment how you would act if you knew that one tiny incident today—bumping into a door or dropping a fork or stubbing your toe or misplacing some key—meant that you would lose a million dollars instead of getting it?

If you had a winning lottery ticket and getting a million bucks was just a matter of taking that ticket down to the local lottery office and claiming your prize, you wouldn't put the ticket down, not even once. You wouldn't let it out of your sight. You would look suspiciously at anyone who came near, and you would guard that ticket with your life.

Suddenly, some tiny action that might jeopardize finding that ticket—misplacing it, putting it in a book or a drawer, sticking it in your wallet—would not seem tiny at all. Every action would be infused with purpose. Nothing you did all day would be done without awareness of the ticket. How many times would you check to make sure it was still in your pocket? You might put plastic around it. Maybe even attach it to something with a sharp edge that would hurt your leg a bit but keep you aware that it was there. Oh yeah, you'd gladly trade a little pain for the added assurance that your million dollar ticket was secure.

You probably get the point and you probably get the sense of how and why a winning coach, or a championship, performer goes about preparing painstakingly for contests that are going to be decided by tiny things, namely a tip-in here, a tap-out there, a deflected ball, a mishandled play.

Three plays. Sometimes fewer. Often that's all that separates greatness from mediocrity. It is this awareness that turns coaches into fanatics, champions into perfectionists, and clichés into wisdom. I mean, isn't it time for you to tighten the screws, to turn your play up a notch, to play like there's no tomorrow, to show what you're made of, to win one for the Gipper, or at least to put your pants on one leg at a time?

Yes of course we coaches get crazy. It's not easy to be sane and laid back and to think like a champion all at the same time.

100.
Underdogs

Remind yourself before the game that all athletes, even huge superstars, have bad days...

There is a lot of talk in sports about underdogs. Either you are the underdog and you're supposed to lose or the other team is the underdog and you're supposed to beat them. For all that talk, every sports fan knows that underdogs often upset favorites. So what does it all mean? In my opinion, all this talk of underdogs and favorites boils down to two simple ideas for an athlete.

1. If you are the favored team you will still have to prove you are better on the field but you have an advantage in that your opponents may truly doubt that they can beat you. If you can jump on them fast and confirm their doubt, you may win a game that otherwise could have turned against you. Their fears—though unspoken and denied—can often work in your favor. As the "over-dog," you may have an opportunity at the beginning of a game to take advantage of your reputation and their doubts. You can never count on it, but it's the favorite's edge.

Every athlete who was ever a favorite (or an underdog) knows how things can level out if the favorite fails to take early advantage. As Rocky said, as the fight wore on and he began to build his confidence, "He ain't so baaad."

As the favorite, you should prepare yourself mentally to take advantage of the underdogs' frame of mind. If you don't, and if you let them get that you-ain't-so-baaad feeling, you could be in for a much tougher struggle.

2. If you are the underdog you have to remind yourself before the game that all athletes, even huge superstars, have bad days, and you have to concentrate on doing everything in your power to help their bad day be today, in their game against you.

Don't bother consoling yourself with statements like, "We have nothing to lose." Of course you have something to lose—the game. That means you have a game to play, and that's what you're there for. Maybe you will win and maybe you will lose. Those are the possibilities whether you are the favorite or the underdog. There are no guarantees in sports. So you go out and give 'em hell. If they beat you, they beat you. But you ought to cut out all the psychological stuff and reaffirm what you're all about. *You* need not be an underdog to anyone. At least you shouldn't bother thinking like one. You are simply an athlete. You are tough, tenacious, and relentless, regardless of whom you are playing. Strive to attain that championship level of consistent performance and let others talk of favorites and underdogs. You should not only avoid talking about it, you should have no need to think about it.

Performance is everything. Whipping up fear of an opponent to avoid being surprised is misdirected effort. So is bolstering yourself with talk about how good you are. Focus strictly on performance and let reporters and fans tell you, after the game, who was favored and who should have won and lost.

"Underdog" is a commentator term, not a concept for champions. Before a game you are neither an underdog nor a favorite. You are just an athlete with an unshakeable commitment to lay it all out there. If you play in that way, practice after practice, game after game, you will enjoy a lot of happy results, regardless of what the commentators call you along the way.

101.
Unfairness

Champions don't want to be treated like everyone else.

Welcoming unfairness is one of the most useful principles in the life of any athlete. Yet I am always struck by how many athletes seem to dwell on fairness when they talk about their sports excellence.

"The coach wasn't fair. The coach did something for him but not for me."

The next time a coach treats you unfairly, thank him and then make the best of the situation.

For many years when I ran a general basketball camp my brother observed a tradition he called "Time to Pee." It was very simple.

I used to begin each camp session explaining the unfairness principle. I told the campers that I planned to treat every athlete unfairly. I would run the camp the way God seems to run the world—arbitrarily. Some people are born rich, some poor. Some tall, some short. Some beautiful, some ugly. Some gifted, others handicapped. Therefore, I told them, at my camp some athletes would be allowed to get drinks when they were thirsty, some would not. Some athletes who asked a question during an activity would be granted their wish but others might be forced to run or do pushups for interrupting. With that, I proceeded to reward some athletes immediately with a candy bar or free T-shirt and punish others by making them run, touch a wall and come back.

With the point made clearly, at the very beginning, we saved a lot of time and misdirected focus the rest of the week. Athletes didn't constantly compare who was getting the most playing time during games, or worry about who was getting special treatment or favoritism in some other way.

During that first year of running the camp my brother and I stayed up very late on the last night, discussing how things had gone. He feared that some kids would go home and tell their parents they had been treated unfairly. He suggested that this might not be good for public relations and the success of future camps. Then he said something like, "Oh well, I guess we'll just see what happens. I have to go and pee."

I agreed. "Wait a minute. I think you're right. We ought to treat everyone fairly, at least on the last night. If I let you go and pee, I ought to let everyone go and pee."

It was three in the morning, but my brother and our college athlete/counselors liked my next instruction.

"Go and wake everyone up and, even if you have to carry them to the urinals, make sure they all pee. I don't want to be accused of unfairness."

That night and every last night of every camp I ran for a decade after, we had the closing "Time to Pee" event. At 3:00 A.M. the counselors would wake everyone (we had all boys back then) one by one and make sure, even if they had to carry someone, that everyone peed in the name of fairness.

It was crazy, it was fun, and it bothered particularly tired athletes who sometimes claimed that they didn't have to pee. But they were always contradicted in very forceful terms by the college athletes standing at their bedsides and ready if necessary to tote them off to the urinals and hold them up while they peed. "One guy peed. Now everyone has to pee. Coach said we have to be fair."

I always hoped that the lesson would get through loud a clear and remain with the athletes forever. Perceived unfairness is so urgently and accusingly pointed out by so many people in so many situations that it's not surprising that athletes, too, can fall into the same trap. Don't let it happen to you.

Desiring fair treatment is the province of the mediocre.

Champions don't want to be treated like everyone else. Champions don't want to be put on an equal plane with others, they welcome the opportunity to show what they are made of under all sorts of conditions. They don't worry what has happened to anyone else. They are eager to demonstrate what they can do.

Hopefully you will not go through life constantly looking to see if you are being treated like others. Instead, focus on making sure you respond famously to whatever treatment you are getting. (Could it be a special test aimed at bringing out something special from you?) Remember, you don't know why the gods seem to favor some over others. In all cases, your best course of action is just to take what comes and make the best of it. I'd like to go on with the explanation, but I can't. I gotta go pee. You have to go, too.

102.
Un-ruffle-ability

If you really can't stand to get hit and not hit back, be a boxer.

This is a word I made up. Don't use it in a school paper, but keep the concept in your head. I think it is a state of mind that every athlete should adopt and be proud of. I think you should walk around your court or field, around any court or field, thinking:

"I am un-ruffle-able. You can't ruffle me. You can't get me mad, you can't get me to start or complete a fight. You can't get me thrown out. You can't get to me. Go ahead, test me. Jab at me. Call me names. Stay up all night thinking. Remember MC Hammer's famous song? You can't touch this. You got it, Baby. Better do your thing on someone else. Your time is wasted on me. I am one incredibly focused son of a bitch."

(You know by reading this far in the book that I don't use many off-color words; in this case I have chosen my words carefully. I believe, when you are thinking about yourself, and thinking about your commitments and your pride and your toughness, you ought to think of yourself as a relentless son of a bitch or as whatever image will stay with you and not go away.)

Why is un-ruffle-ability so great? It puts you in control. Consider the alternative. You could choose instead "not to take any crap from anybody" and you would, by your own choice, force yourself into all sorts of ridiculous behaviors perpetrated by whatever idiots happened to walk into your path. You would have to throw punches at second-string thugs sent into games precisely for the purpose of trading their bodies for yours. You would have to run into the stands to defend your mother's honor against some drunk who had none. You would have to be alert every minute of every day just to make sure no jerk did nothin' to you. What a foolish way to live. What a foolish place to put your pride.

Why not choose un-ruffle-ability? It's tough. It's demanding. But it immediately puts all the petty people below you. You are above them, beyond their reach. Think about it. Gandhi had it. Christ had it. And they weren't the only ones. Every great athlete has it at the end of an important game. Even known hotheads usually won't incur a fifteen-yard retaliation penalty at the end of a big game they are winning. They will let a sore loser hit them and go untouched, rather than risk a penalty that could cost them the game. But why wait till the end of an important game? Why not develop the attitude that works at all times, the true champion's attitude? Focus on yourself, focus on the task at hand, focus on getting the job done in the very best way possible.

If you really can't stand to get hit and not hit back, be a boxer. Otherwise, realize that getting hit sometimes by lesser players and weaker characters is something a champion must learn to accept. Just like criticism, fatigue and injuries must be accepted. They are part of the game. That's all. No big deal.

Un-ruffle-ability. Give it a try. The tougher you are, the more you are going to like it.

103.
Urgency

If you typically give 100 percent, there should be no noticeable change in your effort.

Whenever I attend any sporting event in person, the first thing I notice in the athletes is the degree of urgency they exhibit when they play. It's the obvious sense of urgency that makes championship games, in any sport, so enjoyable to watch. In big games all the athletes feel that sense of urgency. The problem is that most athletes do not exhibit the same urgency in non-championship games and in practice. Those that do usually become champions. By now, you understand this but let me offer a fanciful situation I use each summer at my Point Guard Basketball College to try to give basketball players insight into their efforts on defense.

Most of the athletes with whom I work are very dedicated.

They think they give 100 percent whenever they play; that is their self-image—until I present them with a hypothetical situation and a question.

The Fantasy

Imagine you are watching *Lifestyles of the Rich and Famous* on TV and you hear that very distinctive voice of Robin Leach talking about an eccentric European couple who has the habit of traveling around the world and giving away $10,000 bills to complete strangers in return for meeting small challenges. The man is dressed in a tuxedo and top hat, the woman wears a huge red hat so big it has a bird's nest in it and some hummingbirds buzzing around. What a flamboyant, unforgettable pair.

Then the next day they walk into your gym. Just as the other team is about to bring the ball down the court, the couple walks over to you and says, "We'll give you this $10,000 bill if you stop that other team from scoring this time."

One successful defensive play and you get $10,000. You don't have to be greedy or money-hungry to be motivated by that offer. You are playing a game. You were planning to try to stop that other team anyway. And now you get a $10,000 bill if you are successful just one time.

The Question

How would your defense under these circumstances be different from your typical defense? Would your effort suddenly expand when you got that offer?

If you typically give 100 percent, there should be no noticeable change in your effort. Yet every athlete at my Point Guard program is forced to admit that his or her defense would change. The effort would increase. Feet would move more, determination would intensify, hand and head movements would go hyper. And the vocal chords would flutter. Instructions, reminders, and warnings would fly from the mouth of any athlete suddenly faced with this proposition.

An increased sense of urgency would be noticeable in just about every athlete in the world. But should it?

Though a $10,000 offer may animate you more, a champion must seek to develop that kind of urgency—or come increasingly close to it—on every play of every game, and even in practice.

Whenever you play or practice, get in the habit of asking yourself the $10,000 question. Am I, right now, playing the way I would play if $10,000 were riding on this one play?

104.

Victories—Where?

As an athlete, just like as a citizen on the highways, you have to decide where you want your victories.

You probably come across people nearly every day who get their victories on the highways. They will speed by and cut in front of you in full sight of a red light, knowing they have to come to a quick stop. They will jam on the gas, risk your life, and screech to a stop, all just to get twenty feet ahead of you in a line of traffic at a light. It's a cheap victory. Anyone willing to drive stupidly and exceed the speed limit can beat any driver who has enough common sense not to want to race, risk a wreck, and break a law just to stop and wait one whole car length ahead. But you have to figure that it must be the best they can do during a typical day, these self-crowned champions of crowded city streets. They must not get much gratification from real competition. They must not get much satisfaction from early wins, on level playing fields, against tough competitors. They probably don't compete in any real sports, so they go for cheap victories on the highway against people not even playing their games. You can to tell them to get a life, to put their energies and competitive instincts to better use. But you can't talk to every driver out there.

What you can do is search yourself. (Which incidentally is a good rule of thumb in many aspects of life. When you see something you don't like about someone, instead of thinking about him or her or voicing some complaint to a friend, consider thinking how you may be guilty of similar things and may have the same negative effect on someone else. You can't fix the world, but you can always improve yourself.)

While you may not be guilty of these cheap highway victories, many good athletes are guilty of a similar kind of cheap victory on the practice field. Are you one of those athletes with a tendency to complain in practice about things your teammates do to you? Either they are fouling you in basketball, or holding your jersey in football, or making some kind of illegal contact in hockey. Or maybe you are one of those athletes who enjoys doing those kinds of things to the members of your reserve team. Hey, older players did it to you when you were coming up. Now it's payback time. So you get an advantage here and there, intimidate the junior varsity player trying to compete with you, get a laugh with some of your buddies. It seems harmless enough but these are cheap sources of pride, cheap victories, energy that would better be left for real games against competitors of your ability and experience. *Why get your kicks in practice against the reserve team?*

If this description happens to fit you even occasionally, consider turning the tables on yourself. Tell your younger, less skilled competitors in practice to hold your shirt, hit your arms, break the rules. Invite them to make things tougher for you instead of using your status and greater strength to intimidate them. Rather than complaining about what they're doing, show them how to make it tougher for you. This recommendation does not make practice go easier but it makes your preparation better and your success in games more likely.

As an athlete, just like as a citizen on the highways, you have to decide where you want your victories. If you want applause and admiration in games and the trophies and awards that come from success in sports, you need to consider giving up the laughs that can come from dominating some less experienced kid in practice. What good is winning races to red lights?

105.
"We 'Could-a' Beat Those Guys!"

Veteran coaches, players, and fans can point to dozens of times they have witnessed the seemingly impossible.

These words are usually uttered, often with a kind of surprise, after a loss. And they say something important about the psychology of athletes.

Athletes read press clippings. Athletes get nervous. Athletes begin to believe that another team is especially tough. Sure, they seldom admit it. Athletes learn to act supremely confident. But it is an act, especially when they're about to play an opponent who has already beaten them, or when an undefeated team comes to town, or when the opponent has a big star. Then, regardless of what the athletes' exteriors seem to be saying, there are plenty of worries that "We can't beat those guys."

No, you won't ever hear them say that before a game. Most athletes have already tried a comment like that somewhere in grade school or preschool and their parents or some coach washed their mouths out with soap or made them feel as if they had just stoned a prophet. "No, no way. Don't you *ever* say that again. Do you hear me? You can *always* beat another team. You hear? Hey, look at me. I said look at me. Do you hear me? Don't you ever say that again."

We-can't-beat-those-guys means giving up, and coaches just won't tolerate that kind of talk. Yet, even though most experienced athletes are clear about the importance of never saying they can't beat someone, it is incredible how often these same athletes are surprised when they realize that they *could have* beaten someone they have lost to. Makes you realize that their words do not match their thoughts and that they are frequently going into games that, deep inside, they don't believe they can win. I hope this sinks in. When the game against the big guys is over, nearly always the feeling among the losing team is "they weren't as good as we thought they'd be."

We "could-a" taken those guys. We could've beaten them. Yes. You "could-a." (What made you think you couldn't? What made you think they were going to be so good?) You almost always can beat the other team, except in the case of an overwhelming mismatch in ability. But don't wait until after a game is over to walk off the field with this feeling. You can beat almost anyone, especially in team sports where many intangibles can disappear and appear suddenly. (It's true in individual sports, too.)

Veteran coaches, players, and fans can point to dozens of times they have witnessed the seemingly impossible. The giants against the midgets. David versus Goliath. The undefeated team versus the winless team. It didn't happen once, back in 1902; it happens every season. Bad teams beat good teams. Or come within a point or two. Clearly, they could've beaten them. Surprise is part of sports but to any veteran coach none of this is a surprise. The best teams on paper or by reputation get shocked constantly. If you want to be one of the shockers, it helps to believe from the start.

It's not a matter of developing the habit of chattering that you can beat them, it's a matter of understanding what it takes to win, it's a matter of keeping your objectives in mind play by play, a matter of giving nothing away.

Make them fight for everything they get.

Even big stars are human. No one plays well every game. But to beat the stars or the champs or the undefeated team or the team that whipped you good last time, you have to go into the game scratching and clawing from the beginning—losing with the greatest reluctance.

The next time you walk off a playing field having lost, with the feeling "we could've beaten those guys," stop, think, and regroup. Of course you could've. One reason you didn't is that you probably didn't have the right attitude from the start. You probably spent too much time focusing on their abilities and reputation instead of focusing on what was required to pull off an upset.

106.
Winning Isn't Everything

An athlete needs to compete with the attitude that winning is everything, that it is life-and-death, and that he will do virtually anything to get the job done.

It is and it isn't. Mostly it depends on who is talking. When academic people or philosophers or lazy people talk about sports, they often emphasize ideals that de-emphasize sports.

It's only a game.

There are more important things in life than sports.

You can't win 'em all.

As long as you got good exercise and enjoyed yourself…

To those people, I would say that winning *is* everything and they are missing the special quality of sport with the attitudes they have. If there is too much recognition of the fact that it's only a game or it's just a sport, then there probably isn't enough effort to lift you to championship performance and the real pride and exhilaration that can come from going all-out on a field.

In particular, it is not useful to have the academic's or philosopher's perspective *during* a game.

"Oh well, no use killing myself *this* time. We can't expect to stop 'em every time."

"Oh, so they scored. I did *my* best. You just have to accept that. I mean, you're not going to shut 'em out. What are you getting so excited about, Coach?"

During the action, an athlete doesn't want that perspective except in the back of his mind, the very back. Of course you won't kill to win. Of course you won't intentionally hurt someone. Of course you aren't interested in cheating or gaining some sort of unfair advantage. Those things mock sports the same way a philosopher mocks sports by giving a mediocre effort and claiming he can't expect to stop them every time.

An athlete needs to compete with the attitude that winning is everything, that it is life-and-death, and that he will do virtually anything to get the job done. Is there a contradiction here? Of course, but there is a contradiction every time a person exercises to be fit and healthy while knowing that someday he will die. Philosophers call that the human condition; we have to learn to live to the fullest while recognizing that we can't live forever.

The athlete competes, I think, with that same fervor and same deep-seated ambivalence. Sure you can't win 'em all, sure you are going to have to accept defeat sometimes, sure it's only a sport. But don't talk to me about that now—when I'm lacing up my sneakers and preparing for this opponent or when I'm running down the field and trying to score or prevent a score.

During the action, winning *is* everything. It's not a philosophy class. It's a challenge, a test, commitment.

"Oh well, no use taking any medicine for this cold, I'm going to die someday anyway."

You get the message. While you have your chance to compete and to play a sport, play it like a champion. Play it tough, play it hard, play it all-out. Play it as though losing is unthinkable, a disgrace, a matter of life and death.

If you do lose, you can reevaluate; you can being preparing for the next time. But during the action, anything less than a winning-is-everything attitude will probably doom you to (more frequently than necessary) losing. You can agree with the philosophers in a discussion forum but don't take their perspective into the arena. There you're a gladiator. You can handle both roles. A champion has to.

107.
Work Ethic

Your work ethic can be improved significantly over time, just like any other skill...

A good work ethic is admired not only in sports but in all fields all over the world. Every coach in every sport admires the kind of athlete who comes to practice early, stays late, and works diligently the entire time.

If you are an athlete seeking to be a champion, you must develop a good work ethic and you should know that few people are born with terrific work ethics. Mostly, *an admirable or impressive work ethic is developed over time, just as is any other skill in sports*. You work as hard as you can and you keep trying to improve your ability to work even harder.

Are you lazy? Do you get accused of not working up to your potential? You can change that—if you want to.

Besides concentrating more and constantly urging yourself to work harder, try doing some things that are clearly different from what others are doing. Get up before school and work out. Do some special kind of workout or meditation late at night. Add something unusual to your routine and keep at it long enough to let yourself feel the joy of getting praise for your unexpected efforts. Many so-called lazy athletes have changed and dramatically altered their work ethic after feeling the pride that comes with special recognition from friends, athletes and coaches. Of course this kind of recognition is not likely to come overnight. People will usually have to see you sticking to something for a while before they are likely to praise your efforts. But it isn't that hard to get started and you don't have to start by climbing Mount Everest. Choose something that takes ten or fifteen minutes and just do it at an unusual time. When you start getting some recognition, the effort will get easier.

Remember, your work ethic can be improved significantly over time just like any other skill, and this is one skill you will never regret improving. Any *time spent on improving your work ethic will be useful for the rest of your life*, and admired too. This area cannot be left to chance. You cannot work just to improve your skill level in your sport, you must work to improve your ability to work at improving your skill level. It sounds confusing at first, but every champion knows precisely what this means.

108.
"Working" the Referees

Human nature is more likely to make a referee work against you rather than for you, if you are badgering…

Officials have already been discussed under "Referees and Umpires" but I wanted to hit this "working" aspect especially, because TV commentators are so fond of it and, I think, so wrong about it.

Commentators appear to be enamored with the idea that great coaches have some special knack for "working" referees. Supposedly by badgering and complaining and bending the referees' ears, these coaches get batter calls for their teams.

Don't believe it.

If you understand human nature, you will at least question the wisdom of this thinking. And to make this clear, I am going to offer you one person's human nature—mine—so you know exactly what I am talking about.

If I were officiating a basketball game (I've done it a few times) and a coach kept badgering me to call a three second violation, I can assure you that I would look especially hard and find one of that coach's players who was in the lane for three seconds—or nearly that long—and I would whistle a violation against his team.

If the coach kept telling me his players were getting fouled, would I watch especially closely for fouls committed by his team and I would call one the very next time down the court, if at all possible.

I know I am not alone in this way of thinking. There is a story about the coach of the old Pittsburgh Steelers, maybe fifty or sixty years ago, who once told his quarterback on opening day to drop back to pass on the first play and to throw the ball to the other team.

As you can imagine, the quarterback was flabbergasted. What? To the other team? That of course would go against all the training, all the lectures, all the preparation, and everything that sport is about. But the coach was emphatic. The coach told the quarterback that the owner had instructed him to try a pass on the first play of the game. The coach added, "If that play works, the owner will be sending down another play every time we get the ball."

That would be every coach's nightmare, to have a team owner constantly trying to call plays. Any outstanding coach wants the power to do things his way and then, if he fails, fine. Fire him. But it is completely absurd to have an owner who strolls through practice occasionally, watches the games while conversing with friends, and then decides that he knows just what plays to call at particular times.

Seen in this context you can truly imagine a coach ordering a quarterback to throw an intentional interception. You would hope there would be some other way—an intelligent conversation maybe. But if the coach didn't believe that would work, you can bet he would be willing to trade one interception at the beginning of the season for the opportunity to do things his way for the rest of the games.

A badgered referee is in a position similar to that coach. I think human nature is more likely to make a referee work against you rather than for you, if you are badgering and irritating him in order to get better calls.

There may be some individuals of weak character who would blow the whistle to appease an angry coach but most human beings of any character, if they had a season or two of experience, would soon realize that appeasement is impossible. Give him this call, he's just going to want the next and the next anyway. Plus there are two conflicting sides to appease. How can you win?

A referee wins by ignoring coaches, players, and fans. Failing that, he quiets them with technical fouls, with penalties, and with "take that!" calls that show that he can not be influenced, so the badgering might as well stop. Imagine a referee who really did let a coach get to him. If coaches came to realize that, the badgering would escalate uncontrollably.

For most referees, even bad ones, the easiest way to control the game and get coaches off their backs is to make it clear that badgering will not pay dividends. A referee cannot afford to let a coach get to him, just the way the Steelers coach felt he couldn't afford to let his owner get to him.

And if a badgering coach is not likely to be able to work a referee successfully to get better calls, what chance do you think a player will have? Hopefully you decided long ago to forego that part of the game and focus entirely on yourself. (And hopefully your coach has, too.)

109.
The Unknown Quantity

If you are under pressure enough, you will score some and be called a hero, and you will miss some and be called a goat. There's nothing unknown about that.

The unknown quantity in algebra is X. In sports, it is *you*. Will you have a good game or a bad game? Will you get upset and get thrown out? Will you respond under pressure? Will you make the big play? In sports, there are no guarantees. You never know. But you do know that no star, not even Babe Ruth or Johnny Unitas or Oscar Robertson did everything right all of the time. Ruth struck out hundreds of times, Unitas threw the ball to the wrong team, Robertson got his dribble stolen and missed layups.

Even the greats mess up. Surprisingly often. Yet, knowing that, you still have to hate your own mistakes and strive constantly to eliminate them. You have to push yourself and lift yourself to ever higher levels so you can think of yourself as a champion and not just as a mere participant.

It all boils down to consistent, dynamic, exuberant striving. You're not just out there tolerating conditions, slogging your way through the muck of this or that setback and forcing yourself to go on. There's always a higher plane to be reached. It's not just about overcoming the many obstacles along the way, but also trying to increase your own energy level, enthusiasm, and impact. Not all progress comes at negative moments but you do take your most important steps to championship performance in practice, on fields alone, on rainy, cold days, when something hurts, or when playing with your teammates who are not cooperative, who are not hustling and who are not champions. You usually "get there" when the coach is yelling and angry, when the fans are disappointed and grumbling or maybe even booing their own team, booing you. You get there during those moments when, unexpectedly, the bottom seems to fall out and the fun seems to have gone.

The unknown quantity. The unknown quality. It's not whether or not you score or fail under pressure. If you are under pressure enough, you will score some and be called a hero, and you will miss some and be called a goat. There's nothing unknown about that. That's called percentages. The law of averages. Win some, lose some.

The unknown is how you summon the will and the strength to hold onto a vision of something better, something special, something champion, when you are slogging through that muck of unhappy, tired, injured, or disappointing times.

Champions, everyone knows, are not made on the night of big events but years before, when nondescript, unimpressive little kids make a commitment and begin to carry it out daily. Propelled by their vision, they rise above the inevitable muck they encounter on their way. That's why we so adore true champions. There's always some muck. It's never easy.

How well can you hold onto your vision when it seems as though everything around you is running counter to it? That ability is the unknown quantity or the so-difficult-to-maintain quality. Don't worry about whether or not you have it. Just keep striving for it.

110.

"You can do anything..."

In every major sport, only one team each year reaches the goal of becoming champion.

People in sports often get carried away. A team wins a Little League title and to some people this proves that any dream is possible—that all these little kids can become president of the planet.

There's no need to get carried away. Sports are wonderful and you can learn some valuable lessons and enjoy some terrific experience. But just because you set some goals and win some championships doesn't mean you can do anything you set your mind to. You can't.

Some things simply aren't doable or are not going to get done. Why go around pretending? Just because you beat the other midget league team in your town doesn't suddenly mean you can beat the Atlanta Braves. No matter how hard you try.

It seems necessary to point this out for one important reason: in a very real sense, every new goal is like starting over. Your past accomplishments are fine. They may give you some confidence and the encouragement to tackle new problems and overcome bigger obstacles. Good. But past successes are no guarantee of future successes. There's a lot of failure out there, a lot of frustration, and a lot of other athletes trying to reach the same goals. The fact that things happened to work out for your Little League team doesn't mean that you have all the answers. It just means that you had the right combination of talent and luck to get that job done. A new task may require a whole different set of talents and some luck that never comes. And then?

Does this sound a little gloomy? Maybe it is. But let's look a little more realistically at sports themselves. In every major sport, only one team each year reaches the goal of becoming champion. Are all of the others failures, losers?

Some great pro stars with great attitudes never played on a championship team. Some very good franchises with good players, good managers, good administrators and good people, nevertheless go decades without ever achieving their goals. You can't necessarily do whatever you set your mind to. Some things you flat-out will not do, regardless of what you do with your mind.

Gloomy? I call it realistic. Learn to do things, to try things, to do your best, and to see what happens. Chances are, if you do these things good things will happen. You won't always win championships and you won't always achieve every goal. But you will likely reap rewards from your efforts regardless. Do whatever you set your mind to? No. But get rewards just the same.

It may not be wise to get too caught up in this goal thing. Especially if you fail. Make sure you take the time to evaluate each goal, and make sure that your goals are enabling you to put your ability and efforts into some worthwhile pursuits. If they are, you'll be fine. Even if you don't always win, you could be like Thomas Edison or Abraham Lincoln and fail your way to great success.

Striving for your goals is wonderful if you keep at it and keep moving forward regardless of whether you succeed or fail. But if you get discouraged by failure, be careful. The fault may be in your goal, not in your effort.

You might not accomplish whatever you set your mind to. Big deal. You can do a lot. So, do a lot. I think doing a lot—especially under difficult circumstances—is the mark of a true champion. Not winning every game. And certainly not doing everything you set your mind to. By that definition, there has never been a champion. In other words, relax. Keep moving forward. *Don't get too excited by any particular success, and don't get too discouraged by any particular failure*. A true champion is one who understands how to seek and strive and persist.

111.
Yunno?

Learning to speak clearly and correctly is valued all over the world.

One of the least attractive habits of communication that athletes, along with a lot of other people in America, use too frequently these days is the phrase/question/expletive "you know."

Yunno?

When you get a chance to speak to a newspaper reporter, yunno, or to a teacher, or to a coach, or to a friend, yunno, people like that, yunno, take time to listen to yourself. Yunno what I mean? You'll get a better job, yunno, and things like that. And, yunno, I mean, what does it really mean, yunno?

If they know, yunno, you don't need to say it. Cause they know. Yunno what I mean? And if they don't know, yunno, then no use saying yunno cause they'll have to keep saying no, yunno?

No.

Why bring this up at all? If you're spending so much time and effort to train your body and mind to perform well on an athletic field, you don't want to immediately make a negative impression the moment you open your mouth.

The ability to speak clearly and correctly is valued all over the world. Communication was the characteristic that allowed humans to advance so far as a genus and species, and it continues to be the primary characteristic by which we judge others.

With just a little attention to your speaking habits you can lose the fear of silent pauses in your speech and realize that those pauses typically appear to indicate intelligence, not emptiness. So don't fill those spaces with yunno's. Learn to enjoy the pauses.

Clear thinking and speaking is valuable in almost any endeavor, including the planning and working together that promotes winning in sports. Yes there are people who are able to win and be successful without good speaking habits. But why imitate the occasional exception? Good speech patterns are one of the many factors that help you get ahead in sports and definitely outside of sports. Yunno what I mean? And poor speech patterns can be corrected, like most other things, with practice. So practice if necessary.

Take the time to eradicate yunno from your speaking habits, and do whatever else is necessary to make the kind of impression that says champion about you in every way possible.

Sabes?

112.
Z's, Catching Some

Sometimes you get a great night of sleep and perform poorly the next day. Sometimes you don't get any sleep at all and you perform well.

Many athletes concern themselves excessively with sleep. People talk about the importance of getting a good night's sleep before doing anything important; consequently, athletes spend long nights tossing and turning in bed, thinking excitedly about the game ahead and keeping themselves awake with the worry that they aren't falling asleep and therefore won't have the energy necessary to perform well at the event they are staying awake excitedly to think about.

Does it sound like I'm going in circles? That's exactly what athletes do to themselves on the nights before big events. There are several ways to deal with this problem.

1. Enjoy it! Realize that every athlete has gone through this and many pro stars still do regularly. So you are in good company. Relax. You can perform well on no sleep. Stars do it all the time. You can make up the sleep later.

Naturally it would be nice to be able to sleep ten extra hours on the night before a big event, and to realize a burst of double energy the next day. But, for better or worse, the body just doesn't work that way. Your ability to perform, and the energy at your disposal, doesn't seem to be all that dependent on what happened the night before.

I'm not trying to pretend here that I'm a sleep scientist but I am at least speaking from personal experience and with the benefit of having talked to a lot of athletes about this. From what I have learned, it just doesn't make much of a difference. What probably does matter is the amount of sleep you have gotten over a period of time in relation to what your body needs.

All bodies are not equal. Some people need a lot more sleep than others, and those people don't necessarily have more energy than the others. Not at all.

In other words, you are essentially free to go with your flow. If you can sleep long and peacefully, fine. Do it. And if you can't seem to get to sleep at all, feel free not to, and feel free to perform at your best, regardless. Your body will draw on the sleep it racked up over the past month, supply you with the energy your nutrition and training programs have guaranteed, and let you succeed or fail based on other factors.

When was the last time you heard a losing athlete explain during an interview, "I could have won today but I got all excited last night, couldn't go to sleep, and therefore I just had no energy to run the race today."

It's not that they are afraid to admit this. Not being able to sleep happens frequently to athletes. But performance is rarely affected.

2. A second way to deal with the problem of excited sleeplessness is to get up, acknowledge what is going on, and give into it. Quit tossing and turning and working against what your mind wants to do. Your mind doesn't want to check out yet. It has a few more things to go over.

Turn on the light, sit up, get out your notebook, and write down the things your mind is racing over.

Often, once your mind gets a chance to clear itself out it will relax and permit you to fall asleep. But—and this is a huge but—I realize that it's easy to write solutions in books and make them sound good. What actually happens often doesn't follow the script. I've gotten up dozens of times, written things down, thought about sheep, school, clouds, women...everything, and then turned out the light and went right back to racing thoughts and staying wide awake.

There aren't any guarantees. You try the techniques available. Sometimes they work, sometimes they don't. Sometimes you get a great night of sleep and perform poorly the next day. Sometimes you don't get any sleep at all and you perform well. What's it all mean? To me, it means there's no use getting all flustered about what's happening. If you aren't sleeping, you aren't sleeping. It's not like someone is jabbing a knife into you. You simply are not sleeping. You can still perform well the next day whether you are a skater, a wrestler, or a distance runner.

3. Relax. There isn't a tremendous difference between lying still for a few hours and sleeping for a few hours. Cumulatively there may be a difference over a period of time. But for one night, preparing for one big event...you will be fine if you just lie in bed and let your body relax. You can use progressive relaxation techniques or just lie there and let the thoughts race.

When all the Z's are counted you find out that you can't come to any definite conclusions. The guy with the most Z's isn't declared the winner. It's the guy who trained the best, the hardest, the most intelligently, and it's the guy who had the most ability and took advantage of his opportunities. Sleep just isn't all that important on a short-term basis. So if you're searching for a good excuse for not doing your best, don't plan to use lack of sleep. Better dream up something better than that.

CONCLUSION

I believe the athlete who thinks like a champion is much more likely to perform like a champion and actually be a champion. I hope this book has helped you to think like a champion and put you in a position to win the big one and actually *be* a champion. Best of luck. Win 'em all.

Index

ABOUT THE AUTHOR

Dick DeVenzio gave his life to sports and to a set of beliefs, ideas and convictions mostly related to the intelligent pursuit of excellence in sports. The son of a very successful basketball coach, Dick grew up wanting to be a basketball star. That led to daily schedules and all-day practicing by the time he was in 7th grade. By 10th grade, he was a varsity starter, averaging 20 points a game—at 5′-6″, and the next year he averaged 30—at 5′-9″. In his senior year, he led Ambridge High School to an undefeated state championship, and his team is still considered the best ever to play in Pennsylvania. His name is in the Basketball Hall of Fame, on Parade Magazine's 1967 All-American First Five.

Two years later, at Duke University, Dick was an All-ACC selection, and in 1971, a First Team Academic All-American.

After graduating from Duke, Dick played and coached professional basketball in Europe and South America and founded the now nationally acclaimed Point Guard College.

Considered by many to be a basketball genius and a gifted writer, Dick's writings and basketball programs have inspired and influenced countless coaches and athletes. He died in 2001 at age 52.

OTHER BASKETBALL BOOKS BY PGC FOUNDER

STUFF: Good Players Should Know

Stuff Good Players Should Know may very well be the best book ever written for basketball players. It is conversational and easy to understand, yet filled with subtle insights into the game of basketball. STUFF is page after page of creative concepts, common sense, and special tips that cannot be found anywhere else. STUFF is like having a coach right beside you, in your room, discussing the fine points of the game. Basketball fans will enjoy it, but players won't do without it.

RUNNIN' THE SHOW

Runnin' The Show spells out what it takes to be a real leader on a basketball court. How can a coach get the most out of his players? How can a player make everyone around her better and do the little things that lead to championship performance? Leaders have to sell their dreams, get players to work together, inspire teamwork, and understand people, attitudes and motivation. This is the last book Dick DeVenzio ever published and is a treasure for leaders in all walks of life.

THERE'S ONLY ONE WAY TO WIN

This is not a book of the exact science of basketball X's and O's, but rather a collection of insights into the methods and philosophies of how the game of basketball and life should be played. In every field there are exceptional people whose stories are both fascinating and instructive. This book relates insightful incidents from Coach DV's career and puts his guiding principles into words that can benefit coaches, players, fans, businesspeople, and anyone with a will to succeed.

Interested in transforming your game? Learn more about these 5-star books and explore all our course offerings by visiting https://pgcbasketball.com.